MICRONUTRIENTS IN SOIL AND PLANTS
(*STUDY OF CHICKPEA UNDER RAINFED*)

MICRONUTRIENTS IN SOIL AND PLANTS

(*STUDY OF CHICKPEA UNDER RAINFED*)

By

Dr. Nirmal Kumar Katiyar

Assistant Plant Protection Officer (Chemistry)

Govt. of India

Ministry of Agriculture and Farmers Welfare

Department of Agriculture

Cooperation and Farmers Welfare

Directorate of Plant Protection, Quarantine and Storage

Regional Pesticides Testing Laboratory

Kanpur - 208 022, U.P. (India)

DISCOVERY PUBLISHING HOUSE PVT. LTD.

INDIA

Published by:

Namit Wasan

DISCOVERY PUBLISHING HOUSE PVT. LTD.
4383/4B, Ansari Road, Darya Ganj
New Delhi-110 002 (India)
Phone : +91-11-23279245, 43596064-65
Fax : +91-11-23253475
E-mail : discoverypublishinghouse@gmail.com
namitwasan9@gmail.com
sales@discoverypublishinggroup.com
website: www.discoverypublishinggroup.com

First Edition: **2017**

ISBN: 978-93-5056-876-7

Micronutrients in Soil and Plants
(*Study of Chickpea under Rainfed*)

Printed at:
Infinity Imaging Systems
Delhi

DEDICATED
To My
BELOVED PARENTS
&
MY FAMILY

NIRMAL KUMAR KATIYAR.....

PREFACE

The areas around Chitrakoot are deficient in several macro and micronutrients on acount of high temperature and low moisture conditions. Pulses in general and chickpea in particular rule the area and severe yield losses in these crops are observed due to the deficiencies of micronutrients like zinc, boron and molybdenum. Their supplies balanced with major nutrients, *inter alia*, are most important to proper fertility management. Nevertheless, systematic information regarding the dynamics of these nutrients in plant and soil and their interactive behaviour is meagre. A study entitled "Studies on the dynamics of select micronutrients in soil, plant and their responses on chickpea (*Cicer arietinum* L.) under rainfed conditions", was initiated with the objective of optimizing crop yields with proper balance of major and micronutrients.

Uniform basal doses of N, P, K and S were applied in soil @ 20, 40, 20, 30 kg ha^{-1} respectively. The doses of zinc and boron were 0, 2.5, 5 kg ha^{-1} and 0, 1, 2 kg ha^{-1} and molybdenum 0, 400 g ha^{-1} respectively. The experiment was conducted during the years 2012-13 and 2013-14 on fixed site under factorial RBD using variety Awarodhi on Agricultural Research Farm, Rajaula of the University.

The results showed that Zn; 5 kg ha^{-1}, B; 2 kg ha^{-1} and Mo; 400 g ha^{-1} and their combinations resulted in the highest growth parameters, yield of grain and stover. Plant analysis revealed that concentrations of N, P, K, S, Zn, B, Mo, Cu, Fe and Mn were significantly increased at due to application of Zn, B and Mo. These treatments also gave the maximum uptake values of these nutrients. The best treatment Zn 5 kg ha^{-1}, B 2 kg ha^{-1} and Mo 400 g ha^{-1} gave 2174 kg ha^{-1} yield of grain and 2538 kg ha^{-1} of stover. These yield levels reflected maximized optima under rainfed condition obtaining in the present experimentation. The above treatment also resulted in maximum grain protein content of 20 % and protein yield of 434 kg ha^{-1}. In view of lower availability of nutrients, the crop removal and nutrient mining from the soil was sustainably compensated.

It was concluded that under given set of present experimental conditions combined dose of Zn 5 kg ha^{-1}, B 2 kg ha^{-1} and Mo 400 g ha^{-1} might be recommended for chickpea, for instant adoption by chickpea farmers of that area.

Nirmal Kumar Katiyar

ACKNOWLEDGEMENT

Behind every success there is certainly an unseen power of Almighty GOD, but aim is the external condition of success which is attainable at perfection in everything by who preserve with the association for giving me this unique opportunity to express my heartfelt gratitude to all those who have given me help to make this a study success.

Space does not allow to set fourth my desired extent; words fail to express my feelings of deep gratitude and indebtedness to my Supervisor, Dr. U.S. Mishra, Associate Professor (Soil Science), M.G.C.G.V.V. Chitrakoot, Satna (M.P.), whose blessings, guidance, constant inspiration, conservative criticism and encouragement enabled me to submit his thesis in the present form.

I am extremely grateful to all respected members of my Advisory Committee M.G.C.G.V.V. Chitrakoot, Satna (M.P.) for their constant encouragement and valuable suggestions during this study.

I express my deep sense of gratitude and heartful thanks to Dr. Pawan Sirothia Head, Department of Natural Resource Management, M.G.C.G.V.V. Chitrakoot, Satna for his valuable suggestions learned and critic comments during the research work and his keen personal interest all along the course of investigation.

I also take opportunity to thanks Professor N.C. Gautam, Hon'able Vice-Chancellor, M.G.C.G.V.V. Chitrakoot, Satna (M.P.), and Professor Aroop Kumar Gupta, Dean Faculty of Agriculture for their kindness to provide the facilities during this investigation. Thanks are also rendered to Mr. S.K. Gupta, Assistant Director (Chemistry), and Dr. Virendra Kumar, PPO (PP) Regional Pesticides Testing Laboratory, Kanpur for their Constant moral support.

Most cordial thanks are also expressed to all respected teachers, Ex. Professor & Head Dr. R.K. Pathak, Dr. B.R. Gupta, Dr. D.D. Tiwari, Professor & Head/Senior Pesticide Chemist, Dr. R.C. Nigam, Professor/Residue Analyst, Dr. R.K. Pathak, Dr. A.K. Sachan, Dr. H.C. Tripathi, Dr. R.K. Pandey and Dr. Sushil Dimree Assistant Professor, Department of Soil Science and Agricultural Chemistry, C.S.A.U.A. & T., Kanpur, for their help, fruitful suggestions and generous advice during the course of investigation.

I am also thankful to my seniors, Dr. Ashok Kumar (Assistant Professor, National Sugar Institute, Kanpur), Dr. Anand Kumar Katiyar (Scientist, DRDO, Chandigarh), Dr. Ravi (SS&LUP, New Delhi), Dr. S.P. Yadav (STO, Organic Chemistry, NHRDF, Nashik), Dr. Jagmohan Singh Katiyar and thanks are also due to my affectionate juniors, Dr. S. G. Rajput, Dr. Somraj Rajput, Deependra Sharma, Shiv Mohan Bajpayee,

Rishi Mishra, Sant Kumar Sharma, Anil Aheer, Ramasare Yadav and Pawan Tiwari who rendered their valuable assistance in complication of this manuscript.

I can't forget dear friends Avinash Verma, Roshan Bharadwaj, Akhilesh Kulahade, Pradeep Kumar Rana, Dharmendra Yasona, Rameshwar Ahirwar, Shailesh Kumar Pandey and Atul Kumar Singh for their co-operation, encouragement and valuable criticism during my study.

How can I forget my grandfather Late Shri. Ramchandra Katiyar and my grandmother Late Smt. Kamla Katiyar, my beloved parents, (Respected Shri. Rakesh Kumar Katiyar and Smt. Shiv Vati) and my father in law & mother in law (Shri. Ram Shankar Katiyar and Smt. Usha Katiyar) with regards for their patience, love and sacrifice besides I express thanks and gratitude to Jija Ji Shri. Akhilesh Kumar Katiyar, Didi Smt. Radha Katiyar and nice Swami Saran Singh. Mama Ji (Shri. Raghuveer Sahai Katiyar & Shri. Arun Kumar Katiyar) and my loving younger brother Kaushal, Gaurav, Saurabh, Atul and elder sister Smt. Romi, Rashmi and Shalini Katiyar. I am also thankful to Smt. Sarika Katiyar, my wife and my loving daughter Nivedita Katiyar, whose blessing and love constantly provided me moral support.

Last but not the least, my heartful thanks go to Dr. S.K. Bansal, Director IPRI, Gurgaon (Haryana) and Dr. Arvind K. Shukla, Project Coordinator (MSN), I.I.S.S., Bhopal, (M.P.) whose encouragement enabled me to achieve this lofty goal.

"Act with knowledge, Knowledge is truth,
The path of action is the truth, The path of truth is action"

कर्म करो तुम ज्ञान से, श्रेष्ठ ज्ञान है धर्म ।
कर्मयोग ही धर्म है, धर्मयोग ही कर्म ।।

Nirmal Kumar Katiyar

CONTENTS

LIST OF ABBREVIATIONS USED

S. No.	Full Name	Short Name
1.	Nitrogen	N
2.	Phosphorus	P
3.	Potash	K
4.	Calcium	Ca
5.	Magnesium	Mg
6.	Sulphur	S
7.	Zinc	Zn
8.	Iron	Fe
9.	Boron	B
10.	Manganese	Mn
11.	Molybdenum	Mo
12.	Copper	Cu
13.	Cobalt	Co
14.	Nickel	Ni
15.	Silicon	Si
16.	deci Siemens meter^{-1}	dSm^{-1}
17.	Kilogram	kg
18.	Million hectare	m ha
19.	Milligram per 100 gram	mg 100 g^{-1}
20.	Million tonnes	m tonnes
21.	Kilogram per hectare	kg ha^{-1}
22.	Quintal per hectare	q ha^{-1}
23.	Per cent	%
24.	De oxyribo nucleic acid	DNA
25.	Ribo nucleic acid	RNA
26.	Adenosine diphosphate	ADP
27.	Adenosine triphosphate	ATP
28.	Nitrate	NO_3^-
29.	Phosphate	$PO_4^{=}$

30.	Indole butyric acid	IAA
31.	Parts per million	ppm/mg kg^{-1}
32.	Biological nitrogen fixation	BNF
33.	Phosphorous penta oxide	P_2O_5
34.	Potassium	K_2O
35.	Per plant	$plant^{-1}$
36.	Per pod	pod^{-1}
37.	Power of hydrogen ion	pH
38.	Electrical conductivity	EC
39.	At all	*et al.*
40.	Per hectare	ha^{-1}
41.	Recommended dose of fertilizer	RDF
42.	Per pot	pot^{-1}
43.	Per plot	$plot^{-1}$
44.	Harvest Index	HI
45.	Milligram	mg
46.	Gram per plant	g $plant^{-1}$
47.	Ton per hectare	t ha^{-1}
48.	Degree Celsius	^{o}C
49.	Millimetre	mm
50.	Centimetre	cm
51.	Gram per hectare	g ha^{-1}
52.	Square metre per plot	m^2 $plot^{-1}$
53.	Square metre	m^2
54.	Randomized block design	R.B.D.
55.	Pods per plant	pods $plant^{-1}$
56.	Days after sowing	DAS
57.	Gram	g
58.	Degree fahrenheit	^{o}F
59.	Correction factor	CF
60.	Normal solution	N
61.	Molar solution	M
62.	Millilitre	ml
63.	Nano metre	nm
64.	Number	No.
65.	Critical difference	CD
66.	Standard deviation	SD

67.	Diethylene triamine penta acetic acid	DTPA
68.	Ethylene diamine tetra acetic acid	EDTA
69.	Triethanol amine	TEA
70.	Sodium bicarbonate	$NaHCO_3$
71.	Sulphuric acid	H_2SO_4
72.	Hydrochloric acid	HCl
73.	Nitric acid	HNO_3
74.	Perchloric acid	$HClO_4$
75.	Barium chloride	$BaCl_2$
76.	Barium sulphate	$BaSO_4$
77.	Calcium chloride	$CaCl_2$
78.	Boric acid	H_3BO_3
79.	Calcium carbonate	$CaCO_3$
80.	Sodium tetraborate	$Na_2B_4O_7.5H_2O$
81.	Madhya Pradesh	M.P.
82.	Zinc 0 kg ha^{-1}	Zn_0
83.	Zinc 2.5 kg ha^{-1}	Zn_1
84.	Zinc 5.0 kg ha^{-1}	Zn_2
85.	Boron 0 kg ha^{-1}	B_0
86.	Boron 1 kg ha^{-1}	B_1
87.	Boron 2 kg ha^{-1}	B_2
88.	Molybdenum 0 g ha^{-1}	Mo_0
89.	Molybdenum 400 g ha^{-1}	Mo_1
90.	Per	/
91.	Select micronutrients	Yield limiting micronutrients
92.	Ammonium Molybdate	AM

INTRODUCTION

The green revolution in rice and wheat was ushered in during sixties due to availability of wonder varieties capable of conversion of higher inputs into yield. Unfortunately, there were no such varieties in pulses and the yield of these crops remained low and there is a gap between consumption and production. The pulses are grown under low input conditions by marginal and sub marginal farmers all over the country. The major pulse growing area is under stress conditions particularly under rainfed conditions.

Rainfed agriculture extends over 97m ha comprising of nearly 67 per cent of net cultivated area and has a share of 44 per cent food grain production and supports 40 per cent population. However, recently, the rainfed area has decreased. Among the different crops being grown under rainfed areas pulses alone occupy 22 per cent of net sown area. (Singh *et al.* 1999).

Alfisols and Vertisols are the two major soil types in rainfed areas. Alfisols are low in organic matter with poor fertility. Their moisture holding capacity is low. On account of hard crest on surface the germination is poor. Vertisols are relatively deeper and hold more water but these soils are susceptible to erosion. Inceptisols occupy only smaller areas under rainfed agriculture (Venkateswarlu, 1987).

Pulses play an important role in the human nutrition. Pulses have been functioning as the 'fertilizer factories' on the farmers' fields. In India most of the populations are vegetarian and dependability on the pulse protein is much higher, besides the pulses enrich the soil through symbiotic fixation of atmospheric nitrogen. Pulses are highly adapted to dry land areas. More than 78 per cent areas under pulse are still rainfed. Pulses are the major sources of dietary protein.

Legumes are of considerable importance for providing food and feed world over. In comparison to cereal grains, legume seeds are rich in protein and thus provide highly nutritive food. Legumes are grown on a wide range of soils varying in texture and fertility. Most of the soils of arid and semi-arid regions, being low in soil moisture content, are also low in fertility. So to maximize plant productivity, proper supply of macro - and micro-nutrients to crops is essential. As a general practice, optimal supply of macronutrients to crops is usually ensured but that of micronutrients is ignored.

In view of a plethora of literature, it is now well established that application of micronutrients is effective in alleviating the adverse effects of abiotic stresses such as: salinity and drought. The involvement of micronutrients in different physiological and biochemical activities of the legume plants and are correlated with crop growth and productivity. Use of micronutrients like zinc (Zn), iron (Fe), boron (B), manganese (Mn), molybdenum (Mo), copper (Cu), cobalt (Co) and nickel (Ni) has now become a common practice to increase crop yield especially under adverse environmental conditions. Plants deficient in micronutrients may become susceptible to diseases and abiotic stresses. Rapid leaching of acids in sandy soils tends to produce a deficiency of nutrients such as: Zn, Fe, Cu and B. Therefore, problem soils such as: acid, alkaline or sandy soils are often deficient in one or more micronutrient elements. Micronutrient application not only improves the stress tolerance potential indirectly (because micronutrients deficient plants exhibit an impaired defense response) but also results in improving a number of metabolic phenomena. Thus, application of micronutrients as foliar or soil is recommended to achieve optimum crop productivity from the soils having inherent micronutrient deficiency and low moisture contents.

India contributes to 25 per cent area of pulses in the world and accounts for 16 per cent of total production. Madhya Pradesh has an area of 5327 thousand hectares with production of 5042 thousand tonnes and productivity of 947 kg ha^{-1}. M.P. shares 22.3 per cent area, 28.6 per cent production at national level (Government of MP, 2014). Chickpea is grown in many countries, but India is the largest producer and consumer of chickpea in the world.

Chickpea is one of the most important Rabi pulse crop. It is very nutritious and contains about 18-22 per cent protein, 64 per cent carbohydrate, (47% starch, 6% soluble sugar, 6% crude fiber) and 5 per cent fat. Besides protein and carbohydrates chickpea also contains in P- 340, Ca- 90, Mg- 140 mg 100 g^{-1} and other mineral etc.

Among the pulses Bengal gram or chickpea is the most important. It occupies 7.1 m ha area with a production of 5.75 m tonnes, accounting for 30.9 per cent of total pulse area and 39.9 per cent pulse production at national level. The main chickpea producing areas in the country are located in upper basin Ganga and Yamuna *viz*; Punjab, Haryana, Uttar Pradesh, Bihar and adjoining areas of Central India *viz*; Rajasthan, Madhya Pradesh and Maharashtra (Anonymous, 2006).

Among the different production factors nutrient management is most important and is responsible for 55-60 per cent crop yield. Like other pulses chickpea requires a starter dose of nitrogen (15 to 25 kg ha^{-1} N) for initial growth and nodule formation. Seed treatment with *Rhizobia* is also a gainful practice. In addition application of 40-60 kg ha^{-1} P_2O_5, 40 kg ha^{-1} K_2O, 20 kg ha^{-1} sulphur, 15 kg ha^{-1} zinc sulphate 10 kg ha^{-1} borax, 1kg sodium molybdate and 1 kg iron ha^{-1}, is recommended at national level for higher yields. The average crop yield is 15-20 q ha^{-1} grain.

The present day agriculture mainly depends on chemical fertilizer. Constant depletion of plant nutrients in soil due to intensive cultivation has compelled the farmers to use higher doses of chemical fertilizer particularly in sub tropical soils, where the organic matter content in very low. The huge drain of nutrients from the soil will continue to deplete the soil nutrients status unless replenished by natural or artificial sources. In such condition, the country has to look for an alternative source of plant nutrients both for augmentation and sustainability of crop production. In modern agriculture the increasing use of high analysis NPK fertilizers generally devoid of secondary and micronutrient such as: sulphur, zinc, boron and molybdenum, have further complicated the situation. Considering the critical limit deficiencies of 0.60, 0.20, 4.50, and 2.00 mg kg^{-1} in DTPA-Zn, DTPA-Cu, DTPA-Fe and DTPA-Mn. Taking the critical limit of 0.50 mg kg^{-1} for hot water extractable (Katyal and Rattan 2003) elements.

Zinc is one of the most important micronutrient in present day agriculture. About 50 per cent soils of the country are deficient in zinc. It is a constituent of several enzymes *viz;* carbonic anhydrase, alcoholic dehydrogenase and super oxide dismutase. Zinc is required in very small quantities for the growth of the plants. Zinc influences translocation and transport of P in plant. Zinc is essential for proper utilization of other micronutrients like: Cu and Mn. Zinc plays an important role in auxin (IAA) and protein synthesis. Most of the farmers are not very much familiar with zinc fertilization. At present requirement of zinc fertilizer is increasing year after year but not much research has been done on zinc fertilization in pulses. Therefore, we need to rationalize zinc doses on pulses, especially chickpea which is major pulse crop in our country.

The zinc which is available to plants is that present in the soil solution, or is adsorbed in a labile (easily desorbed) form. The soil factors affecting the availability of zinc to plants are those which control the amount of zinc in the soil solution and its sorption-desorption from/into the soil solution. These factors include: the total zinc content, pH, organic matter content, clay content, calcium carbonate content, redox conditions, microbial activity in the rhizosphere, soil moisture status, concentrations of other trace elements, concentrations of macronutrients, especially phosphorus and climate. Sandy soils and acid highly leached soils with low total and plant-available zinc concentrations are highly prone to zinc deficiency. Availability of zinc decreases with increasing soil pH due to increased adsorptive capacity of exchange complex the formation of hydrolyzed forms of zinc, possible chemisorptions on calcium carbonate and coprecipitation in iron oxides.

Alkaline, calcareous and heavily limed soils tend to be more prone to zinc deficiency than neutral or slightly acid soils., When rapidly decomposable organic matter, such as: manure, is added to soils, zinc may become more available due to the formation of soluble organic zinc complexes which are mobile and also probably capable of absorption into plant roots. Available zinc concentrations in soils with high organic matter contents (peat and muck soils) may be low due to either an inherently low total concentration in these organic materials and/or due to the formation of stable organic complexes with the solid-state organic matter. High levels of phosphorus may decrease the availability of zinc or the onset of zinc deficiency associated with phosphorus\fertilization may be due to plant physiological factors, Some forms of phosphatic fertilizers, such as: superphosphate, contain significant amounts of zinc as impurities and also have an acidifying effect on soils.

Nitrogen fertilizers, can have a combined beneficial effect on the nutrition of crop plants by both supplying nitrogen, and also an increase in zinc availability through the acidification of the soil resulting in desorption of zinc, and through improved root growth (and hence an increased volume of soil explored by roots) in the more vigorously growing plant. Where topsoil has been removed, often as a result of leveling fields for irrigation, crops grown on the subsoil can be highly prone to zinc deficiency, especially in calcareous soils. The topsoil contains the most organic matter and when removed there are shortages of macronutrients as well as micronutrients. However, N, P and K fertilizers usually address to the macronutrient requirements but the zinc status of these 'cut' soils also needs to be considered.

In the time since 1932, zinc has been found to be a vitally important micronutrient in crop production and deficiencies of this element have been shown to be more widespread throughout the world than those of any other micronutrient Brown *et al.* (1993). In plants, zinc does not undergo valency changes and its predominant forms are: low molecular weight complexes, storage metalloproteins, free ions and insoluble forms associated with the cell walls. Zinc can become inactivated within cells by the formation of complexes with organic ligands or by complexation with phosphorus. Depending on the plant species, between 58 per cent and 91 per cent of the zinc in a plant can be in a water-soluble form (low molecular weight complexes and free ions). This water-soluble fraction is widely considered to be the most physiologically active and is regarded as a better indicator of plant zinc status than total zinc contents Brown *et al.* (1993).

Boron is unique, not only in its chemical properties, but also in its roles in biology. Since boron discovery as essential plant nutrient, the importance of B as an agricultural chemical has grown very rapidly and its availability in soil and irrigation water is an important determinant of agricultural production. Boron deficiency is the most common and widespread, which impairs plant growth and reduces yield. Normal healthy plant growth requires a continuous supply of B, once it is taken up and used in the plant; it is not translocated from old to new tissue. That is why, deficiency symptoms starts with the youngest growing tissues. Therefore, adequate B supply is necessary for obtaining high yields and good quality of agriculture crops.

Boron is directly or indirectly involved in several physiological and biochemical processes during plant growth and metabolism. Boron deficiency causes reduction in cell enlargement in growing tissues because of its structural role. Its deficiency is responsible for creating male sterility and inducing floral abnormalities (Sharma, 2006). Several physiological and biochemical functions of B in plants are summarized below:-

Carbohydrate metabolism and transport of sugar, phenol and auxin metabolism, tissue development and formation of cell walls, reproduction and disease resistance, root elongation and nucleic acid metabolism, nitrogen fixation and nitrate assimilation, water relations.

Boron is not efficiently remobilized in many plant species that is why B deficiency occurs in young parts of the plant and toxicity in mature parts of plants. In many plant species, plants exposed to deficiency maintain B concentration in old mature leaves, whereas young portions of plants do not receive sufficient B to support growth.

Deficient and toxic levels of B are associated with plant disorders and reduction in the yield of crops. Boron deficiency and toxicity levels depend on types and species of crops, as dicotyledons need more B than monocotyledons (Gupta, 1993). Boron requirements vary with plant type; in monocotyledons species, leaf content ranges from 1 to 6 mg kg^{-1}; in most dicotyledons from 20 to 70 mg kg^{-1} and in dicotyledons with latex systems from 80 to 100 mg kg^{-1}. Crops such as: sugar beet, celery, apple, pear and grape have higher B requirement (Benton, 2003). Thus, excessive and deficient levels could be encountered during the same season (Mortvedt and Woodruff, 1993). Boron levels in rice plant tissue are considered deficient if concentration is < 5 mg kg^{-1}, sufficient if concentration is about 6-15 mg kg^{-1} and toxic if concentration is > 30 mg kg^{-1} (Dobberman and Fairhurst, 2000). Average B content in most plants is 20 mg kg^{-1} on dry weight basis. Boron is unevenly distributed within plants and highest levels are found in reproductive structures such as: anthers, stigma and ovaries.

Commonly occurring B deficiency symptoms include chlorosis and death of the growing points, distortion thickening and cracking of stems, formation of rosettes, growth of auxiliary buds, bushy growth and multiple branching (Anonymous, 2003). Root may become thick, twisted and do not develop properly, roots may show excessive branching, root crops often fail to develop edible portions or affected by the presence of dark colored corky areas.

Boron in the soil is exists in five categories; primary minerals such as: tourmaline and B rich micas; in secondary minerals within the clay mineral lattice; adsorbed on clays, hydrous oxide surfaces and organic matter; in solution as boric acid and borate anions; and in organic matter and the microbial biomass (Argust, 1998). Soil parent materials differ widely in their B content. Granite-derived soils often carry B deficient crops and these soils contain on average 0.07-0.15 mg hot water soluble B kg^{-1}, soils derived from basalt contain 0.25-0.35 mg kg^{-1} B and soils from sedimentary rocks have B up to 0.50 mg kg^{-1}. Soils derived from granite and other igneous rocks, gneiss and sandstone are particularly low in both total and water soluble B, whereas soil derived from loess contains more B. Boron is lost during metamorphism, some contributing to tourmaline formation but most of it is released to the environment (Shorrocks, 1997). Total soil B content can range from around 10 to 100 mg kg^{-1}; however only a small fraction of this amount that is about 3 to 5 per cent is available to the crop. A large amount of the total soil B is present as a component of highly insoluble mineral tourmaline. Boron available forms for plants include inorganic borate complexes of Ca, Mg, and Na, plus various organic compounds formed from plant and microbial decomposition (Hou *et al.* 1994). Tourmaline is a common B containing mineral but it is very resistant to chemical breakdown in the weathering and thus accumulates in the clastic fraction of sediments and sedimentary rocks. In igneous, metamorphic and sedimentary rocks, B occurs as borosilicate, which are resistant to weathering and not readily available to plants (Zerrari *et al.* 1999).

Plant available B in agricultural soils varies from 0.05 to 5 mg kg^{-1}, most of the available B in soil is derived from sediments and plant materials (Gupta, 1993). Boron has complex chemistry and is capable of bond in combination with hydrogen. In aqueous solution, the element has a charge of 3+, an ionic radius of 0.023 nm, with an electro negativity of 2.0 on the pauling scale and around 50 per cent ionic character of bond with oxygen. Boron occurs as boric acid, H_3BO_3 in aqueous solution and hydrolyse reversibly to the borate ion (Goldberg, 1997).

$B(OH)_3 + H_2O = B(OH)_4 + H+ \leftrightarrow pKa = 9.2$ The most common B species are $B(OH)_4^-$, $B_2O(OH)_5^-$, $B_3O_3(OH)_4^-$ and $B_4O_5(OH)_4$.

Boron occurs in combination with oxygen in 3-fold and 4-fold coordination (Evans and Sparks, 1983). The principal B sources in soils are H_3BO_3 and $B(OH)_4$. The neutral species H_3BO_3 are predominant in soil solution. It is only above pH 9.2 that the species $B(OH)_4$ become predominant (Keren and Bingham, 1985).

Boron content of Indian soils varies from 16 to 630 mg kg^{-1} with an average of 38 mg kg^{-1}. But Berger and Trong available B is very small. High boron content is found in arid and semi-arid soils, particularly in salt affected soils. Boron deficiency is of wide occurrence in soils of Bihar, Karnataka, Madhya Pradesh, Uttar Pradesh and West Bengal. (Tandon, 2002).

Molybdenum is the only heavy transition metal taken up by the plants as molybdate ions (MoO_4^{2-}). A healthy Mo-sufficient plant contains 0.1 to 2 mg $kg-^{1}$ of molybdenum. In the plant system under oxidative environments, it exists as Mo (VI) and undergoes reduction to Mo (V) and Mo (IV) forms. Ability of molybdenum too exist in variable valence states imparts it a biochemical role. Molybdenum is involved in protein biosynthesis through its effect on ribonuclease and alanine aminotransferase activity. It affects the formation and viability of pollens and development of anthers. Legumes, grains are good sources of Mo, while fruits, root, stem vegetables and muscle meat are poor ones.

Molybdenum chemistry largely resembles that of P in soils. All soil factors which increase availability of phosphorous also do molybdenum as well. For example, Mo availability is very low in acid soils. Molybdenum gets fixed in iron and aluminium compounds as well as on silicates at low pH. The fixed molybdate can be made available to crops phosphate application to soil which releases fixed molybdate ions by anion exchange, indicating that the fixation sites on soil colloids for phosphates and molybdate are the same. The following antagonistic effects have been established on the uptake of micronutrients by crop: Excess of S and Cu induces Mo-deficiency in crops.

Molybdenum is associated with the prosthetic group of the enzyme nitrate reductase and nitrogenase and thus plays important role in nitrogen metabolism. Molybdenum deficiency causes chlorotic interveinal mottling of the older leaves; flower formation is inhibited and causes whiptail disease in cauliflower plants (Jain, V.K. 2011).

Molybdenum is also deficient in about 11-12 per cent soils of the above states albeit, it has a great nutritional significance in pulses for its role in nodulation, BNF and protein systems. Thus management of Zn, B and Mo is most crucial. Molybdenum is present in nitrogenase (Nitrogen fixation) and nitrate reductase enzymes, essential for nitrogen fixation and nitrogen assimilation (Brady, 1995). Deficiencies of molybdenum are reported to be of wide variation mainly alfisols and inceptisols in states like: Bihar 55 per cent, Gujarat 10 per cent, Madhya Pradesh 18 per cent and Haryana 28 per cent (Dhane 2011).

Significant increase in protein, P, Fe, Mo and Zn content in grain and stover has been observed in chickpea due to molybdenum application (Singh *et.al.* 2004). Pulses respond well to molybdenum application because of its essential role in growth grain yield and protein content combined application of S, Mo and Rhizobium increased the vegetative growth, nodules number grain and stover yield in black gram (Singh *et.al.* 2008). (Valenciano *et.al.* 2010) reported a significant increase in chickpea yield due to positive interaction Zn x B x Mo., (Bozoglu *et.al.* 2007) reported the optimum doses of zinc and molybdenum as 2 mg kg^{-1} and 0.05 mg kg^{-1} respectively in chickpea.

Excessive amounts of Mo are toxic, especially to grazing cattle. High-Mo forage may occur on wet, high-pH, and high-OM soils. Molybdenosis, a disease in cattle, is caused by an imbalance of Mo and Cu in the diet when the Mo content of the forage is >5 mg kg^{-1}. Mo toxicity causes stunted growth and bone deformation in the animal and can be corrected by oral feeding of Cu, injections of Cu, or the application of $CuSO_4$ to the soil. Other practices used to decrease Mo toxicity are application of S or Mn and improvement of soil drainage (Tisdale and Nelson 2012).

The significance of these nutrients in plant is described. Since most of pulse growing soils are deficient in all the three micronutrients (Zn, B and Mo) the cumulative deficiencies of these elements tell upon yield and quality of pulses. So for the literature is meagre on their conjoint use in pulses and particularly in the chickpea. It was a need based realization to undertake research under the project entitled, 'Studies on the dynamics of select micronutrients in soil, plant and their responses on chickpea (*Cicer arietinum* L.) under rainfed conditions', with the following objectives:

1. Analysis of surface soil of experimental plot for Zn, B and Mo before and after the crop.
2. Conducting the field scale experiments to see the effect of Zn, B and Mo application on the growth and yield of chickpea.
3. Analysis of plants for Zn, B and Mo contents to calculate the total uptake of nutrients.
4. To study the effect of Zn, B and Mo and their interactions on the grain and straw yields.
5. To see the effect of Zn, B and Mo and their interaction on the nodulation of the crop.

PRESENT SCENARIO OF MICRONUTRIENTS

The research work relating to relevant aspects of the problem, and envisaged objectives of study present entitled "Studies on the dynamics of select micronutrients in soil, plant and their responses on chickpea (*Cicer arietinum* L.) under rainfed conditions", is reviewed here as under:

Nilnond *et al.* (1986) reported that in soils with moderate to severe phosphorus deficiency the P responses were 50-87 per cent. The deficiencies in several soils were observed for N, P, K, S, Cu, Zn, Mn, Mo, Mg, B and Fe. The study suggested that soil fertility evaluation must be bases on holistic approach to reveal the response of a particular nutrient.

(Singh *et al.* 1999) the rainfed agriculture extends over 97 m ha which is nearly 67 per cent of the net cultivated area of the country. It has a share of 44 per cent food grain production and supports 40 per cent population. Extension of irrigation facilities over the years has significantly reduced the rainfed area. The most important crops which are grown under unirrigated areas are rice, wheat, pulses, oilseeds, cotton, sorghum pearlmillet, maize etc. Pulses alone are grown on 22 per cent of net sown area under rainfed conditions.

Blevin (1999) described that phosphorus is second most important macronutrient required by all plants for growth, development and production. Many important biochemicals in the plants contain phosphorus. Phospholipids are the primary structural component of membranes that surround each plant cell and organelles. Inside the cell, genetic information in the form of DNA and RNA molecules contain P as an integral structural component. These genetic informational molecules guide the synthesis of proteins.

Blevin (1999) further reported that even though the total P may be high P is tightly bound to organic and inorganic soil constituents and become unavailable for uptake by plants. Association with mycorrhizal fungi their hyphae penetrate in soil and extract P. Some plants secrete organic acids (citric and malic) which form complexes with Al and Fe releasing P for root uptake. Roots also secrete special enzymes like: phosphatases which break down the organic P.

Once proteins are made, when and where work may be regulated by events that again involve P. Much of the metabolism inside the cell is controlled by phosphorylation and dephosphorylation of certain proteins *i.e.,* enzymes. The addition and removal of phosphate then becomes a key signally mechanism for what is happening inside the plant cell. The source of phosphate for signal events is ATP, which also serves as the major energy currency in the cell.

Photosynthesis is one of the key to biochemical phenomenon life on earth to harvest to sustain energy from sunlight and trap it in the form of high energy phosphate bonds to finally build the carbohydrates. Phosphorus in plants is involved in many ways *i.e.,* synthesis of trioses and hexose phosphates. Phosphate must also enter the chloroplast in order to get triose phosphate out of chloroplast for use in other plant processes. This phosphate/triose phosphate exchange reaction is critical for movement of sugars. In soybean leaves that are deficient in P, small sugars cannot exit chloroplast properly. The small sugars accumulate in large molecules of starch which eventually cause structural damage to chloroplast and shutdown photosynthesis.

Water movement through xylem is like an open piping system for movement of water and nutrients from root to leaf. The system is very responsive to P and increases with high level of P. Several phosphoteins undergo phosphorylation and dephosphorylation in a gated system and their opening and closing depends upon phosphorylation to tone up this system specially in water deficient conditions also controls the flow of Ca, Mg and water through xylem controlled by ATP. At the end of maturity P is reimmobilized is seed and store genetic information in RNA and DNA. P is stored in phytic acid containing 6 P^- charge for attracting K, Ca, Mg, Cu, Zn and Fe.

Singh (2001) the combined figures of Uttar Pradesh and Madhya Pradesh show that boron was most deficient 68 per cent and the next are zinc deficiency 46 per cent. This shows that far augmenting the mungbean production supply of zinc and boron is crucial. There are a number of reports that the crop response there nutrients have been positive under various situations.

Thiyagarajan (2003) reported that nutrient imbalance is one of the major abiotic constraints limiting productivity of pulses. The inbuilt mechanism of biological N_2 fixation enable pulse crops to meet 80-90 per cent of their nitrogen requirements, hence a small dose of 15-25 kg N ha^{-1} is sufficient to meet out the requirement of most of the pulse crops. However, in emerging cropping systems like: rice, chickpea; a higher dose of N (30·40 kg ha^{-1}) had shown beneficial effect - phosphorus deficiency in soils is wide spread and most of the pulse crops have shown good response to 20-60 kg P_20_5 ha^{-1} depending upon nutrient status of soil, cropping system and moisture availability. Response to potassium application is location specific. In the recent years, use of sulphur (20-30 kg ha^{-1}) and some of the micronutrients such as: Zn, B, Mo and

Fe have improved productivity of pulse crops considerably in many pockets. Band placement of phosphatic fertilizers and use of bio-fertilizers enhance the efficiency of applied as well as native P. Foliar nutrition of some micronutrients proved quite effective. The amount and mode of application is determined by indigenous nutrient supply, moisture availability and genotypes. Balanced nutrition is indispensable for achieving higher productivity. At the same time, in view of increasing nutrients demand, there is immense need to exploit the alternate source of nutrients *viz*; organic materials and bio-fertilizers to sustain the productivity with more environment friendly nutrient management systems. The environmental issues and other hazards emerging out of the imbalanced use of nutrients should also be addressed properly.

Anonymous (2006) indicated that in overall management of pulses under water stress conditions is the choice of crop is of special significance in a given ecosystem. From this point of view bengalgram or chickpea is foremost choice. Chickpea is most important pulse crop in India and occupies 7.1 million ha area with a production of 5.75 million tons accounting for 30.9 per cent and 39.9 per cent of total pulse area and production, respectively. Bengal gram growing areas in the country are upper basin of Ganga and Yamuna *viz*; Punjab, Haryana, Uttar Pradesh, Madhya Pradesh, Bihar and adjoining areas of Central India *viz*; Rajasthan, Madhya Pradesh and Maharashtra. Being capable of fixing nitrogen, it requires small dose of nitrogen for initial growth and nodule formation. Seed treatment with *Rhizobia* culture is beneficial in this respect. About 15 to 20 kg N and 40-60 kg P_2O_5 ha^{-1} is a general dose. Use of phosphate solubilizing organisms is beneficial. In addition, application of 40 kg K_2O, 20 kg sulphur 15 kg zinc sulphate, 10 kg borax, 1 kg sodium molybdate and 1 kg iron ha^{-1} is also recommended. Under optimum conditions the average yield of chickpea is 1500 to 2000 kg grain ha^{-1}.

Begum *et al.* (2007) reported that inclusion of legume crop in a cropping system is an important component of integrated nutrient management. Legume is supposed to supply sufficient amount of nitrogen to succeeding crop. The yields of legumes are poor specially under low fertilizer conditions and water scarcity. Application of phosphorus under such situations might result in considerable increase in yields of legume crop and succeeding non legume a crop.

Shukla (2011) reported that micronutrient deficiencies are now frequently observed in intensively grown oilseeds, pulses and vegetable crops. Analysis of a large number soil samples has indicated that 49 per cent of soils of India are potentially deficient in Zn, 12 per cent in Fe, 5 per cent in Mn, 3 per cent in Cu and 33 per cent in B and 11 per cent in Mo. He further reported that balanced application of micronutrients along with NPK in system productivity enhanced the yield of crops in the system considerably. The average system productivity of wheat based cropping systems enhanced by 6.61 per cent due to addition of micronutrients in balanced NPK fertilizer schedule ranging from 5.32 per cent in sesame-wheat to 7.82 per cent in pigeon pea, wheat system.

Zinc

This topic was extensively reviewed by Brown *et al.* (1993) and the following section is mainly based on their review and individual papers which they used have not been referred to in this brief coverage of the subject. Readers seeking more details are recommended to the chapter by Brown *et al.* in 'zinc in soils and plants' edited by A.D. Robson (1993) Brown *et al.* (1993, the review by Welch (1995) 'Micronutrient Nutrition of Plants' Welch, R.M. (1995), or the second edition (1995) of Marchner's book 'Mineral Nutrition of Higher Plants' Marschner, H. (1995). A biological requirement for zinc was first identified by Raulin in 1869 when the common bread mould *(Aspergillus niger)* was found not to be able to grow in the absence of zinc. However, its essentiality was not established until 1926 and it was only in 1932 that zinc deficiency was first identified under field conditions (in Californian apple orchards and South Australian citrus trees).

Graham *et al.* (1992) comment that it would appear that there is a critical level required for zinc in the soil before roots will either grow into it or function effectively. According to Marschner, H. (1995). the metabolic functions of zinc are based on its strong tendency to form tetrahedral complexes with N-, O- and particularly S- ligands and it thereby plays both a functional (catalytic) and a structural role in enzyme reactions. Although more than 70 metalloenzymes containing zinc have been identified, these only account for a relatively small proportion of the total zinc in a plant Brown *et al.* (1993).

Zinc appears to be absorbed by roots primarily as Zn^{2+} from the soil solution and its uptake is mediated by a protein with a strong affinity for zinc. Kochian (1993) proposed that the transport of zinc across the plasma membrane was towards a large negative electrical potential so that the process is thermodynamically passive. This negative electrical potential of the plasma membrane is the driving force for zinc by means of a divalent cation channel in dicotyledons and monocotyledons other than the poaceae.

Singh, K.B. and Saxena, M.C. (1999) (World average yield 1990-94 = 0.7 t ha^{-1}) although acute zinc deficiency is not very commonly seen, the symptoms are: yellowing, then bronzing and necrosis of lower and middle leaves. Foliar sprays with 0.5 per cent zinc sulphate mixed with 0.25 per cent calcium hydroxide are often used to treat the deficiency.

Mishra (2001) studied the salt tolerance of chickpea cultivars due to zinc application and found that zinc resulted in improved grain formation and narrowed down the Na/K and Na/Ca, Na/Ca=Mg ratio and induced salt tolerance in the crop.

Khan, *et al.* (2003) reported that under rainfed conditions, application of zinc increased the vegetative growth, yields and water use efficiency in chickpea.

Hafiz (2004) reported that effect of the biofertilizer, phosphorin (phosphate-dissolving bacteria) and foliar spraying of chelated Zn (0, 400 or 800 mg kg^{-1} as 14 per cent Zn EDTA) on the yield, yield components and quality of chickpea grown on newly reclaimed sandy soil. The application of phosphorin significantly enhanced the evaluated parameters except the number of seeds pod^{-1}, increase plant height, number of branches, number of pods, seed $plant^{-1}$, weight of pods and seed $plant^{-1}$, 100 seed weight, number of seed pod^{-1}, biological yields and seed protein contents of chickpea. The foliar application of chelated Zn upto 800 mg kg^{-1} significantly improved the yield attributes, seed, yields, and quality.

Karwasra and Anil Kumar (2007) observed that application of P and Zn increased yield attributes like: number of secondary branches $plant^{-1}$, dry matter weight and uptake of P and Zn of chickpea.

Among the micronutrients, zinc is most important and its deficiency is widespread throughout the country. Dhane (2011) reported that Inceptisols, Entisols, Adisols, Alfisols Mollisols of Haryana 61 per cent, Punjab 47 per cent and UP 45 per cent and Vertisols, Alfisols, Inceptisols and Ultisols of Madhya Pradesh, Tamilnadu, Andhra Pradesh 51-63 per cent, Bihar 52 per cent were deficient in zinc. The incidence of these deficiencies is on increase with time. The zinc fertilization is therefore essential to sustainable crop production.

Boron

Harris and Gilman (1950) observed marked increase in the yield of groundnut by application of boron as borax. This increase in yield besides other factors was due to increase in nodulation and chlorophyll content of leaves.

Knowledge of status and distribution of boron in soils is essential for proper management of soils with regard to its deficiency, sufficiency or toxicity. The range of its sufficiency is very narrow and its application in the form of fertilizer is still not in vogue. The toxic concentration of boron has been found to occur either naturally in arid region (Reeve *et al.* 1955) or may develop due to long term use of irrigation water containing high amounts of boron (Singh and Kanwar, 1963).

Ashokan and Raj (1974) reported that increased level of boron fertilization *i.e.* 0, 0.3, 0.6 and 0.8 mg kg^{-1} B ha^{-1} increased the plant height, nodulation and yield of groundnut.

Role of boron in plant nutrition is of vital importance. Its deficiency retards meristematric activity and causes the death of growing apices of stem and root, inhibits the assimilation of calcium, retards the formation of root nodules in leguminous plants, causes stunted growth, inhibits the bud formation and development of new leaves and finally causes the death of plant. These effects of boron deficiency are attributed to its effect on protein synthesis. Deficiency of boron in fleshy organs causes browning of internal tissues causing brown heart in vegetables. The dry heart rot of sugarbeet, internal browning and cork formation in apples and the brown areas in cauliflower are the other examples of boron deficiency (Kochher, 1977).

Katyal and Randhawa (1983) worked out the critical limits of boron as 0.5 B mg kg^{-1} soil for deficiency, 0.5 mg to 1.0 mg kg^{-1} for medium and above 1.0 mg kg^{-1} for sufficiency. They reported that about 17 per cent of irrigated soils were deficient in boron. The values for rainfed were 61, 36 and 3 per cent.

Dugger (1983) observed that legumes require higher amounts of boron that non-legume crops. Under boron deficiency, the leaves have low sink activity and accumulation of simple sugars due to failure of synthesis of higher carbohydrates and retarded lignifications of plants. Decrease in RNA concentration and increase RNAase activity were also observed due to boron deficiency.

Saxena and Mehrotra (1984) observed the response of applied boron on groundnut and noted that plant concentration and dry matter yields were increased in normal soils. The results were marked when applied with P and Ca.

Boron deficiency is of great concern in the areas receiving plentiful rainfall while toxicity may be a problem in the soils of arid region. Its toxicity appears to be associated mostly with the use of irrigation water high in B content (Keren and Bigham, 1985).

Marschner (1986) reported that boron availability in soil is related to soil pH, being most available in acid soils. When pH is increased by liming boron availability is decreased being the lowest between pH 7 and 9. The element is fixed or bound by soil colloids as the pH increases, resulting in lime-induced deficiency. Boron is also absorbed by humus and organic matter which serves as the major reservoir of boron in many soils. The availability of boron is also impaired by long dry spells. Deficiencies are common calcareous Aridisol and neutral to alkaline soils that are high in pH.

Das (1988) further classified the nutrients according to their biochemical functions, and placed P, B and sodium tetraborate ($Na_2B_4O_7.5H_2O$ in one group and the select biochemical roles of three nutrients is esterification with negative alcohol groups in plants. The phosphate esters are involved in energy transfer reactions. The role of boron was underlined in causing the mobility and availability of calcium and keeping K/Ca ratio within appropriate range. It helps in the absorption of nitrogen, causes precipitation of excess cations, buffering action, regulation of the other nutrients, development of new meristematic cell, proper pollination and fruit setting, augmenting translocation of sugars, starches, phosphate amino acid synthesis and protein formation, helps in the formation and development of nodules in leguminous plants.

Gupta (1993) reported that boron availability is influenced by soil characteristics, crop and cropping system.

Tisdale *et al.* (1993) described the various aspects of soil boron. It was expressed that boron is the only non-metal among the micronutrients. It occurs in concentration in the earth crest and in most igneous rocks upto 10 mg kg^{-1} to 100 mg kg^{-1}, present mainly in clay minerals. Less than 5 per cent of total boron in soils is available to plants. Release of boron is quite slow. Increasing B deficiency suggests that it is incapable of supplying B matching to plant requirement under prolonged heavy cropping. Boron toxicity is uncommon in most arable soils, unless it is added in excessive amounts in fertilizers. The availability and movement of boron is influenced by soil texture, amount and type of clay, pH, liming organic matter and interrelationship with other elements. The most common fertilizer of B is sodium tetra borate ($Na_2B_4O_7.5H_2O$). Boron can be applied as spray or dust directly to foliage, broadcast or band placement. The general recommendation of B application in different crops varies from 0.5 to 3 kg ha^{-1}.

According to Tiwari (1995) boron is such a micronutrient that is required in very low concentration and its amount is very low in soil and plant. Generally 1 mg kg^{-1} of boron is considered sufficient for plants. Any excess than 2 mg kg^{-1} in plants becomes toxic. However, the toxic concentration differs in different crops. Plants absorb boron in the form of borate ion. With regards to its metabolic functions, boron is not a constituent of any enzyme but is known to activate several metabolic enzymes like: catalase, oxidase, peroxidase, sucrose and other enzymes related to protein and carbohydrate metabolism specially redox enzymes. Role of boron is less understood because of the lack of suitable isotope. Water absorption, ionion transportation and uptake and many other processes are governed by boron. Synthesis of nucleic acid and pectic substances of cell wall as well as phosphate utilization are accelerated by boron.

New alluvial soils of north Bihar, soils of Himachal Pradesh, Punjab, Haryana, Uttar Pradesh, red soils and yellow soils of Orissa arc specially in the grip of boron deficiency. On the other hand in some parts of Haryana, Punjab and Rajasthan the soils contain toxic concentration of boron. In the areas of low and deficient rainfall the well waters contain such a high concentration of boron, that the wells and bore well waters become unfit for irrigation. (Tiwari, 1995).

Sakal *et al.* (1996) reported the optimum dose of B in calcarious and heavy textured soils in the range of 1.5 to 2.0 kg ha^{-1} and in light soils it varied from 1.0 to 1.5 kg ha^{-1}. Borax was suitable for soil application and boric acid for foliar spray. Among pulses, chickpea was highly responsive to B application, with an average increase in yield of 5.4 q ha^{-1}. Other pulse crops had lentil 2.6 q ha^{-1} black gram 2.7 q ha^{-1} pigeon pea 3.4 q ha^{-1} Soil application of borax and foliar spray of boric acid in these crops was suitable. Available B in post harvest soil increased with increasing B levels. Foliar spray of 0.2 and 0.4 per cent boric acid solution was optimum for lentil crop.

Das (1999) reported that boron in small concentrations was essential for plant but its presence in higher concentration in irrigation water was detrimental to plants. Irrigation water with 100 mg kg^{-1} boron was the safe limit for several crops.

Tandon (2002) reported that B content of Indian soils ranges from 16 mg kg^{-1} to 630 mg kg^{-1}, with an average of 38 mg kg^{-1}. Available B is generally 0.5 per cent of total B. High boron content is found in arid and semi-arid soils, particularly those suffering from salinity and alkalinity, where it can reach harmful toxic levels. Boron occurs in organic and mineral forms, both of which are in equilibrium with each other. Being an anion it can easily be leached out from soil, making arid soils prone to B deficiency. Boron deficiency is of wide occurrence in Bihar, Karnataka, Madhya

Pradesh, Uttar Pradesh and West Bengal. Light acidic soils are susceptible to B deficiency, which can be overcome by spraying of Borax in the concentration of 0.1 to 0.2 per cent, on leaves. Problem of B deficiency is more acute in Tarai regions.

Asad *et al.* (2002) conducted experiment in green gram sunflower cropping system in black soil fertilized by fertilizer alone and in combination with manure might have influence on available B. As boron is an essential micronutrient its response was reflected on the growth flowering and seed setting of sunflower. Boron availability is maintained for long periods in soils receiving FYM or B with fertilizer. Further, soil characteristics *viz*; organic carbon, cation exchange capacity and $CaCO_3$ had significant influence, shown by significant positive correlation coefficients in controlling the B availability, (Murthy, 2006).

Chaudhary and Shukla (2004) studied the boron status of Rajasthan soils and observed that boric acid (H_3BO_3) is the main constituent of soluble B in soils. This form of B is present in non-ionised product in soil solution, and is leached easily from soil under humid condition. The availability of B is greatly influenced by pH, EC, organic carbon, texture, free Fe and Al oxides and calcium content. Super availability of B in irrigated soils of Western Rajasthan was observed. In rainfed soils the availability was much less than irrigated soils, but in former case B was present at toxic level.

Arora *et al.* (2004) reported the effect of ionic strength of NaCl and $CaCl_2$ electrolytes and observed that boron adsorption increased with increase in ionic strength of supporting electrolytic solution in soils of North-Western India. Berger and Pratt (1963) reported that the major part of boron in soil is associated with organic matter in tightly bound compounds which is released in available form by microbial action.

Ceyhan, *et al.* (2007) tried 4 levels of boron 0, 1, 3, 6 kg B ha^{-1} in soils deficient in B (0.19 mg B kg^{-1}) on chickpea cultivars. The results showed that plant height, pods $plant^{-1}$, grain yield, protein content, protein yield, thousand seed weight and leaf B concentration, the grain yield of genotypes increased significantly. The yield and yield attributing characters were increased significantly by correcting B deficiency.

The pH is the most important factor affecting B adsorption in soils, with increasing soil solution pH, B fixation also increases and maximum adsorption is near pH 8 to 9, further increase in solution pH decreases the adsorption. Boron adsorption surfaces in the soil are oxides, clay minerals, calcium carbonate and organic matter (Goldberg 2007).

Guhey *et al.* (2008) observed the effect of boron on the germination, nodulation, flower drop and yield of chickpea genotypes was studied at Varanasi, Uttar Pradesh, India during 1996-97. Boron as a basal application of borax 10 kg ha^{-1} and foliar application of boric acid at 300 mg kg^{-1} ha^{-1} at pre flowering stage was given. Germination, chlorophyll content, nodulation, flower drop and seed yield was established. The results showed that boron spray reduced the flower drop and increased the pod setting contributing to higher yields.

Gitanjali *et al.* (2010) reported that boron deficient plants exhibited visible deficiency systems in addition to reduced number of pods and seeds resulting in lowered biomass and economic yield. Boron deficiency lowered the B concentration in leaves and seeds, photosynthesis pigments, hill reaction activity, starch (in leaves and seeds) and protein and protein-N (in seeds), whereas phenols sugars (in leaves and seeds) and non protein-N (in seeds) were elevated. The specific activity of acid peroxidase (POX) increased in leaves and pod wall and decreased in seeds, while activity of acid phosphate and ribonuclease were stimulated in leaves, seeds and pod wall in B-deficient chickpea.

Saleem *et al.* (2011) reported that boron is unique, not only in its chemical properties, but also in its roles in biology. Since boron discovery as essential plant nutrient, the importance of B element as an agricultural chemical has grown very rapidly and its availability in soil and irrigation water is an important determinant of agricultural production. Boron deficiency is the most common and widespread micronutrient deficiency problem, which impairs plant growth and reduces yield. Normal healthy plant growth requires a continuous supply of B, once it is taken up and used in the plant; it is not translocated from old to new tissue. That is why, deficiency symptoms starts with the youngest growing tissues. Therefore, adequate B supply is necessary for obtaining high yields and good quality of agriculture crops.

Plants respond to the B concentration which is present in soil solution as a primarily uncharged boric acid H_3BO_3. Generally it is absorbed as molecular boric acid in a physical process regulated by the diffusion due to differences in B content (Bingham *et al.* 1981). Plant B uptake is correlated with the concentration of H_3BO_3 in soil solution because leaf B increased in a linear fashion as the B concentration of the nutrient solution increased (Tariq *et al.* 2005). Boric acid uptake by the roots is carried out by different molecular mechanisms (Tanaka and Fujiwara, 2008). Boron uptake is a passive processes B transport rate is in proportion to the concentration gradients. This is due to the high permeability of boric acid to lipid bilayers because boric acid is a non-charged molecule (Brown and Shelp, 1997). After taken up by roots, B is loaded to xylem for upward transport to shoots. The long distance translocation of solutes in the xylem depends on transpiration as B is transported along the transpiration streams. This long distance transport has been considered passive because B accumulates at the site of high transpiration rate such as: margins of large mature leaves (Brown and Shelp, 1997).

It was also found that B concentration in young leaves was higher than that of old leaves in these plant species (Brown and Shelp, 1997; Brown and Hu, 1998). This pattern of distribution cannot be explained by B distribution along transpiration stream. These species commonly produce a significant amount of sugar alcohols including mannitol and sorbitol and use them for the phloem translocation of photosynthate, in place of sucrose. Sugar alcohols contain cis-hydroxyl groups, and thus, it can readily bind to boric acid (poly- B complex) and is likely to allow B to be transported through the phloem (Brown *et al.*, 1999). Recent evidences suggest that non-sugar alcohol producing plants can transport boric acid to young tissues, including arabidopsis, canola and sunflower (Takano *et al.* 2001; Noguchi *et al.* 2000). This translocation was detected under B limitation, but not under conditions of normal B supply. It can be concluded that even plants without the capacity to synthesize sugar alcohols have mechanisms to transport B to sink tissues. Boron transporters and channels may be involved in this translocation (Stangolius *et al.* 2001).

Boron concentration in the soil solution is controlled by B adsorption reactions. These reactions restrict the amount of water-soluble B available for plant uptake, because plants respond directly to the B concentration in soil solution and only indirectly to the amount of B attached to soil surfaces. Thus, the soil adsorption complex acts as both a source and a sink for dissolved B (Chen *et al.* 2002; Keren and Bingham 1985). The pH is the most important factor affecting B adsorption in soils, with increasing soil solution pH, B fixation also increases and maximum adsorption is near pH 8 to 9, further increase in solution pH decreases the adsorption. Boron adsorption surfaces in the soil are oxides, clay minerals, calcium carbonate and organic matter (Goldberg 2007).

Soil Factors Affecting B Availability to Plants: Boron nutrition to crop is influenced by many soil and plant factors. Among the most important are soil pH, soil texture, organic matter, soil moisture, lime application and plant physiological factors.

Plant Factors Affecting B Availability: Plant species exhibit a wide range of response to B. Cruciferous crops is very responsive to fertilization. Dicotyledonous crops have higher B requirement than monocotyledonous. Boron uptake is a passive process, after taken up by roots; it is loaded to xylem for upward transport to shoots. The long distance translocation of solutes in the xylem depends on transpiration, and B is transported along the transpiration streams (Brown and Shelp 1997).

Plants are classified into two categories; one category includes species with restricted B mobility and other one with significant mobility. In the former case, water is the translocation agent for the movement of B. The B uptake is proportional to its concentration and water flow. In the later case, B shows rapid and significant phloem mobility in species for which sorbitol is the primary photosynthetic product (Brown and Hu, 1998). The pattern of B concentration in plants and symptoms of B deficiency or toxicity are correlated with leaf ventilation. Boron in leaves can be mobile and accumulated at the sites of the termination of leaf veins (Matoh and Ochiai, 2005). Boron may react with organic compounds which prevent its translocation to other tissues. Plant ability to adopt at high or low concentrations of B may depend on the germplasma, physiological mechanisms and genetic diversity of species (Bolanos *et al.* 2004).

Molybdenum

Deo, *et al.* (2002) a field experiment was laid out during three consecutive years of 1997-98 to 1999-2000 on loamy sand soil (typic ustipsamment) of the state of

Rajasthan in India in rabi season to investigate the effect of modes of application and different levels of molybdenum (Mo) on grain yield, protein content and number of nodules plant^{-1} of chickpea *Cicer arietinum* L.; Variety RSG-44). Doses applied were: 0.5, 1.0 and 1.5 kg Mo ha^{-1} as ammonium molybdate for soil application, and 1.75, 3.5 and 5.25 g sodium molybdate kg^{-1} seed for seed treatment. The six treatments with one control were replicated thrice in a randomized block design. The physicochemical characteristics of the soil were: pH-8.1, EC 0.11 dSm^{-1} and OC 0.12 per cent. Available N, P and K were 158, 20 and 216 kg ha^{-1}, respectively. The Mo status of soil was 0.06 mg kg^{-1}. The three years' pooled data revealed that application of Mo either by soil application or through seed treatment, significantly increased the grain yield of chickpea. Soil application of 1.0 kg Mo ha^{-1} and seed treatment with 3.5 g sodium molybdate kg^{-1} seed increased the grain yield by 13.13 per cent and 16.76 per cent over the yields 24.4 and 24.5 q ha^{-1}, respectively at lower doses while it was at par with yields at higher doses of Mo. Protein content of grain, number of nodules plant^{-1} of chickpea and available nitrogen in soil also increased with increasing doses of Mo under both the modes of application.

Gupta, *et al.* (2012) a field experiment was conducted during rabi 2007-08 and 2008-09 in a medium black soil to study the effect of molybdenum and iron in combination with *Rhizobium* and PSB inoculation on 'JG-130' variety of chickpea (*Cicer arietinum* L.). Eight treatment combinations comprising recommended dose of fertilizers (RDF as control), RDF+ *Rhizobium* + Phosphate solubilizing bacteria (PSB), RDF + *Rhizobium* + PSB + 0.5 and 1 kg ammonium molybdate (AM) ha^{-1} as soil application, RDF + *Rhizobium* + PSB + 0.5 and 1.0 g AM kg^{-1} seed as seed treatment, RDF + *Rhizobium* + PSB + 1.0 g FeSO4 + 0.5 and 1.0 g AM kg^{-1} of seed as seed treatment were tried in RBD with three replications. Application of AM either as soil application or through seed treatment in combination with *Rhizobium* + PSB + RDF significantly increased number and dry weight of nodule, branch plant^{-1}, plant height, flowers and pods plant^{-1}, N and P uptake, chlorophyll content in leaves and protein content in chickpea over control (RDF alone). Soil application of 1.0 kg AM ha^{-1} along with *Rhizobium* + PSB + RDF and seed treatment with 1.0 g AM kg^{-1} seed along with *Rhizobium* + PSB + RDF also increased the grain yield by 39.9 and 32.4 per cent respectively over RDF alone (1253 kg ha^{-1}); and both of these treatments on AM were statistically on par. However, seed treatment of 1.0 g AM along with *Rhizobium* + PSB + RDF was found to be highly remunerative and viable as compared to others.

Nadia Gad; and M.R. Abd El-Moez (2013) two field experiments were carried out to evaluate the effect of different levels of molybdenum on nodules efficiency, growth, yield quantity and quality of cowpea plants. The experiments were conducted at Research and Production station, National Research Centre, EL- Nobaria site, Beheara Governorate, Delta Egypt, under drip irrigation system during 2011 and 2012 seasons. The obtained results are summarized in the following: Molybdenum enhance cowpea root nodules efficiency, growth, minerals composition, yield quantity and quality compared with control plants. Molybdenum at 16 mg kg^{-1} resulted in maximum growth, nodules number and weight, nitrogenase activity, pods and seeds yield as well as nutritional and chemical content. Increasing molybdenum levels more than 16 mg kg^{-1} decreased the molybdenum promotive effect on cowpea.

Zinc, Boron and Molybdenum Interaction

Singh *et al.* (1988) reported that fertilizer is now widely used in dry land areas. The crops grown in Alfisols and Vertisols respond to moderate doses of phosphorus and some micronutrients including boron. It is important that the amount applied and their ratios with nitrogen and phosphorus are the major issues, in the above conditions.

Tandon, H.L.S. (1992) in India agriculturally important interactions include: $N_X P$, $P_X K$, P_X Ca (lime), $P_X S$, $P_X Zn$, $P_X Fe$, $P_X Mn$, $P_X Cu$, $P_X B$ and $P_X Mo$.

Brady (1995) reported has significant role in plant metabolism. It activates dehydrogenase enzymes vital for translocation of sugars, synthesis of nucleic acidic and plant hormone.

Tiwari and Tiwari (1996) reported that boron plays a key role in the development of root nodule in legume crops. The plants are not the able to utilize nitrogen under boron deficiency the plant nutrient transport system does not work well under suboptimal leaf tissue level of boron. It also regulate K/Ca ratio and calcium uptake is hampered due to deficiency of boron. In light acidic soils B deficiency can be overcome by spray of borax in the concentration of 0.16 to 0.20 per cent leaves. Problem of B deficiency is more acutic in Trari regions.

The high intensity cropping through improved production technology and use of high analysis fertilizers has rendered the soil prone to deficiencies of single or multiple micronutrients. Pulse crops are respond well to application of micronutrients like: Zn, B, Mo and Fe. Each and every micronutrient has an essential role in growth, grain yield and quality (protein content) of pulse crop (Thyiyagarajan *et al.* 2003).

Shil, N.C. *et al.* (2007) field experiments on chickpea (cv. BARI Chola-5) were carried out in calcareous dark grey floodplain soil under AEZ 11 at Jessore and non calcareous grey floodplain soil under AEZ 13 at Rahmatpur during the rabi season of 2001-2002 and 2002-2003. The objective was to find out the optimum dose of boron and molybdenum for yield maximization. Four levels each of boron (0, 1, 2 and 2.5 kg ha^{-1}) and molybdenum (0, 1, 1.5 and 2 kg ha^{-1}) along with a blanket dose of $N_{20} P_{25} K_{35} S_{20} Zn_2$ kg ha^{-1} and cowdung 5 t ha^{-1} were applied in this study. The combination of $B_{2.5} Mo_{1.5}$ kg ha^{-1} and $B_{2.5} Mo_1$ kg ha^{-1} produced significantly higher yield in both the years of study at Jessore and Rahmatpur, respectively. The said treatments produced the highest mean yields of 2.10 and 1.49 t ha^{-1} for Jessore and Rahmatpur, respectively, which was around 53 per cent higher over control ($B_0 M_0$). The combined application of both boron and molybdenum were found superior to their single application even though boron played major role in augmenting the yield. However, from the regression analysis, the optimum treatment combination was calculated as $B_{2.34} Mo_{1.44}$ kg ha^{-1} for Jessore and $B_{2.20} Mo_{1.29}$ kg ha^{-1} for Rahmatpur.

Bozoglu *et al.* (2007) a field experiment was conducted in Amasya conditions in Northern Turkey for two years in order to determine the effect of zinc and molybdenum fertilization on chickpea following a completely randomized block design with three replications. Doses of zinc (Zn_0 : 0, Zn_1 : 1 mg kg^{-1}, Zn_2 : 2 mg kg^{-1}) and molybdenum (Mo_0 : 0, Mo_1 : 0.05 mg kg^{-1}, Mo_2 : 0.1 mg kg^{-1}) were applied on leaf when the plants were in vegetative stage. Variation of years on all investigated characters was statistically significant. Applied zinc or molybdenum failed to show any significant effect on any parameter. It was found that effect of Zn × Mo interaction was statistically significant ($p < 0.01$) on the seed yield. The highest seed yield resulted from Zn_2 (2 mg kg^{-1}) × Mo_0 interaction. This was followed by Zn_1 (1 mg kg^{-1}) × Mo_1 (0.05 mg kg^{-1}) and Zn_1 × Mo_2 doses showing no statistical differences from each other.

Srinivasarao, *et al.* (2008) observed that little attention had been paid to the diagnosis of deficiencies of micronutrients such as: Zinc and Boron and secondary nutrients such as: sulphur in rainfed systems. The authors evaluated Zn, B and S status of 1617 farmers' fields in 14 districts of semiarid tropical India. The results showed that most of the soil samples were low to medium in organic carbon contents. The zinc deficiency ranged from 2 to 100 per cent, B deficiency ranged from 0 to 100 per cent and S deficiency ranged from 40 to 100 per cent. On farm trials were conducted to study the responses of rainfed crops to Zn, B and S application and the residual effects of B and S. Significant responses in finger millets, maize, sunflower, soybean, groundnut and chickpea to application of Zn, B and S were observed.

Valenciano *et al.* (2010) Spain is the main chickpea (*Cicer arietinum*) producing country in Europe, despite there are few studies on micronutrient application to chickpea. The response of chickpea to the applications of Zn, B and Mo was studied in pot experiments with natural conditions and acidic soils in northwest Spain from 2006 to 2008 following a factorial statistical pattern (5 × 2 × 2) with three replicates. Five concentrations of Zn (0, 1, 2, 4 and 8 mg Zn pot^{-1}), two concentrations of B (0 and 2 mg B pot^{-1}), and two concentrations of Mo (0 and 2 mg Mo pot^{-1}) were added to the pots. Chickpea responded to the Zn, B and Mo applications. There were differences between soils. The mature plants fertilized with Zn, with B and with Mo had a greater total dry matter production. Harvest Index (HI) improved with the Zn application and with the Mo application. The highest HI was obtained with the Zn_4× B_2 × Mo_2 treatment 60.30 per cent while the smallest HI was obtained with the Zn_0 × B_0 × Mo_0 treatment 47.65 per cent. The Zn, B and Mo applications improved seed yield, mainly due to the number of pods per plant. This was the yield component that had the most influence on, and the most correlation with seed yield. The highest seed yield was obtained from the Zn_4 × B_2 × Mo_2 treatment 4.00 g plant^{-1} while the lowest was obtained from the Zn_0 × B_0 × Mo_0 treatment 2.31 g plant^{-1}. There was a low interaction between the three micronutrients. The Zn application was more efficient when it was applied with both B and Mo.

Abraham and Abraham (2011) field experiments were conducted during the rabi seasons of 2003-04 and 2004-05 at Allahabad, Uttar Pradesh, to evaluate the effect of different methods of P application, bioinoculants and micronutrients (Mo + B) on growth and yield of kabuli chickpea (*Cicer kabulium*) var. Pragati. The experiments were laid out in split-split plot design with three replications. Main plot consisted of four different methods of P application, sub-plots consisted of bioinoculants and sub-sub-plots comprised of micronutrients. The experimental results revealed that Band placement (basal) recorded significantly higher dry weight 30.04 g plant^{-1}, pods plant^{-1} 47.95, pod yield 12.01 g plant^{-1}, seed weight plant^{-1} (13.09 g) and seed yield 35.03 q ha^{-1}. Among the bio-inoculants, the performance of dual inoculation of Trichoderma + PSB was the best having recorded significantly superior growth, yield attributes and yield. Increase in grain yield in Trichoderma + PSB was 10.75 per cent and 12.79 per cent over single inoculation of Trichoderma and PSB. Application of molybdenum + boron also significantly influenced nodulation 23.1 and 32.9 at 60 and 80 DAS, dry weight 32.0 g plant^{-1}, yield attributes and yield 32.72 q ha^{-1}.

Valenciano *et al.* (2011) in Spain Europe's leading chickpea producing country chickpea (*Cicer arietinum*) is mainly cultivated on non-irrigated soils with low native fertility. This study was carried out from 2006 to 2008 in the province of Leon, Spain, under acid soil field conditions, with the aim of determining whether the application of zinc (Zn), boron (B) and molybdenum (Mo) improved chickpea growth and yield on acid soils. A split-split-plot design with three replications was used. Chickpea responded only to the Zn and Mo applications. At maturity, plants fertilized with Zn and with Mo had a greater total dry matter production and seed yield, mainly due to an increment in pod dry matter. For Zn, the highest yield was obtained with 2 mg Zn plant^{-1} (6.80 g plant^{-1}) whereas for Mo the highest yield was obtained with 1 mg Mo plant^{-1} (6.73 g plant^{-1}). Interaction was observed between B and Mo, interpreted as indicating that Mo can counteract the effect of B application.

Quddus *et al.* (2011) an experiment was carried out in Calcareous Low Ganges River Floodplain Soil (AEZ 12) at Pulses Research Sub-Station (PRSS), Madaripur during Kharif I of 2008 and 2009.The objectives were to evaluate the effect of zinc (Zn) and boron (B) on the yield and yield contributing characters of mungbean (*Vigna radiata* L. Wilczek) and to find out the optimum dose of Zn and B for yield maximization. There were four levels of zinc 0, 0.75, 1.5, and 3.0 kg ha^{-1} and boron 0, 0.5, 1.0, and 2 kg ha^{-1} along with a blanket dose of $N_{20} P_{25} K_{35} S_{20}$ kg ha^{-1}. The experiment was laid out in RCBD with three replications. Results showed that the combination of $Zn_{1.5}B_{1.0}$ produced significantly higher yield 3058 kg ha^{-1} and 2631 kg ha^{-1}, in the year 2008 and 2009, respectively. The lowest yield 2173 kg ha^{-1} and 1573 kg ha^{-1}, were found in control (Zn_0B_0) combination. The combined application of zinc and boron were observed superior to their single application in both the years. Therefore, the combination of $Zn_{1.5}B_{1.0}$ might be considered as suitable dose for mungbean cultivation in Bangladesh. But from regression analysis, the optimum treatment combination was $Zn_{1.87}$ $B_{1.24}$ kg ha^{-1} for Madaripur.

Das *et al.* (2012) the field investigation was carried out to improve the inoculated *Rhizobium* efficiency by applying different micronutrients on nodulation, growth and uptake of N and P and yield of chickpea during *Rabi* seasons of 2006-07 at the Crop Research Centre, G. B. Pant University of Agriculture and Technology, Pantnagar. Fourteen treatments consisting combinations of micronutrients *viz;* Zinc, Boron and Molybdenum, with and without *Rhizobium* sp. inoculation, were laid out in randomized block design (RBD) in triplicates. *Rhizobium* sp. inoculation gave significant increases of 33.72, 26.11 and 4.56 per cent in nodule dry weight and 15.59, 14.25 and 1.90 per cent in plant dry weight at 45, 75 and 120 DAS, respectively. Among the two levels of $ZnSO_4$, 25 kg $ZnSO_4$ ha^{-1} was found superior to 10 kg $ZnSO_4$ ha^{-1} for different studied parameters. Application of 10 kg Borax ha^{-1} was found better than 5 kg Borax ha^{-1} for chickpea. Seed treatment of Mo with 0.5 kg Na_2MoO_4 ha^{-1} was found sufficient to meet the crop need. *Rhizobium* inoculation in combination with different micronutrients recorded higher nodulation, plant dry weight, grain and straw yield and uptake of N and P than the treatments of only micronutrients or *Rhizobium* alone. The highest nodule dry weight of 235, 616 and 1476 mg $plant^{-1}$ was recorded with treatment of 5 kg Borax ha^{-1} + *Rhizobium* at 45, 75 and 120 DAS, respectively. The treatment with 0.5 kg Na_2MoO_4 ha^{-1} + *Rhizobium* gave the highest plant dry weight of 4.22, 9.12 and 11.35 g $plant^{-1}$ at 45, 75 and 120 DAS, respectively. The highest grain yield of 2977 kg ha^{-1} and straw yield 7111 kg ha^{-1} was recorded due to inoculation with *Rhizobium* + 10 kg Borax ha^{-1} and *Rhizobium* + 5 kg Borax ha^{-1}, respectively. Significant variations in total N and P uptake due to *Rhizobium* inoculation and application of micronutrients were also observed and it varied from 122.83 kg ha^{-1} and 10.67 kg ha^{-1} in uninoculated control to 203.90 kg ha^{-1} and 22.02 kg ha^{-1} in 5 kg Borax ha^{-1} + *Rhizobium*, respectively.

Pingoliya *et al.* (2014) the role of micronutrients in crops is well known in the present context. Research already proved the micronutrient deficiency in various crops as well as in the human beings and which results as drastic reduction in crop yield. Chickpea is an important grain legume crop in the world, and being a rich and cheap source of protein can help people to improve the nutritional quality of their diets. It is also the premier food legume crop in India, ranks first among all pulse crops. Iron (Fe) play vital role in several enzymatic reactions and metabolism in plants. A little amount of Fe enhanced the chickpea yield and quality. Application of Fe fertilizer for crop production also reduces the malnourishment in human and animals. At present, more emphasis is on biofortification aspect through agronomic as well as breeding techniques. Application of Fe fertilizer in chickpea crop production may be a better sustainable option to overcome these problems in the future. This review article described the Fe role in yield, quality and nutrient uptake by chickpea.

Khan *et al.* (2014) the present study was based on the hypothesis that the applied molybdenum and iron influence the nodulation, nitrogen fixation and yield by chickpea genotypes. For this purpose a field experiment was conducted to study the influence of different levels of molybdenum and iron on the nodulation, nitrogen fixation and yield of chickpea genotypes (*Cicer arietinum* L.) growing two different genotypes such as: Desi (Sheenghar) and Kabuli (Karak-II) during, 2011-12 at Malakandher Farm, The University of Agriculture, Peshawar. Different levels of molybdenum and iron were applied at the rate of 0, 0.25 and 0.50 and 0, 2 and 5.0 kg ha^{-1}, respectively along with a basal dose of 25 N, 60 P_2O_5 and 60 K_2O in randomized complete block design with split plot arrangement and replicated three times. Results revealed that maximum yield and yield parameters, numbers of root nodules and nitrogen concentration were observed in those treatment plots where Mo 0.5 and Fe 2.0 kg ha^{-1} were applied simultaneously for both genotypes. The grain yield, nodulation and nitrogen concentration were recorded significantly more in Kabuli (Karak-II) as compared to Desi (Sheenghar) of chickpea genotypes, perhaps due to the formation of maximum nodulation and nitrogen concentration by plants. Results revealed that with increasing the levels of Mo and Fe in soil, the concentration of Fe and N in plant leaves were significantly increased in both genotypes at flowering stage. Moreover, in the present study the number of nodules were correlated with N concentration of plants for both genotypes and found as the nodules formation increases the plant N concentration linearly increased and showed close relationship with one another. Similarly, the Fe-concentration increases in plant leaves, N-concentration also increases in a similar fashion, indicated that Fe-played a vital role in N-fixation by chickpea genotypes. The present study suggests that the application of Mo 0.5 and Fe 2.0 kg ha^{-1} is important which play a significant role in getting the maximum yield, nodules and nitrogen concentration in chickpea genotypes.

METHODOLOGY OF NUTRIENTS APPLICATION

The relevant information regarding the materials used and methodology adopted to carry out the present investigation on envisaged programme are given below:

Experimental Site

A field experiment was conducted at Agricultural Research Farm, Rajaula of Mahatma Gandhi Chitrakoot Gramodaya Vishwavidyalaya Chitrakoot, Satna (M.P.) during 2012-13 and 2013-14 Rabi season.

Geographical Situation

Geographically, Chitrakoot is situated at 25°15' to 25°15' North latitude 80°52' East longitude. The altitude of place is nearly 190-210 meter above mean sea level.

Meteorological Characteristics

The climatic conditions are semi-arid with extremes of summer and winter. The average minimum temperature prevails around 4.5°C to 5.0°C and maximum temperature is averaged between 46°C and 47°C. The annual rain fall average is about 950 mm with major precipitation between first week of October to last week of April. Chitrakoot spreads over a total geographic area of 14345 ha and is located in Kymore Plateau in Madhya Pradesh. The main geographic units are hills, pediments, alluvial plain, ravines, etc. Within pediments a number of rocky hills are also found Table 3.1(a) and Fig. 3.1(a) and Table 3.1(b) and Fig. 3.1(b).

Soil Characteristics of the Experimental Field

Random soil samples were collected from the experimental field to a depth of 0-15 cm prior to sowing of chickpea crop. The composite soil sample was analyzed for its physico-chemical properties. The detail physico-chemical properties of experimental field are given in Table 3.2.

Climate and Weather

Table 3.1(a): Meteorological conditions during experimental period in Rabi season (2012-13)

Months	S.W.	Minimum Temp. (°C)	Maximum Temp. (°C)	Relative Humidity Average (%)	Rainfall (mm)
October 2012	42	16.58	32.17	62.21	0.00
	43	30.57	31.64	60.35	0.00
November	44	11.85	29.28	61.71	0.00
	45	10.35	28.81	59.06	0.00
	46	9.67	27.60	60.35	0.00
	47	8.42	27.25	58.78	0.00
December	48	7.00	26.21	59.06	0.00
	49	6.24	26.90	57.21	0.00
	50	11.25	26.37	68.49	0.25
	51	5.08	22.62	64.64	0.00
	52	3.54	19.51	73.28	0.25
January 2013	1	3.30	19.41	67.71	0.00
	2	2.52	21.58	62.99	0.00
	3	9.87	25.47	65.92	0.00
	4	1.42	20.60	64.50	0.00
February	5	4.68	24.18	61.28	0.00
	6	8.85	24.45	66.64	8.75
	7	11.18	23.50	74.00	61.75
	8	10.28	24.98	69.78	7.50
March	9	11.14	27.63	62.43	0.00
	10	10.23	30.67	56.57	0.00
	11	15.29	32.84	55.14	1.25
	12	15.71	34.41	51.56	4.50
	13	16.74	33.10	57.49	3.25
April	14	15.95	35.74	43.93	0.00
	15	20.98	38.80	34.71	0.00

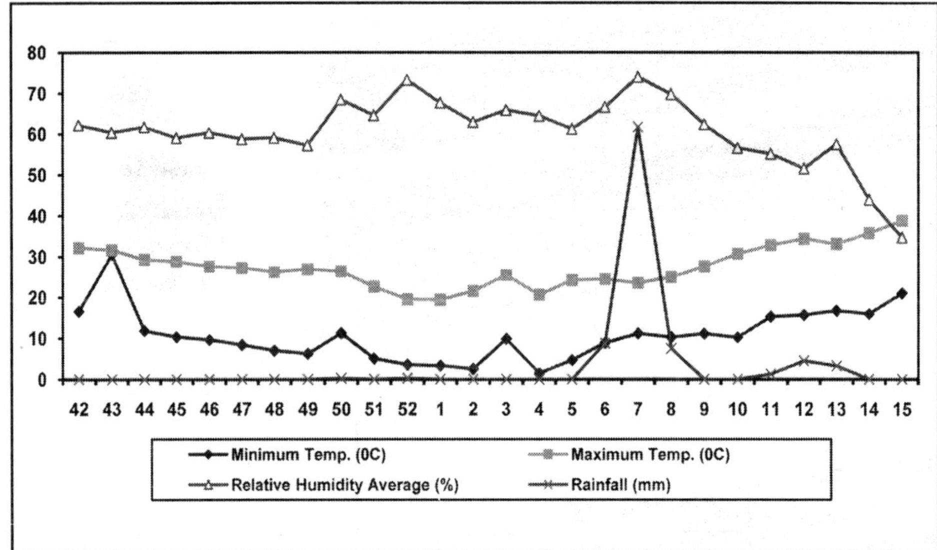

Fig. 3.1(a): Meteorological conditions during experimental period in Rabi season 2012-13

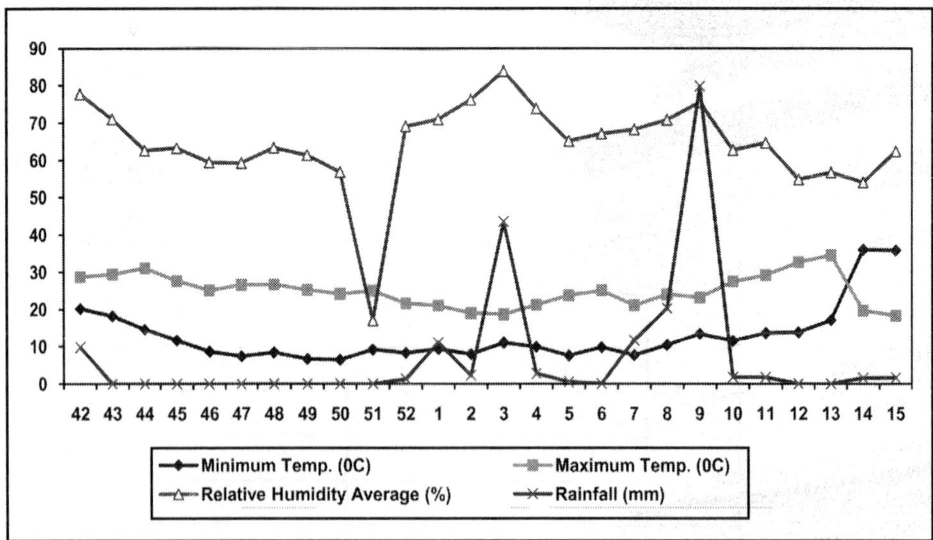

Fig. 3.1(b): Meteorological conditions during experimental period in Rabi season 2013-14

Table 3.1(b): Meteorological conditions during experimental period in Rabi season (2013-14)

Months	S.W.	Minimum Temp. (°C)	Maximum Temp. (°C)	Relative Humidity Average (%)	Rainfall (mm)
October 2013	42	20.18	28.72	77.64	9.75
	43	18.22	29.45	71.00	0.00
November	44	14.64	31.12	62.64	0.00
	45	11.64	27.70	63.28	0.00
	46	8.64	25.12	59.43	0.00
	47	7.41	26.62	59.28	0.00
December	48	8.38	26.71	63.35	0.00
	49	6.68	25.28	61.35	0.00
	50	6.44	24.18	56.86	0.00
	51	9.17	24.97	17.07	0.00
	52	8.28	21.61	69.05	1.25
January 2014	1	9.34	21.00	70.93	11.00
	2	7.92	19.02	76.14	2.25
	3	11.01	18.67	83.79	43.50
	4	9.91	21.22	73.78	2.75
February	5	7.54	23.74	65.14	0.50
	6	9.78	25.04	67.07	0.00
	7	7.64	21.07	68.21	11.75
	8	10.40	24.02	70.78	20.25
March	9	13.45	23.20	75.50	79.75
	10	11.54	27.45	62.71	1.75
	11	13.67	29.18	64.64	1.75
	12	13.87	32.62	54.86	0.00
	13	17.11	34.51	56.71	0.00

Experimental Details

The following treatments are experimental design and were executed to achieve the objectives.

Table 3.2: Physico-chemical properties of the experimental soil

S. No.	Soil Properties	Initial Values
1.	Soil Texture	Sandy loam
	Sand(%)	57.0
	Silt(%)	29.0
	Clay(%)	14.0
2.	pH (1:2 Soil: Water)	7.20
3.	EC	0.21
4.	Organic Carbon (%)	0.25
5.	Available N (kg ha^{-1})	173.00
6.	Available P (kg ha^{-1})	8.00
7.	Available K (kg ha^{-1})	176.00
8.	Available S (ppm)	7.96
9.	DTPA extractable Zn (ppm)	0.54
10.	DTPA extractable Cu (ppm)	0.43
11.	DTPA extractable Fe (ppm)	4.64
12.	DTPA extractable Mn (ppm)	20.08
13.	Available B (ppm)	0.35
14.	Available Mo (ppm)	0.042

Treatments

(a) Zn_0 = Without Zn (b) B_0 = Without B (c) Mo_0 = Without Mo

(a) Zn_1 = 2.5 kg ha^{-1} (b) B_1 = 1 kg ha^{-1} (c) Mo_1 = 400 g ha^{-1}

(a) Zn_2 = 5 kg ha^{-1} (b) B_2 = 2 kg ha^{-1}

Treatment Combinations

	Mo_0		**Mo_{400}**
T_1	$Mo_0 + Zn_0 + B_0$	T_{10}	$Mo_1 + Zn_0 + B_0$
T_2	$Mo_0 + Zn_0 + B_1$	T_{11}	$Mo_1 + Zn_0 + B_1$
T_3	$Mo_0 + Zn_0 + B_2$	T_{12}	$Mo_1 + Zn_0 + B_2$
T_4	$Mo_0 + Zn_1 + B_0$	T_{13}	$Mo_1 + Zn_1 + B_0$
T_5	$Mo_0 + Zn_1 + B_1$	T_{14}	$Mo_1 + Zn_1 + B_1$
T_6	$Mo_0 + Zn_1 + B_2$	T_{15}	$Mo_1 + Zn_1 + B_2$
T_7	$Mo_0 + Zn_2 + B_0$	T_{16}	$Mo_1 + Zn_2 + B_0$
T_8	$Mo_0 + Zn_2 + B_1$	T_{17}	$Mo_1 + Zn_2 + B_1$
T_9	$Mo_0 + Zn_2 + B_2$	T_{18}	$Mo_1 + Zn_2 + B_2$

Experimental Design and Layout

The experiment was laid out in factorial randomized block design with three replications Fig. 3.2 as given below:

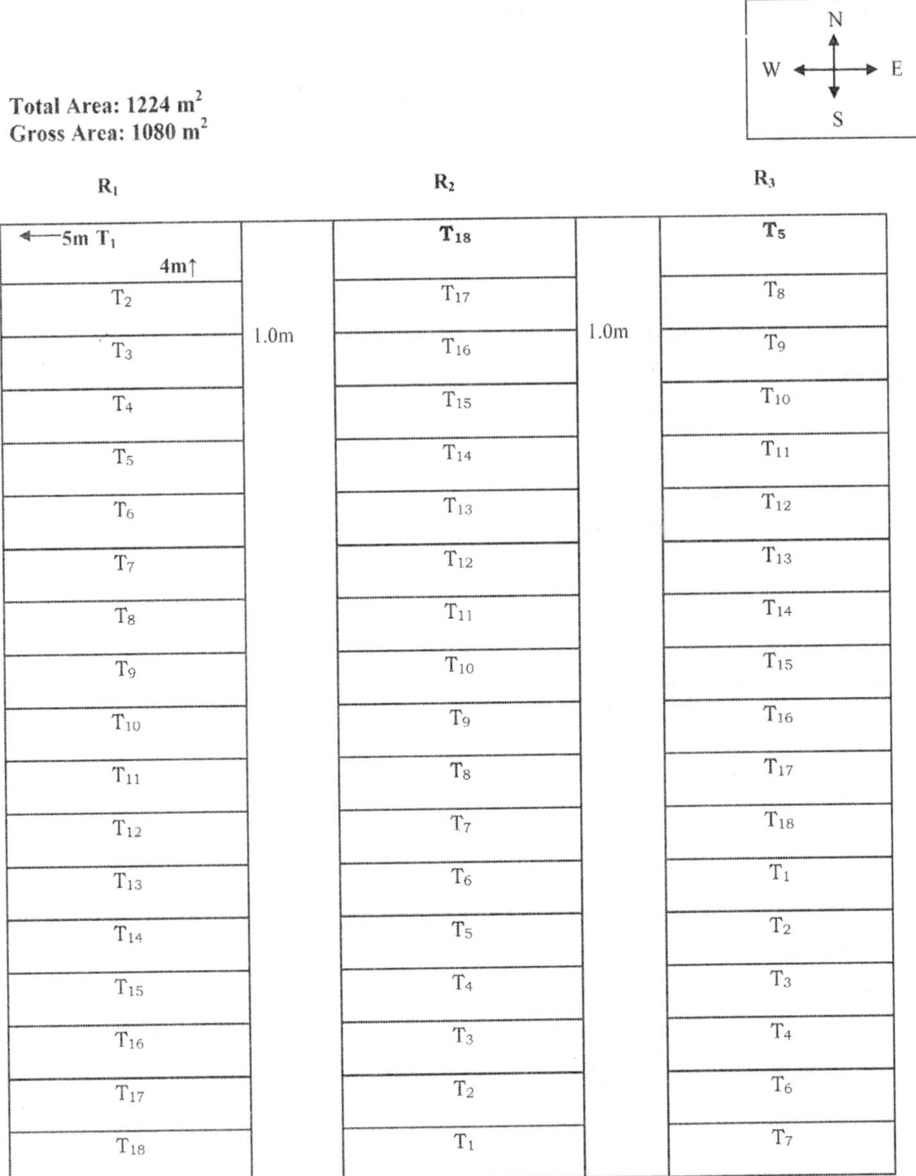

Fig. 3.2: Experimental Layout

The description of experimental design is as follows:

Field experiment on chickpea was conducted with the following details:

Design	:	Factorial R.B.D.
Replications	:	3
No. of Treatments	:	18
Plot Size	:	$5 \times 4 = 20$ m^2 plot^{-1}
Total No. of plots	:	$18 \times 3 = 54$
Total Plot Area	:	$54 \times 20 = 1080$ m^2
Crop	:	Chickpea
Variety	:	Awarodhi
Row to row spacing	:	30 cm.
Seed rate	:	80 kg ha^{-1}

General Description of Treatments

Control

Control plot are same as other treatment without molybdenum and with molybdenum.

Preparation of Experimental Field

The experimental plots of chickpea were prepared by one pass of harrowing, two pass of cultivator and one planking, cultivator and finally leveled by plunked.

Sowing

Sowing was done by manually spacing 30 cm grains and depth 8-10 cm., application of basal doses of fertilizer was done manually.

Fertilizer Application

1. Nitrogen : 20 kg ha^{-1} applied basal uniformly as urea.
2. Phosphorus : 40 kg ha^{-1} applied basal uniformly as DAP.
3. Potassium : 20 kg ha^{-1} applied basal uniformly as muriate of potash.
4. Sulphur : 30 kg ha^{-1} applied basal uniformly as elemental sulphur.
5. Zinc : 0, 2.5 and 5.0 kg ha^{-1} notations Zn_0, Zn_1 and Zn_2 levels applied as zinc sulphate (monohydrate 33% Zn).
6. Boron : 0, 1.0 and 2.0 kg ha^{-1} notations B_0, B_1 and B_2 levels applied as borax.
7. Molybdenum : 0 and 400 g ha^{-1} notations Mo_0 and Mo_1 levels applied as ammonium molybdate.

Weed Management

First weeding was done after 30 days of sowing and there after second weeding was done depending upon the weed intensity and plants were kept weed free the crop growth.

Harvesting

Table 3.3: Details of operational dates of crops

Operation	Date		Remarks
	2012-13	2013-14	
	Preparation of experimental field		
Harrowing	15.10.2012	12.10.2013	Tractor drawn disc harrow as per treatment description
Cultivator ploughing and planking	17.10.2012	13.10.2013	Tractor drawn Cultivator and planker as treatment description
Pre-soil sampling	19.10.2012	14.10.2013	Soil Auger
Sowing	20.10.2012	17.10.2013	Grain were shown manually with spacing of 30 cm
	Fertilizer application		
Basal application	20.10.2012	17.10.2013	At the time sowing
	Weed Control		
Hand Weeding 1st 2nd	20.11.20 1219.12.2012	10.11.2013 25.12.2013	
	Observations Recorded		
First 30 DAS	20.11.2012	17.11.2013	
Second 60 DAS	20.12.2012	17.12.2013	
Third 90 DAS	20.01.2013	17.01.2013	
No. of pods plant^{-1}	20.01.2013	17.01.2014	
Harvesting	31.03 2013	08.04.2014	
Grain and Stover sampling	02.04.2013	09.04.2014	
Threshing	03.04.2013	10.04.2014	
Soil sampling at harvest	04.04.2013	11.04.2014	Soil Auger

Observations recorded for the following:

(A) Growth and yield attributes:

1. Plant height.
2. Number of branch plant$^{-1.}$
3. Number of nodules plant^{-1}
4. Nodules dry weight (mg) plant$^{-1.}$
5. Number of pods plant$^{-1.}$
6. Number of grains pod$^{-1.}$
7. Test weight (weight of 100 grains in g).

} at 30, 60 and 90 DAS.

8. Grain yield (kg ha^{-1}).
9. Stover yield (kg ha^{-1}).
10. Harvest Index (%).

Harvest index was calculated as below:

$$\textit{Harvest index} (\%) = \frac{\textit{Economic yield}}{\textit{Biological yield}} \times 100$$

or

$$\textit{Harvest index} (\%) = \frac{\textit{Grain yield}}{\textit{Grain + Stover yield}} \times 100$$

(B) Physical and Chemical analysis:

Collection of Soil Samples

The soil samples from 0-15 cm., depth from each plot were collected with the help of steel tube auger, air-dried and ground with pestle and mortar to passing through 2 mm. sieve. These samples were analyzed for various physico-chemical properties. It was mixed thoroughly in order to make it homogeneous before use. The mechanical composition and physiochemical characteristics of the soil are given below.

Particle Size Analysis

The relative proportion of sand, silt and clay in soil sample was determined by using Bouyoucos hydrometer method as describing by Bouyoucos, (1962).

pH

It was measured in 1:2.5 soil-water suspension by Elico digital pH meter. (Jackson, 1967).

EC

It was determined by conductivity meter (Jackson, 1967) in the soil-water suspension of which pH was measured. The electrical conductivity was expressed as deci Siemens meter^{-1} (dSm^{-1}).

Organic Carbon

It was determined by Walkley and Black's rapid titration method as described by (Jackson, 1973).

Available Nitrogen in Soil

The available nitrogen was determined by distilling the soil with alkaline potassium permanganate solution 0.32 per cent (Subbiah and Asija, 1956).

Available Phosphorus in Soil

The available phosphorus content of soil was determined (Olsen's reagent) 0.5 M $NaHCO_3$, pH 8.5 extractant is used by estimation read the intensity of blue colour on a photometric colorimeter using 660 nm red filter method described by Olsen *et al.* (1954).

Available Potassium in Soil

It was extracted by 1N NH_4OAC (pH 7.0) solution and in the extract available K was determined flame photometrically (Jackson, 1967).

Available Sulphur in Soil

Available sulphur in soil was determined by the turbidimetric method, in the soil extract with 0.15 per cent $CaCl_2$ at 420 nm on Spectronic 20, (Chesnin and Yien, 1951).

Available DTPA Extractable Zn, Cu, Fe and Mn in Soil

Available zinc content in soil was be extracted with 0.005 M-DTPA, 0.01 M $CaCl_2$ and 0.1 M Triethanol amine (TEA) adjusted to pH 7.3 and analyzed on atomic absorption spectrophotometer (AAS-4141) (Lindsay and Norvell, 1978).

Available Boron in Soil

Hot water soluble boron in soil was determination by Azomethane -H reagent and intensity of colour measure absorbance at 420 nm on Spectronic 20 were taken on method (Berger and Truog 1939).

Available Molybdenum in Soil

Available molybdenum in soil was extracted with perchloric acid and Grigg's reagent ammonium oxalate (pH 3.3) estimated absorbance of the green complex is then measured at 475 nm on a colorimeter (Grigg, J.L. 1953).

Plant Analysis

Preparation of Plant Samples

The grain and stover samples were processed for chemical analysis. The stover samples were first air-dried and kept in oven at 60-70°C for drying till the 12 hours to become free from moisture. The samples were ground in a willey mill and stored in clean polythene bags. Similarly, dried grain samples were also ground oven dried, passed through 60 mesh sieve and stored in the sample bottles.

Nitrogen

It was determined by Micro-Kjeldahl method by digesting and distilling the ground material as described by (Jackson, 1973).

Phosphorus

Well ground grain and stover samples were digested in a diacid mixture of HNO_3 and $HClO_4$ (3:1) and P concentration in extract will be transmittance or absorbance of solution after 30 minutes at 420 nm with colorimeter using blue filter colorimetrically as Vandomolybadate yellow colour method (Jackson, 1973).

Potassium

Well ground grain and stover samples were digested in a diacid mixture through wet ashing (described under phosphorous). Potassium was determined by flame photometer as described by Jackson (1967).

Sulphur

Total sulphur in the digest was determined turbidimetrically as described by Chaudhary and Cornfield (1966). The absorbance or transmittance of the solution is read with Spectronic 20 at 420 nm.

Zn, Cu, Fe and Mn

Zinc content in grain and stover was determined in diacid mixture having HNO_3 and $HClO_4$ (3:1) ratio. The intensity of Zn, Cu, Fe and Mn in solution was measured by Atomic Absorption Spectrophotometer (AAS - 4141) (Lindsay and Norvell, 1978).

Boron

One gram of the plant material was taken in 100 ml flask 15 ml mixture of di-acid (3:1 of AR grade HNO_3: $HClO_4$) was added to each flask and whole mass was digested on a hot plate to get white solution. The digest was collected in the 50 ml. volumetric flask and volume was made upto the mark with distilled water was colorimetric determination by Azomethane -H reagent and intensity of colour measure absorbance at 420 nm on Spectronic 20 were taken on method (Berger and Truog 1939).

Molybdenum

Molybdenum content in plant samples were washed with tap water rinsed with distilled water and dried in an oven at 60-70°C. The plant samples were wet digested in di-acid (HNO_3 : $HClO_4$) mixture and analyzed for molybdenum content by thiocyanate method (Jackson, 1973).

Protein

Nitrogen content in grains was determined by Kjeldahl's method, and then the protein content was obtained by multiplying the nitrogen content with the factor 6.25 (AOAC, 1970).

Grain Protein Yield (kg ha^{-1})

Grain protein yield kg ha^{-1} was calculated by multiplying nitrogen per cent content in to grain yield kg ha^{-1}.

$$\text{Protein harvest (kg ha}^{-1}) = \frac{\text{Protein content (per cent)} \times \text{Grain yield (kg ha}^{-1})}{100}$$

Nutrient Uptake

The uptake of nutrients (NPK) in kg ha^{-1} by plant and seed at harvest will be obtained by fallowing formula.

$$\text{Uptake of nutrient (kg ha}^{-1}) = \frac{\text{Nutrient content (\%)} \times \text{Yield (kg ha}^{-1})}{100}$$

or

$$\text{Uptake of nutrient (g ha}^{-1}) = \frac{\text{Nutrient content (mg kg}^{-1}) \times \text{Yield (q ha}^{-1})}{10}$$

Statistical Analysis

The data were statistically analysed by standard method (Chandel, 1990).

$$SE(m) \pm = \sqrt{\frac{V_E}{r}}$$

$$SEd \pm = \sqrt{\frac{2V_E}{r}}$$

CD (P = 0.05) = SEd± × $t_{0.5}$ at.....d.f.

Anova Table **Source of Variation**	**Degree of Freedom**	**Sum of Squares**	**Mean Sum of Squares**	**F cal**	**Significance**
Replications					
Factor Zn					
Factor B					
Factor Zn × B					
Factor Mo					
Factor Zn × Mo					
Factor B × Mo					
Factor Zn × B × Mo					
Error					
Total					

OBSERVATIONS, FINDINGS OF NUTRIENTS APPLICATION

The problem "Studies on the dynamics of select micronutrients in soil, plant and their responses on chickpea (*Cicer arietinum* L.) under rainfed conditions", was conducted in pursuit of the following defined objectives:

1. Analysis of surface soil of experimental plot for Zn, B and Mo before and after the crop.
2. Conducting the field scale experiments to see the effect of Zn, B and Mo application on the growth and yield of chickpea.
3. Analysis of plants for Zn, B and Mo contents to calculate the total uptake of nutrients.
4. To study the effect of Zn, B, Mo and their interactions on the grain and straw yields.
5. To see the effect of Zn, B, Mo and their interaction on the nodulation of the crop.

The encompasses the following growth parameters, yield of grain and stover, concentrations and uptake of N, P, K, S, Zn, B, Mo, Cu, Fe and Mn grain analysis for the protein content.

The salient findings are described as below:

Growth Parameters

(a) Plant Height (cm)

The data relating to plant height at all the three stages of crop growth for both the years of study are shown in Table 4.1 and 4.2. During first year (2012-13) Table 4.1 plant height varied from 12.53 to 14.43 cm and 13.70 to 14.90 cm in case of without and with molybdenum, respectively and these values were given by B_2Zn_2 in former and Zn_0B_2 in latter cases. The main effect of Zn, B and Mo and interaction Zn × Mo resulted significant increase in plant height at 30 DAS.

At 60 DAS the ranged of 23.73 to 24.60 cm was observed in without molybdenum treatment and the lowest and the highest values were given by Zn_0B_0 and Zn_2B_2 on addition of molybdenum the minimum and maximum values were observed at 24.66 to 25.96 cm and these values were observed in Zn_1B_0 and Zn_2B_2 respectively. At 60DAS during first year only the main effects of Zn and Mo were significant and the rest of variables did not show significant increase in plant height.

At 90 DAS the lowest and the highest values in without molybdenum were 35.13 and 36.93 cm in treatments Zn_0B_0 and Zn_1B_2 respectively. On molybdenum treatment the plant height varied from 36.00 to 36.98 cm in Zn_0B_0 and Zn_1B_2 respectively. At this stage only the main effect of zinc and molybdenum were significant and other variable were not significant.

The plant height varied with the advancement in the age of plant. The mean plant height in without molybdenum was 13.48 and that in 13.95 cm, in molybdenum treatment at 30 DAS. At 60 DAS the mean plant height was 23.92 cm in without molybdenum and 25.21 cm with molybdenum. Similarly at 90 DAS the mean plant height was 36.15 cm in without molybdenum and 36.62 cm in presence of molybdenum during first year Table 4.1.

During second year (2013-14) plant height varied from 12.65 to 14.56 cm and 13.73 to 15.00 cm in case of without and with molybdenum respectively and these values were given by B_2Zn_2 in former and Zn_0B_2 in latter cases. These main effect of Zn, B and Mo and interaction Zn × Mo resulted significant increase in plant height at 30 DAS.

At 60 DAS the ranged of 23.35 to 25.68 cm was observed in without molybdenum treatment and the lowest and the highest values were given by Zn_0B_0 and Zn_2B_2 on addition of molybdenum the minimum and maximum values were observed at 24.93 to 26.55 cm and these values were observed in Zn_0B_0 and Zn_2B_2 respectively. At 60DAS only the main effects of Zn, B and Mo were significant and their interactions did not show significant increase in plant height.

At 90 DAS the lowest and the highest values in without molybdenum were 35.13 and 37.67 cm in treatments Zn_0B_0 and Zn_2B_2 respectively on molybdenum treatment the plant height varied from 36.25 to 38.46 cm in Zn_0B_0 and Zn_2B_2 respectively. At this stage the main effect of zinc and molybdenum were significant and other variable were not significant.

The plant height varied the advancement in the age of plant. The mean plant height in without molybdenum was 13.60 and 14.05 cm in molybdenum treatment at 30 DAS. At 60 DAS the mean plant height was 24.74 cm in without molybdenum and 25.73 cm with molybdenum. Similarly at 90 DAS the mean plant height was 36.48 cm in without molybdenum and 37.29 cm in presence of molybdenum during second year Table 4.2. The trends of variation in plant height at different stages of crop growth are shown in (Fig. 4.1).

Table 4.1: Effect of Zn, B and Mo levels on plant height (cm) 2012-13 in Chickpea

Treatments	30 DAS				60 DAS				90 DAS			
	Without Molybdenum				Without Molybdenum				Without Molybdenum			
	Zn_0	Zn_1	Zn_2	Mean	Zn_0	Zn_1	Zn_2	Mean	Zn_0	Zn_1	Zn_2	Mean
B_0	12.53	12.86	13.80	13.06	23.73	23.86	24.06	23.88	35.13	36.20	36.13	35.82
B_1	13.20	13.60	13.93	13.58	24.53	23.20	24.26	24.00	36.20	36.46	35.93	36.20
B_2	13.42	13.56	14.43	13.80	23.93	23.13	24.60	22.89	36.60	36.93	35.80	36.44
Mean	13.05	13.34	14.05	13.48	24.06	23.40	24.31	23.92	35.98	36.53	35.95	36.15
	With Molybdenum				With Molybdenum				With Molybdenum			
B_0	13.70	13.64	13.83	13.72	24.80	24.66	25.53	25.00	36.00	36.83	36.53	36.45
B_1	14.40	13.68	13.96	14.01	24.93	25.26	25.80	25.33	36.60	36.86	36.26	36.57
B_2	14.90	13.66	13.78	14.11	24.66	25.28	25.96	25.30	36.80	36.98	36.73	36.84
Mean	14.33	13.66	13.86	13.95	24.80	25.07	25.76	25.21	36.47	36.89	36.51	36.62
	S.E.(d)		C.D.(P=0.05)		S.E.(d)		C.D.(P=0.05)		S.E.(d)		C.D.(P=0.05)	
Zn	0.147		0.299		0.278		0.565		0.213		0.433	
B	0.147		0.299		0.278		N.S.		0.213		N.S	
Mo	0.120		0.244		0.227		0.461		0.174		0.354	
Zn×B	0.255		N.S.		0.482		N.S.		0.369		N.S.	
B×Mo	0.208		N.S.		0.393		N.S.		0.301		N.S.	
Zn×Mo	0.120		0.423		0.393		N.S.		0.301		N.S.	
Zn×B×Mo	0.361		N.S.		0.681		N.S.		0.522		N.S.	

Table 4.2: Effect of Zn, B and Mo levels on plant height (cm) 2013-14 in Chickpea

Treatments	30 DAS				60 DAS				90 DAS			
	Without Molybdenum				Without Molybdenum				Without Molybdenum			
	Zn_0	Zn_1	Zn_2	Mean	Zn_0	Zn_1	Zn_2	Mean	Zn_0	Zn_1	Zn_2	Mean
B_0	12.65	12.98	13.93	13.19	23.35	24.19	24.53	24.02	35.13	36.35	37.24	36.24
B_1	13.32	13.72	14.05	13.70	24.65	25.05	25.65	25.12	35.52	36.41	37.30	36.41
B_2	13.52	13.68	14.56	13.92	24.67	24.87	25.68	25.07	35.89	36.78	37.67	36.78
Mean	13.16	13.46	14.18	13.60	24.22	24.70	25.29	24.74	35.51	36.51	37.40	36.48
	With Molybdenum				With Molybdenum				With Molybdenum			
B_0	13.80	13.73	13.93	13.82	24.93	25.06	25.40	25.13	36.25	37.14	38.03	37.14
B_1	14.50	13.78	14.06	14.11	25.73	25.92	26.52	26.06	36.25	37.20	38.08	37.18
B_2	15.00	13.76	13.88	14.21	25.75	25.74	26.55	26.01	36.72	37.52	38.46	37.57
Mean	14.43	13.76	13.96	14.05	25.47	25.57	26.16	25.73	36.41	37.29	38.19	37.29
	S.E.(d)		C.D.(P=0.05)		S.E.(d)		C.D.(P=0.05)		S.E.(d)		C.D.(P=0.05)	
Zn	0.176		0.358		0.198		0.403		0.362		0.735	
B	0.176		0.358		0.198		0.403		0.362		N.S.	
Mo	0.144		0.292		0.162		0.329		0.295		0.600	
Zn×B	0.305		N.S.		0.343		N.S.		0.626		N.S.	
B×Mo	0.249		N.S.		0.280		N.S.		0.512		N.S.	
Zn×Mo	0.249		0.506		0.280		N.S.		0.512		N.S.	
Zn×B×Mo	0.431		N.S.		0.485		N.S.		0.886		N.S.	

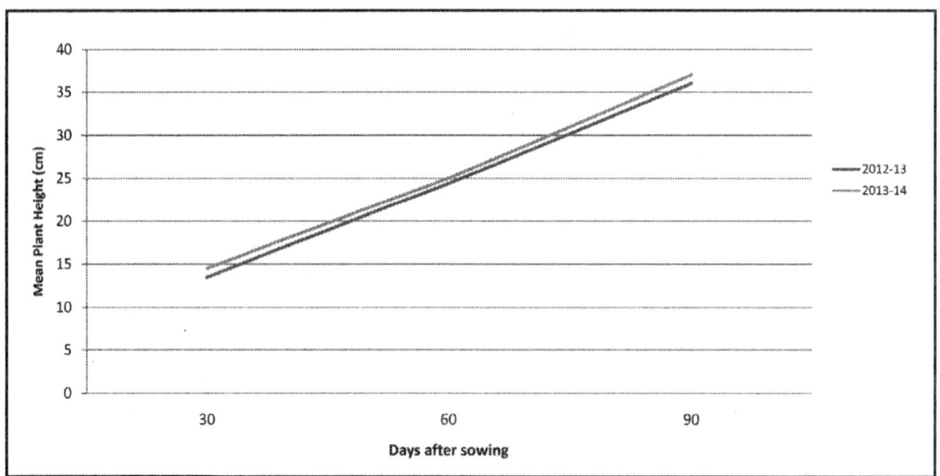

Fig. 4.1: Trends showing the effect of three different growth stages on plant height (cm) of Chickpea

(b) Number of Branches Plant^{-1}

The results of the effect of different treatments on number of branches are shown in Table 4.3. During first year (2012-13) varied from 3.67 to 4.40 and 4.00 to 4.53 branches plant^{-1} in case of without and with molybdenum respectively and these values were given by Zn_2B_1 in former and Zn_2B_1 in latter cases. Only main effect of Zn and interaction Zn × B resulted significant increase in number of branches plant^{-1} at 30 DAS.

At 60 DAS it ranged from 9.15 to 12.67 branches plant^{-1} in without molybdenum treatment and the lowest and the highest values were given by Zn_0B_0 and Zn_2B_1. On addition of molybdenum the minimum and maximum values were observed from 12.00 to 12.89 branches plant^{-1} and these values were observed in Zn_0B_0 and Zn_1B_2 respectively. At 60DAS (2012-13) these main effects of Zn, B and Mo and interactions Zn × B, B × Mo and Zn × Mo were significant and the rest of variables did not show significant increase in number of branches plant^{-1}.

At 90 DAS the lowest and the highest values in without molybdenum were 12.33 and 14.40 branches plant^{-1} in treatments Zn_0B_0 and Zn_2B_2 respectively. On molybdenum treatment, the number of branches plant^{-1} varied from 13.67 to 14.80 branches plant^{-1} in Zn_0B_0 and Zn_2B_2 respectively. At these stages the main effect of Zn, B and Mo were significant and other variable were not significant. The trends of variation in number of branches due to different treatments were similar during both the years.

The number of branches plant^{-1} varied with the advancement in the age of plant. The mean number of branches plant^{-1} in without molybdenum was 4.15 and 4.24 branches plant^{-1} and in molybdenum treatment at 30 DAS. At 60 DAS the mean number of branches plant^{-1} was 11.75 branches plant^{-1} in without molybdenum and 12.65

branches plant^{-1} in with molybdenum. Similarly at 90 DAS the mean number of branches plant^{-1} was 13.76 branches plant^{-1} in without molybdenum and 14.33 in presence of molybdenum during first year (Table 4.3).

During second year (2013-14) number of branches plant^{-1} varied from 3.76 to 5.38 branches plant^{-1} and 4.10 to 5.60 branches plant^{-1} in case of without and with molybdenum respectively and these values were given by Zn_2B_2 in former and Zn_2B_2 in latter cases. These main effects of Zn, B and Mo resulted significant and interaction did not show significant increase in number of branches plant^{-1} at 30 DAS.

At 60 DAS, the range was observed of 9.23 to 12.75 branches plant^{-1} in without molybdenum treatment and the lowest and the highest values were given by Zn_0B_0 and Zn_2B_1 on addition of molybdenum the minimum and maximum values were observed at 12.10 to 12.99 branches plant^{-1} and these values were observed in Zn_0B_0 and Zn_1B_2 respectively. At 60DAS (2013-14) only the main effects of Zn, B and Mo and interactions Zn × B, B × Mo and Zn × Mo were significant and the rest of variables did not show significant increase in number of branches plant^{-1}.

At 90 DAS the lowest and the highest values in without molybdenum were 12.40 and 14.48 branches plant^{-1} in treatments Zn_0B_0 and Zn_2B_2 respectively. On molybdenum treatment the number of branches plant^{-1} varied from 13.74 to 14.88 in Zn_0B_0 and Zn_2B_2 respectively. At this stage the main effect of Zn, B and Mo were significant and other variable were not significant.

The number of branches plant^{-1} varied with the advancement in the age of plant. The mean number of branches plant^{-1} in without molybdenum was 4.79 and 5.03 branches plant^{-1} and in molybdenum treatment at 30 DAS. At 60 DAS the mean number of branches plant^{-1} was 11.83 branches plant^{-1} in without molybdenum and 12.75 branches plant^{-1} with molybdenum. Similarly at 90 DAS the mean number of branches plant^{-1} was 13.81 branches plant^{-1} in without molybdenum and 14.41 branches plant^{-1} in presence of molybdenum during second year Table 4.4. Treatment effects were similar during both the years of study. The trends of showing the effect of three different stages on number of branches plant^{-1} of chickpea shown in (Fig. 4.2).

(c) Number of Nodules Plant^{-1}

As shown in Table 4.5 during the first year (2012-13) the number of nodules plant^{-1} varied from 4.00 to 5.20 nodules plant^{-1} and 4.33 to 5.55 nodules plant^{-1} in case of without and with molybdenum, respectively and these values were given by Zn_2B_2in former and Zn_2B_2 in latter cases. The main effect of Zn, B and Mo in a resulted significant increase in number of nodules plant^{-1} at 30 DAS.

At 60 DAS the ranged of 8.33 to 10.43 in without molybdenum treatment and the lowest and the highest values were given by Zn_0B_0 and Zn_2B_2. On addition of molybdenum the minimum and maximum values were observed at 9.33 to 11.67 and these values were observed in Zn_0B_0 and Zn_2B_2 respectively. At 60DAS (2012-13) only the main effects of Zn, B and Mo were significant and the rest of variables did not show significant increase in number of nodules plant^{-1}.

Table 4.3: Effect of Zn, B and Mo levels on number of branches plant[-1] 2012-13 in Chickpea

Treatments	30 DAS				60 DAS				90 DAS			
	Without Molybdenum				Without Molybdenum				Without Molybdenum			
	Zn_0	Zn_1	Zn_2	Mean	Zn_0	Zn_1	Zn_2	Mean	Zn_0	Zn_1	Zn_2	Mean
B_0	3.67	4.33	4.33	4.11	9.15	11.33	12.33	10.94	12.33	13.33	13.67	13.11
B_1	4.33	4.00	4.40	4.24	10.67	12.33	12.67	11.89	13.67	14.33	14.38	14.13
B_2	4.00	4.00	4.30	4.10	12.33	12.36	12.60	12.43	13.33	14.36	14.40	14.03
Mean	4.00	4.11	4.34	4.15	10.72	12.01	12.53	11.75	13.11	14.01	14.15	13.76
	With Molybdenum				With Molybdenum				With Molybdenum			
B_0	4.00	4.33	4.43	4.25	12.00	12.33	12.87	12.40	13.67	14.20	14.42	14.10
B_1	4.33	4.08	4.53	4.31	12.60	12.80	12.68	12.69	14.20	14.38	14.50	14.36
B_2	4.05	4.10	4.33	4.16	12.83	12.89	12.83	12.85	14.40	14.40	14.80	14.53
Mean	4.13	4.17	4.43	4.24	12.48	12.67	12.79	12.65	14.09	14.33	14.57	14.33
	S.E.(d)		C.D.(P=0.05)		S.E.(d)		C.D.(P=0.05)		S.E.(d)		C.D.(P=0.05)	
Zn	0.087		0.177		0.190		0.386		0.208		0.422	
B	0.087		N.S.		0.190		0.386		0.208		0.422	
Mo	0.071		N.S.		0.155		0.315		0.170		0.345	
Zn×B	0.151		0.307		0.329		0.669		0.360		N.S.	
B×Mo	0.123		N.S.		0.269		0.546		0.294		N.S.	
Zn×Mo	0.123		N.S.		0.269		0.546		0.294		N.S.	
Zn×B×Mo	0.213		N.S.		0.465		N.S.		0.509		N.S.	

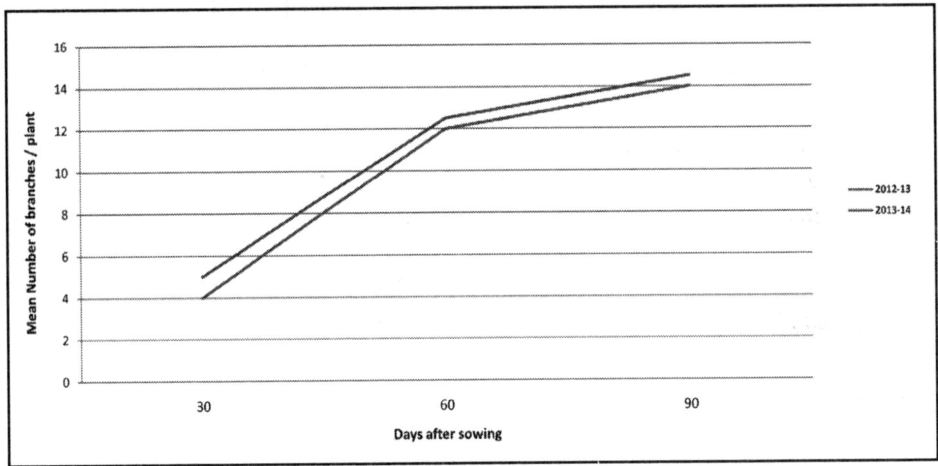

Fig. 4.2: Trends showing the effect of three different growth stages on number of branches plant^{-1} of Chickpea

At 90 DAS the lowest and the highest values in without molybdenum were 2.33 and 3.83 nodules plant^{-1} treatments Zn_0B_0 and Zn_2B_2 respectively. On molybdenum treatment the number of nodules plant^{-1} varied from 2.33 to 3.93 nodules plant^{-1} in Zn_0B_0 and Zn_2B_2 respectively. At this stage only the main effects of Zn, B and Mo and interaction affect Zn × B were significant and other variable were not significant.

The number of nodules plant^{-1} varied with during first year (2012-13) the increasing in the age of plant. The mean number of nodules plant^{-1} in without molybdenum was 4.55 and 4.93 nodules plant^{-1} in molybdenum treatment give the ranges at 30 DAS. At 60 DAS the mean number of nodules plant^{-1} was 9.40 nodules plant^{-1} in without molybdenum and 10.87 nodules plant^{-1} with molybdenum. Similarly at 90 DAS the mean number of nodules plant^{-1} was 2.95 nodules plant^{-1} in without molybdenum and 3.10 nodules plant^{-1} in presence of molybdenum Table 4.5.

During second year (2013-14) number of nodules plant^{-1} varied from 4.20 to 5.30 nodules plant^{-1} and 4.40 to 5.60 nodules plant^{-1} in case of without and with molybdenum respectively and these values were given by Zn_2B_2 in former and Zn_2B_2 in latter cases. The main effect of Zn, B and Mo resulted significant increase in number of nodules plant^{-1} at 30 DAS.

At 60 DAS the ranged of 8.50 to 10.61 nodules plant^{-1} was observed in without molybdenum treatment and the lowest and the highest values were given by Zn_0B_0 and Zn_2B_2. On addition of molybdenum the minimum and maximum values were observed at 9.50 to 11.85 nodules plant^{-1} and these values were observed in Zn_0B_0 and Zn_2B_2 respectively. At 60 DAS (2013-14) only the main effects of Zn, B and Mo were significant and the rest of variables did not show significant increase in number of nodules plant^{-1}.

Table 4.4: Effect of Zn, B and Mo levels on number of branches plant^{-1} 2013-14 in Chickpea

Treatments	30 DAS				60 DAS				90 DAS			
	Without Molybdenum				Without Molybdenum				Without Molybdenum			
	Zn_0	Zn_1	Zn_2	Mean	Zn_0	Zn_1	Zn_2	Mean	Zn_0	Zn_1	Zn_2	Mean
B_0	3.76	4.49	4.69	4.31	9.23	11.41	12.41	11.02	12.40	13.40	13.75	13.18
B_1	4.52	5.15	5.35	5.01	10.75	12.41	12.75	11.97	13.74	14.40	14.30	14.15
B_2	4.55	5.18	5.38	5.04	12.41	12.44	12.68	12.51	13.40	14.44	14.48	14.11
Mean	4.28	4.94	5.14	4.79	10.80	12.09	12.61	11.83	13.18	14.08	14.18	13.81
	With Molybdenum				With Molybdenum				With Molybdenum			
B_0	4.10	4.73	4.91	4.58	12.10	12.43	12.97	12.50	13.74	14.27	14.50	14.17
B_1	4.76	5.39	5.57	5.24	12.70	12.90	12.78	12.79	14.27	14.48	14.58	14.44
B_2	4.79	5.42	5.60	5.27	12.93	12.99	12.93	12.95	14.47	14.47	14.88	14.61
Mean	4.55	5.18	5.36	5.03	12.58	12.77	12.89	12.75	14.16	14.41	14.65	14.41
	S.E.(d)		C.D.(P=0.05)		S.E.(d)		C.D.(P=0.05)		S.E.(d)		C.D.(P=0.05)	
Zn	0.047		0.096		0.178		0.361		0.236		0.480	
B	0.047		0.096		0.178		0.361		0.236		0.480	
Mo	0.039		0.078		0.145		0.295		0.193		0.392	
Zn×B	0.082		N.S.		0.308		0.626		0.409		N.S.	
B×Mo	0.067		N.S.		0.251		0.511		0.334		N.S.	
Zn×Mo	0.067		N.S.		0.251		0.511		0.334		N.S.	
Zn×B×Mo	0.116		N.S.		0.435		N.S.		0.579		N.S.	

At 90 DAS the lowest and the highest values in without molybdenum were 3.33 and 4.83 nodules plant^{-1} in treatments Zn_0B_0 and Zn_2B_2 respectively on molybdenum treatment the number of nodules plant^{-1} varied from 3.34 to 4.93 in Zn_0B_0 and Zn_2B_2 respectively. At this stage the main effects of Zn, B and Mo and interaction effect Zn × B were significant and other variable were not significant during second year (2013-14).

The number of nodules plant^{-1} varied with the advancement in the age of plant. The mean number of nodules plant^{-1} in without molybdenum was 4.60 and 4.93 nodules plant^{-1} in molybdenum treatment at 30 DAS. At 60 DAS the mean number of nodules plant^{-1} was 9.58 nodules plant^{-1} in without molybdenum and 11.04 nodules plant^{-1} with molybdenum. Similarly at 90 DAS the mean number of nodules plant^{-1} was 3.95 nodules plant^{-1} in without molybdenum and 4.10 nodules plant^{-1} in presence of molybdenum Table 4.6. The trends of showing the effect of three different stages on number of nodules plant^{-1} and without and with molybdenum of chickpea shown in Fig. 4.3 (a) and 4.3 (b).

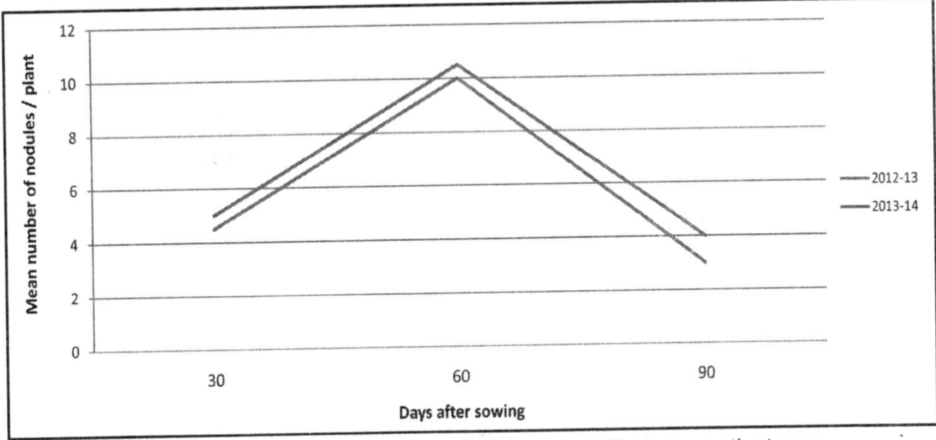

Fig. 4.3(a): Trends showing the effect of three different growth stages on number of nodules plant^{-1} of Chickpea

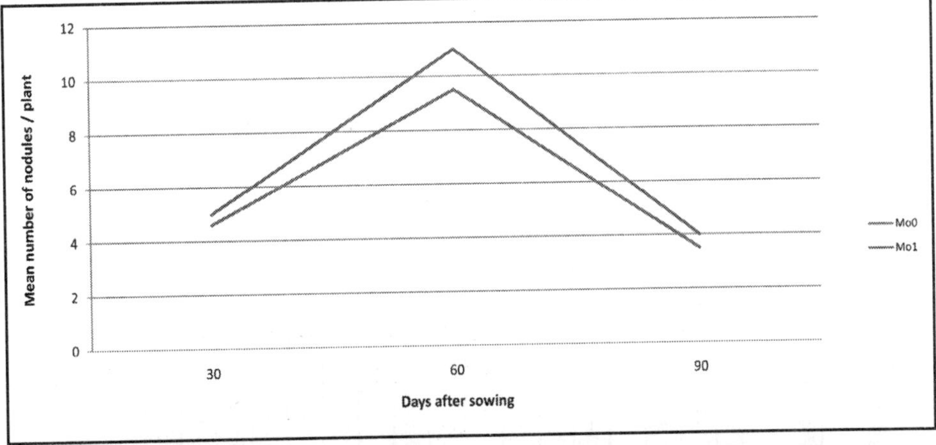

Fig. 4.3(b): Trends showing number of nodules plant^{-1} at three different stages of sowing with and without molybdenum of Chickpea

Table 4.5: Effect of Zn, B and Mo levels on number of nodules plant^{-1} 2012-13 in Chickpea

Treatments	30 DAS				60 DAS				90 DAS			
	Without Molybdenum				Without Molybdenum				Without Molybdenum			
	Zn_0	Zn_1	Zn_2	Mean	Zn_0	Zn_1	Zn_2	Mean	Zn_0	Zn_1	Zn_2	Mean
B_0	4.00	4.30	4.80	4.37	8.33	9.00	10.00	9.11	2.33	2.67	2.83	2.61
B_1	4.20	4.33	4.98	4.50	8.48	9.40	10.33	9.40	3.00	3.00	3.33	3.11
B_2	4.50	4.60	5.20	4.77	9.00	9.67	10.43	9.70	2.67	2.87	3.83	3.12
Mean	4.23	4.41	4.99	4.55	8.60	9.36	10.25	9.40	2.67	2.85	3.33	2.95
	With Molybdenum				With Molybdenum				With Molybdenum			
B_0	4.33	4.63	5.20	4.72	9.33	10.68	11.43	10.48	2.33	2.83	3.00	2.72
B_1	4.67	4.83	5.40	4.97	10.00	11.23	11.50	10.91	3.10	3.33	3.67	3.37
B_2	4.83	4.93	5.55	5.10	10.67	11.33	11.67	11.22	2.67	3.00	3.93	3.20
Mean	4.61	4.80	5.38	4.93	10.00	11.08	11.53	10.87	2.70	3.05	3.53	3.10
	S.E.(d)		C.D.(P=0.05)		S.E.(d)		C.D.(P=0.05)		S.E.(d)		C.D.(P=0.05)	
Zn	0.081		0.164		0.242		0.491		0.058		0.118	
B	0.081		0.164		0.242		0.491		0.058		0.118	
Mo	0.066		0.134		0.197		0.401		0.047		0.096	
Zn×B	0.140		N.S.		0.419		N.S.		0.101		0.205	
B×Mo	0.114		N.S.		0.342		N.S.		0.082		N.S.	
Zn×Mo	0.114		N.S.		0.342		N.S.		0.082		N.S.	
Zn×B×Mo	0.198		N.S.		0.592		N.S.		0.142		N.S.	

Table 4.6: Effect of Zn, B and Mo levels on number of nodules plant[-1] 2013-14 in Chickpea

Treatments	30 DAS				60 DAS				90 DAS			
	Without Molybdenum				Without Molybdenum				Without Molybdenum			
	Zn_0	Zn_1	Zn_2	Mean	Zn_0	Zn_1	Zn_2	Mean	Zn_0	Zn_1	Zn_2	Mean
B_0	4.20	4.30	4.80	4.43	8.50	9.17	10.17	9.28	3.33	3.67	3.83	3.61
B_1	4.30	4.40	5.00	4.57	8.65	9.57	10.50	9.57	4.00	4.00	4.33	4.11
B_2	4.50	4.60	5.30	4.80	9.17	9.84	10.61	9.87	3.67	3.88	4.83	4.13
Mean	4.33	4.43	5.03	4.60	8.77	9.53	10.43	9.58	3.67	3.85	4.33	3.95
	With Molybdenum				With Molybdenum				With Molybdenum			
B_0	4.40	4.60	5.20	4.73	9.50	10.85	11.61	10.65	3.34	3.83	4.00	3.72
B_1	4.50	4.80	5.40	4.90	10.17	11.40	11.68	11.08	4.10	4.33	4.67	4.37
B_2	4.90	5.00	5.60	5.17	10.84	11.50	11.85	11.40	3.67	4.00	4.93	4.20
Mean	4.60	4.80	5.40	4.93	10.17	11.25	11.71	11.04	3.70	4.05	4.53	4.10
	S.E.(d)		C.D.(P=0.05)		S.E.(d)		C.D.(P=0.05)		S.E.(d)		C.D.(P=0.05)	
Zn	0.137		0.278		0.198		0.402		0.070		0.142	
B	0.137		0.278		0.198		0.402		0.070		0.142	
Mo	0.112		0.227		0.161		0.328		0.057		0.116	
Zn×B	0.237		N.S.		0.342		N.S.		0.121		0.246	
B×Mo	0.194		N.S.		0.280		N.S.		0.099		N.S.	
Zn×Mo	0.194		N.S.		0.280		N.S.		0.099		N.S.	
Zn×B×Mo	0.335		N.S.		0.484		N.S.		0.171		N.S.	

(d) Nodules Dry Weight (mg) Plant^{-1}

As shown in Table. 4.7 nodules dry weight mg plant^{-1} varied from 9.16 to 12.37 mg plant^{-1} and 9.92 to 11.91 mg plant^{-1} in case of without and with molybdenum respectively and these values were given by Zn_2B_2 in former and Zn_2B_2 in latter cases. The main effect of Zn and B resulted significant increase in nodule dry weight (mg plant^{-1}) at 30 DAS during first year (2012-13). The interaction Zn x Mo was significant.

At 60 DAS the range of 20.83 to 26.08 mg plant^{-1} was observed in without molybdenum treatment and the lowest and the highest values were given by Zn_0B_0 and Zn_2B_2 on addition of molybdenum the minimum and maximum values were observed at 23.33 to 29.18 mg plant^{-1} and these values were observed in Zn_0B_0 and Zn_2B_2 respectively. At 60DAS (2012-13) only the main effects of Zn, B and Mo and interaction Zn × Mo were significant and the rest of variables had no significant effect.

At 90 DAS the lowest and the values varied from 6.43 to 9.19 mg plant^{-1} in without molybdenum in treatments Zn_0B_0 and Zn_2B_2 respectively. On molybdenum treatment the nodule dry weight varied from 6.43 to 10.13 mg plant^{-1} in Zn_0B_0 and Zn_2B_2 respectively. At this stage only the main effect of Zn, B and Mo were significant and other variable were not significant.

The nodules dry weight mg plant^{-1} varied the advancement in the age of plant. The mean nodule dry weight in without molybdenum was 10.82 and 10.56 mg plant^{-1} and in molybdenum treatment at 30 DAS during first year. At 60 DAS the mean nodule dry weight was 23.52 mg plant^{-1} in without molybdenum and 26.96 mg plant^{-1} with molybdenum. Similarly at 90 DAS the mean nodules dry weight mg plant^{-1} was 7.98 mg plant^{-1} in without molybdenum and 8.46 mg plant^{-1} in presence of molybdenum during 2012-13 Table. 4.7.

During second year (2013-14) nodules dry weight varied from 8.95 to 12.14 mg plant^{-1} and 10.08 to 12.82 mg plant^{-1} in case of without and with molybdenum respectively and these values were given by Zn_2B_2 in former and Zn_2B_2 in latter cases. The main effects of Zn, B and Mo resulted in significant increase in nodules dry weight at 30 DAS.

At 60 DAS the ranged of 21.25 to 26.53 mg plant^{-1} was observed in without molybdenum treatment and the lowest and the highest values were given by Zn_0B_0 and Zn_2B_2 on addition of molybdenum the minimum and maximum values were observed at 23.75 and 29.63 mg plant^{-1} and these values were observed in Zn_0B_0 and Zn_2B_2 respectively. At 60DAS (2013-14) only the main effects of Zn, B and Mo were significant and the rest of variables did not show significant increase in nodules dry weight.

At 90 DAS the lowest and the highest values in without molybdenum were 9.19 and 13.33 mg plant^{-1} in treatments Zn_0B_0 and Zn_2B_2 respectively. On molybdenum treatment the nodule dry weight varied from 9.22 to 13.61 mg plant^{-1} in Zn_0B_0 and Zn_2B_2 respectively. At this stage the main effect of Zn, B and Mo and interaction effect Zn × B were significant and other variable were not significant.

Table 4.7: Effect of Zn, B and Mo levels on nodules dry weight (mg) plant[-1] of 2012-13 in Chickpea

Treatments	30 DAS				60 DAS				90 DAS			
	Without Molybdenum				Without Molybdenum				Without Molybdenum			
	Zn_0	Zn_1	Zn_2	Mean	Zn_0	Zn_1	Zn_2	Mean	Zn_0	Zn_1	Zn_2	Mean
B_0	9.16	11.06	11.29	10.50	20.83	22.60	25.00	22.81	6.43	7.36	7.81	7.20
B_1	9.62	10.60	11.91	10.71	21.20	23.50	25.83	23.51	8.28	8.28	9.19	8.58
B_2	10.31	11.06	12.37	11.25	22.50	24.18	26.08	24.25	7.37	7.92	9.19	8.16
Mean	9.70	10.91	11.86	10.82	21.51	23.43	25.64	23.52	7.36	7.85	8.73	7.98
	With Molybdenum				With Molybdenum				With Molybdenum			
B_0	9.92	9.85	10.99	10.25	23.33	26.70	26.58	25.54	6.43	7.81	8.28	7.51
B_1	10.69	9.92	11.40	10.67	25.00	28.08	28.75	27.28	8.56	9.19	10.13	9.29
B_2	9.85	10.53	11.91	10.76	26.68	28.33	29.18	28.06	7.37	8.28	10.13	8.59
Mean	10.15	10.10	11.43	10.56	25.00	27.70	28.17	26.96	7.45	8.43	9.51	8.46
	S.E.(d)		C.D.(P=0.05)		S.E.(d)		C.D.(P=0.05)		S.E.(d)		C.D.(P=0.05)	
Zn	0.201		0.408		0.266		0.540		0.200		0.407	
B	0.201		0.408		0.266		0.540		0.200		0.407	
Mo	0.164		N.S.		0.217		0.441		0.164		0.333	
Zn×B	0.348		N.S.		0.460		N.S.		0.347		N.S.	
B×Mo	0.284		N.S.		0.376		N.S.		0.283		N.S.	
Zn×Mo	0.284		0.577		0.376		0.764		0.283		N.S.	
Zn×B×Mo	0.491		N.S.		0.651		N.S.		0.491		N.S.	

Table 4.8: Effect of Zn, B and Mo levels on nodules dry weight (mg) plant[-1] of 2013-14 in Chickpea

Treatments	30 DAS				60 DAS				90 DAS			
	Without Molybdenum				Without Molybdenum				Without Molybdenum			
	Zn_0	Zn_1	Zn_2	Mean	Zn_0	Zn_1	Zn_2	Mean	Zn_0	Zn_1	Zn_2	Mean
B_0	8.95	9.85	10.99	9.93	21.25	22.93	25.43	23.20	9.19	10.13	10.57	9.96
B_1	10.13	10.08	11.45	10.55	21.63	23.93	26.25	23.94	11.29	11.04	11.95	11.43
B_2	10.31	10.53	12.14	10.99	22.93	24.60	26.53	24.69	10.13	10.71	13.33	11.39
Mean	9.80	10.15	11.53	10.49	21.94	23.82	26.07	23.94	10.20	10.63	11.95	10.93
	With Molybdenum				With Molybdenum				With Molybdenum			
B_0	10.08	10.53	11.91	10.84	23.75	27.13	29.03	26.64	9.22	10.57	11.04	10.28
B_1	10.31	10.99	12.37	11.22	25.43	28.50	29.20	27.71	11.32	11.95	12.89	12.05
B_2	11.22	11.45	12.82	11.83	27.10	28.75	29.63	28.49	10.13	11.04	13.61	11.59
Mean	10.54	10.99	12.37	11.30	25.43	28.13	29.29	27.61	10.22	11.19	12.51	11.31
	S.E.(d)		C.D.(P=0.05)		S.E.(d)		C.D.(P=0.05)		S.E.(d)		C.D.(P=0.05)	
Zn	0.226		0.459		0.310		0.631		0.164		0.333	
B	0.226		0.459		0.310		0.631		0.164		0.333	
Mo	0.184		0.375		0.253		0.515		0.134		0.272	
Zn×B	0.391		N.S.		0.537		N.S.		0.284		0.577	
B×Mo	0.319		N.S.		0.439		N.S.		0.232		N.S.	
Zn×Mo	0.319		N.S.		0.439		N.S.		0.232		N.S.	
Zn×B×Mo	0.553		N.S.		0.760		N.S.		0.401		N.S.	

The nodules dry weight mg plant^{-1} varied the increase in the age of plant. The mean nodules dry weight mg plant^{-1} in without molybdenum was 10.49 and 11.30 mg plant^{-1}. In molybdenum treatment at 30 DAS. At 60 DAS the mean nodules dry weight was 23.94 in without molybdenum and 27.61 mg plant^{-1} with molybdenum. Similarly at 90 DAS the mean nodules dry weight mg plant^{-1} was 10.93 mg plant^{-1} in without molybdenum and 11.31 mg plant^{-1} in presence of molybdenum during second year Table 4.8. The trends of showing the effect of three different stages on nodules dry weight mg plant^{-1} and without and with molybdenum of chickpea shown in Fig. 4.4(a) and 4.4(b).

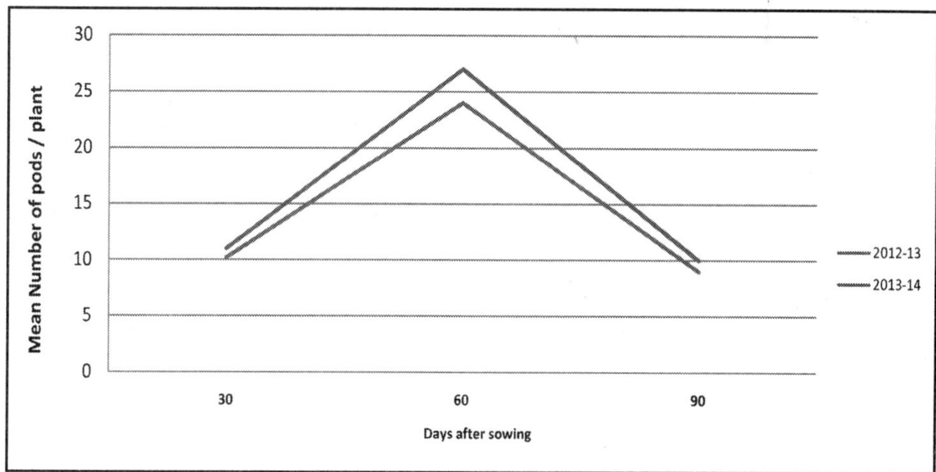

Fig. 4.4(a): Trends showing effect of three different growth stages on nodules dry weight (mg) plant^{-1} of Chickpea

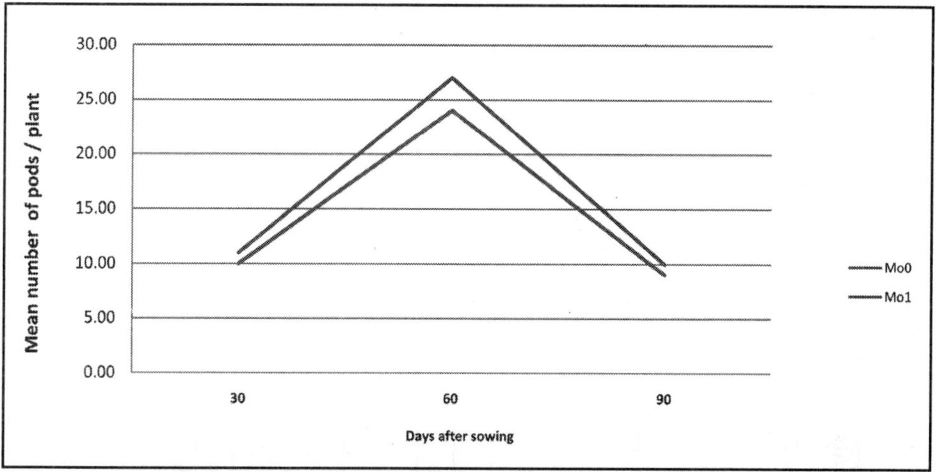

Fig. 4.4(b): Trends showing nodules dry (mg) plant^{-1} at three different stages of sowing without and with molybdenum of Chickpea

Table 4.9: Effect of Zn, B and Mo levels on number of pods plant^{-1} in Chickpea

Treatments	2012-13				2013-14			
	Without Molybdenum				Without Molybdenum			
	Zn_0	Zn_1	Zn_2	Mean	Zn_0	Zn_1	Zn_2	Mean
B_0	65.67	79.00	83.33	76.00	68.17	81.50	85.83	78.50
B_1	71.00	78.00	84.50	77.83	73.50	80.50	87.00	80.33
B_2	78.67	85.33	85.20	83.07	81.17	87.83	87.70	85.57
Mean	71.78	80.78	84.34	78.97	74.28	83.28	86.84	81.47
	With Molybdenum				With Molybdenum			
B_0	70.67	82.33	84.00	79.00	73.07	84.73	86.40	81.40
B_1	84.00	83.00	85.20	84.07	86.07	85.40	87.68	86.38
B_2	78.83	86.33	85.90	83.69	81.23	88.73	88.30	86.09
Mean	77.83	83.89	85.03	82.25	80.12	86.29	87.46	84.62
	S.E.(d)		C.D.(P=0.05)		S.E.(d)		C.D.(P=0.05)	
Zn	0.636		1.293		0.949		1.929	
B	0.636		1.293		0.949		1.929	
Mo	0.520		1.056		0.775		1.575	
Zn×B	1.102		2.240		1.644		3.341	
B×Mo	0.900		1.829		1.342		2.728	
Zn×Mo	0.900		1.829		1.342		2.728	
Zn×B×Mo	1.559		3.168		2.324		N.S.	

Table 4.10: Effect of Zn, B and Mo levels on number of grains pod^{-1} in Chickpea

Treatments	2012-13				2013-14			
	Without Molybdenum				Without Molybdenum			
	Zn_0	Zn_1	Zn_2	Mean	Zn_0	Zn_1	Zn_2	Mean
B_0	1.24	1.34	1.39	1.32	1.26	1.29	1.31	1.29
B_1	1.42	1.43	1.50	1.45	1.43	1.45	1.40	1.43
B_2	1.46	1.41	1.49	1.45	1.47	1.49	1.52	1.49
Mean	1.37	1.39	1.46	1.41	1.39	1.41	1.41	1.40
	With Molybdenum				With Molybdenum			
B_0	1.35	1.41	1.42	1.39	1.42	1.42	1.45	1.43
B_1	1.45	1.48	1.51	1.48	1.49	1.50	1.55	1.51
B_2	1.51	1.53	1.58	1.54	1.52	1.55	1.65	1.57
Mean	1.44	1.47	1.50	1.47	1.48	1.49	1.55	1.51
	S.E.(d)		C.D.(P=0.05)		S.E.(d)		C.D.(P=0.05)	
Zn	0.024		0.048		0.021		N.S.	
B	0.024		0.048		0.021		0.043	
Mo	0.019		0.039		0.017		0.035	
Zn×B	0.041		N.S.		0.037		N.S.	
B×Mo	0.034		N.S.		0.030		N.S.	
Zn×Mo	0.034		N.S.		0.030		N.S.	
Zn×B×Mo	0.058		N.S.		0.052		N.S.	

(e) Number of Pods Plant^{-1}

It shown in Table 4.9 number of pods plant^{-1} varied from 65.67 to 85.33 and 70.67 to 86.33 pods plant^{-1} in case of without and with molybdenum respectively and these values were given by Zn_1B_2 in former and Zn_1B_2 in latter cases. The main effect of Zn, B and Mo and interactions Zn × B, Zn × Mo, B × Mo and Zn × B × Mo were also significant increase in number of pods plant^{-1} at during first year (2012-13).

Number of pods plant^{-1} varied from 68.17 to 87.83 and 73.07 to 88.73 pods plant^{-1} in case of without and with molybdenum respectively and these values were given by Zn_1B_2 in former and Zn_1B_2 in latter cases. The main effect of Zn, B and Mo and interaction Zn × B, B × Mo and Zn × Mo resulted significant increase in number of pods plant^{-1} at during second year (2013-14).

The number of pods plant^{-1} varied the increasing age of plant. The mean number of pods plant^{-1} in without molybdenum was 78.97 and 82.25 pods plant^{-1} in molybdenum treatment at first year. Similarly at the mean number of pods plant^{-1} was 81.47 pods plant^{-1} in without molybdenum and 84.62 pods plant^{-1} in presence of molybdenum second year Table 4.9. The trends of showing the effect of zinc and boron levels on number of pods plant^{-1} without and with molybdenum of chickpea shown in Fig. 4.5(a) and 4.5(b).

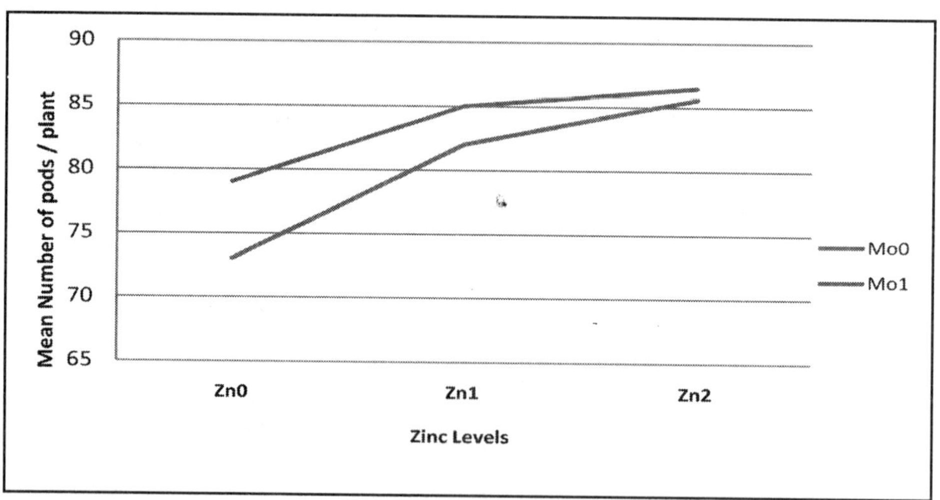

Fig. 4. 5(a): Trends showing the effect zinc levels on number of pods plant^{-1} with and without molybdenum of Chickpea

(f) Number of Grains Pod^{-1}

The data on number of grains pod^{-1} are given in Table 4.10. It is observed that number of grains pod^{-1} varied from 1.24 to 1.50 and 1.35 to 1.58 grains pod^{-1} in case of without and with molybdenum respectively and these values were given by Zn_2B_1 in former and Zn_2B_2 in latter cases. These main effects of Zn, B and Mo results significant increase in number of grains pod^{-1} at during first year *i.e.* 2012-13.

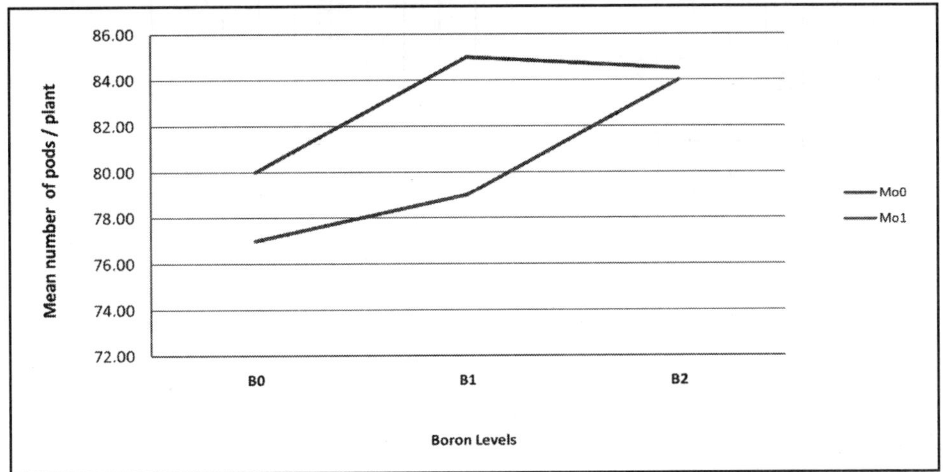

Fig. 4.5 (b): Trends showing the effect boron levels on number of pods plant^{-1} with and without molybdenum of Chickpea

Number of grains pod^{-1} varied from 1.26 to 1.52 and 1.42 to 1.65 grains pod^{-1} in case of without and with molybdenum respectively and these values were given by Zn_2B_2 in former and Zn_2B_2 in latter cases. These main effect of B and Mo resulted significant increase in number of grains pod^{-1} at second year (2013-14).

The number of grains pod^{-1} varied the increasing age of plant. The mean number of grains pod^{-1} in without molybdenum was 1.41 and 1.47 grains pod^{-1} in molybdenum treatment at (2012-13). Similarly at the mean number of grains pod^{-1} was 1.40 grains pod^{-1} in without molybdenum and 1.51 grains pod^{-1} in presence of molybdenum second year Table 4.10.

(g) Test Weight g of 100 Grains

Test weight varied from 18.20 to 20.80 and 18.71 to 21.00 g in case of without and with molybdenum respectively and these values were given by Zn_2B_2 in former and Zn_2B_2 in latter cases. These main effects of Zn and B resulted significant increase in test weight during first year.

Test weight varied from 18.22 to 20.86 and 18.73 to 21.06 g in case of without and with molybdenum respectively and these values were given by Zn_2B_2 in former and Zn_2B_2 in latter cases. These main effect of Zn, B and Mo resulted significant increase in test weight at (2013-14).

Test weight varied the advancement in the age of plant. The mean test weight in without molybdenum was 19.63 and 20.06 g in molybdenum treatment at (2012-13). Similarly at the mean test weight was 19.68 g in without molybdenum and 20.12 g in presence of molybdenum second year Table 4.11. The trends of results were somewhat similar during both the years and addition of Zn, B and Mo increased the test weight. The trends of showing the effect of zinc and boron levels on test weight (100 grains) without and with molybdenum of chickpea shown in Fig. 4.6(a) and 4.6(b).

Table 4.11: Effect of Zn, B and Mo levels on test weight (g) of 100 seeds in Chickpea

Treatments	2012-13				2013-14			
	Without Molybdenum				Without Molybdenum			
	Zn_0	Zn_1	Zn_2	Mean	Zn_0	Zn_1	Zn_2	Mean
B_0	18.20	19.14	19.34	18.89	18.22	19.20	19.40	18.94
B_1	18.71	20.47	20.53	19.90	18.73	20.52	20.59	19.95
B_2	18.82	20.67	20.80	20.10	18.84	20.72	20.86	20.14
Mean	18.58	20.09	20.22	19.63	18.60	20.15	20.28	19.68
	With Molybdenum				With Molybdenum			
B_0	18.71	19.46	19.42	19.20	18.73	19.48	19.48	19.23
B_1	19.86	20.51	20.80	20.39	19.88	20.76	20.86	20.50
B_2	19.83	20.93	21.00	20.59	19.85	20.96	21.06	20.62
Mean	19.47	20.30	20.41	20.06	19.49	20.40	20.47	20.12
	S.E.(d)		C.D.(P=0.05)		S.E.(d)		C.D.(P=0.05)	
Zn	0.289		0.588		0.170		0.346	
B	0.289		0.588		0.170		0.346	
Mo	0.236		N.S.		0.139		0.283	
Zn×B	0.501		N.S.		0.295		N.S.	
B×Mo	0.409		N.S.		0.241		N.S.	
Zn×Mo	0.409		N.S.		0.241		N.S.	
Zn×B×Mo	0.708		N.S.		0.417		N.S.	

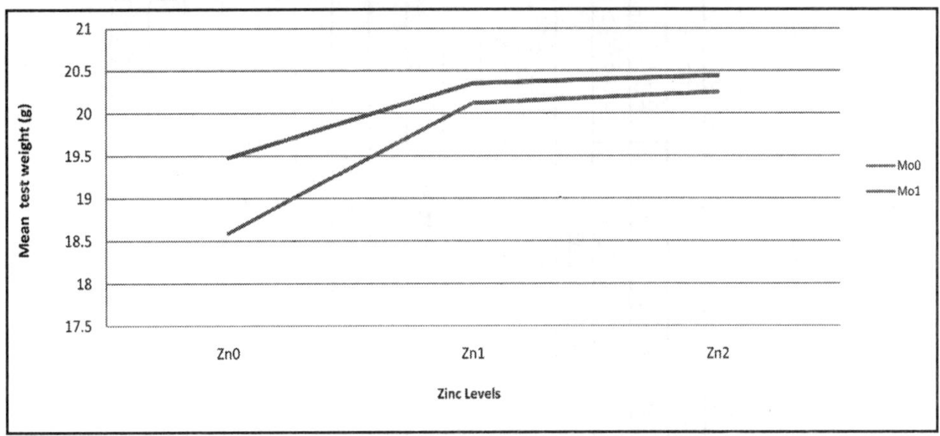

Fig. 4.6(a): Trends showing the effect zinc levels on test weight (100 seeds) with and without molybdenum of Chickpea

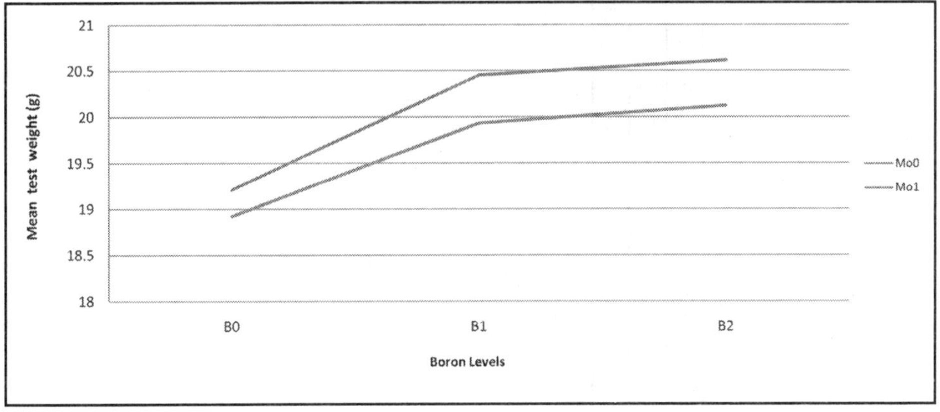

Fig. 4.6(b): Trends showing the effect boron levels on test weight (100 seeds) with and without molybdenum of Chickpea

Yields

(a) Grain Yield

Table 4.12 shows the effect of Zn, B and Mo levels on grain yield of chickpea expressed as kg ha^{-1}. On the whole the yield levels were found to be satisfactory irrespective of treatments. It was further indicated that the yield levels in general during second year were somewhat higher than those of first year. In case of Mo_0 yield varied from 1800.00 to 2260.00 kg ha^{-1} and in case of Mo_1 it varied from 1950.00 to 2325.00 kg ha^{-1}. In case of no molybdenum, Zn_1 and Zn_2 where at par and there existed no significant difference between the two levels. But both the levels (Zn_1 and Zn_2) were significantly superior to Zn_0 during first year. In case of boron (B_1 and B_2) did not differ from each other significantly. However, both the levels were significantly superior to control. B_2 was numerically superior to B_1.

Table 4.12: Effect of Zn, B and Mo levels on grain yield (kg ha^{-1}) in Chickpea

Treatments	2012-13				2013-14			
	Without Molybdenum				**Without Molybdenum**			
	Zn_0	**Zn_1**	**Zn_2**	**Mean**	**Zn_0**	**Zn_1**	**Zn_2**	**Mean**
B_0	1800.00	2130.00	2140.00	2023.33	1805.00	2135.00	2145.00	2028.33
B_1	1980.00	2250.00	2250.00	2160.00	1985.00	2255.00	2255.00	2165.00
B_2	2020.00	2260.00	2260.00	2180.00	2020.00	2260.00	2265.00	2181.67
Mean	1933.33	2213.33	2216.67	2121.11	1936.67	2216.67	2221.67	2125.00
	With Molybdenum				**With Molybdenum**			
B_0	1950.00	2205.00	2210.00	2121.67	1955.00	2210.00	2215.00	2126.67
B_1	2180.00	2325.00	2320.00	2275.00	2185.00	2330.00	2325.00	2280.00
B_2	2175.00	2315.00	2325.00	2271.67	2175.00	2315.00	2330.00	2273.33
Mean	2101.67	2281.67	2285.00	2222.78	2105.00	2285.00	2290.00	2226.67
	S.E.(d)		C.D.(P=0.05)		S.E.(d)		C.D.(P=0.05)	
Zn	27.704		56.317		22.722		46.189	
B	27.704		56.317		22.722		46.189	
Mo	22.620		45.983		18.552		37.713	
Zn×B	47.985		N.S.		39.355		N.S.	
B×Mo	39.180		N.S.		32.133		N.S.	
Zn×Mo	39.180		N.S.		32.133		N.S.	
Zn×B×Mo	67.861		N.S.		55.657		N.S.	

On molybdenum treatment during first year, the yield level was increased by 8.70 per cent over no molybdenum control, irrespective of Zn and B levels on mean basis. Thus the yield levels were increased by molybdenum treatment and on the whole Zn_2B_2 came out to be the yielding highest yield combination in case of both without and with molybdenum during first year (2012-13).

The main affects of zinc, boron and molybdenum were significant but their interactions were not significant in both, without and with molybdenum during first year.

During second year (2013-14) it indicated that the yield levels in general during second year where somewhat higher than those of first year. Addition of molybdenum increased the yield by 4.8 per cent over no molybdenum control. The treatment effects during this year were similar to those of first year *i.e.,* the main affects of Zn, B and Mo were significant but the interactions of these nutrient elements were not significant. Zn_2B_2 again emerged to be the highest yielding treatment both in presence and absence of molybdenum.

The yield varied from 1805.00 to 2265.00 kg ha^{-1} and 1955.00 to 2330.00 kg ha^{-1} in case of without and with molybdenum respectively, during second year. In the treatments Zn_0B_0 addition of molybdenum alone increased the yield by 8.31 per cent. The main affects of Zn, B and Mo were significant but their interactions were not significant. The effect of zinc and boron levels on grain yield kg ha^{-1} without and with molybdenum of chickpea shown in Fig. 4.7(a) and 4.7(b).

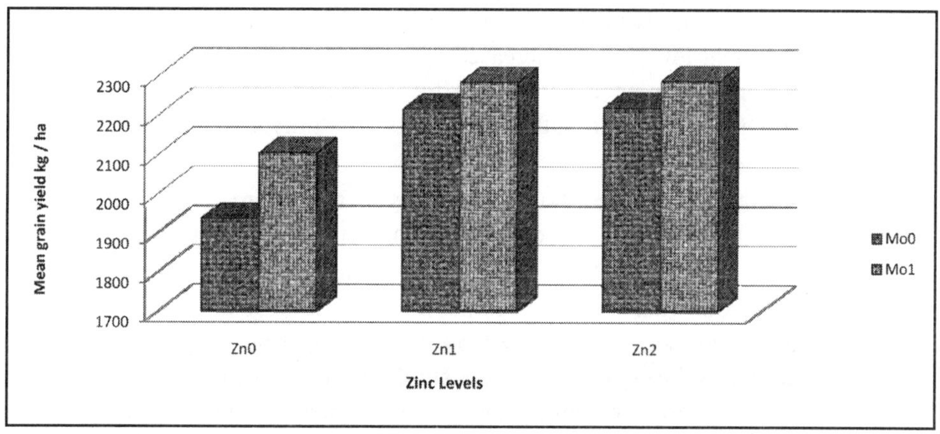

Fig. 4.7(a): The effect of zinc levels on grain yield kg ha^{-1} with and without molybdenum of Chickpea

(b) Stover Yield

Table. 4.13 showed the effect of Zn, B and Mo levels on stover yield of chickpea. The yield levels were found to the satisfactory regardless of treatments. It was observed that the yield levels in general during second year where somewhat higher than those of first year. In case of Mo_0 yield varied from 1980.00 to 2725.00 kg ha^{-1} and in case of Mo_1 it varied from 2145.00 to 2930.00 kg ha^{-1}. In case of no molybdenum, Zn_1 and

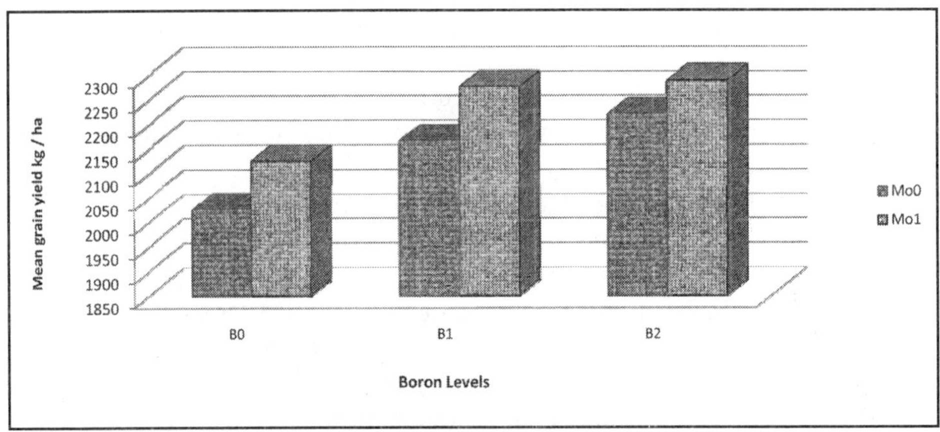

Fig. 4.7(b): The effect of boron levels on grain yield kg ha^{-1} with and without molybdenum of Chickpea

Zn_2 where at par and there was no significant difference between the two levels. But both the levels (Zn_1 and Zn_2) were significant superior to Zn_0 during first year. In case of boron (B_1 and B_2) did not differ from each other significantly. However, both the levels were significantly superior to control. B_2 was numerically superior to B_1.

On molybdenum treatment during first year, the yield level was increased by 6.70 per cent over no molybdenum control, irrespective of Zn and B levels on mean basis. Thus the yield levels were increased by molybdenum treatment on the whole the treatments appeared to have increasing effect on biological yield Zn_2B_2 the highest yielding combination in case of both without and with molybdenum during first year (2012-13).

The main affects of zinc, boron and molybdenum were significant but their interactions were not significant in both without and with molybdenum during first year.

During second year (2013-14) it was further indicated that the yield levels in general during second year where somewhat higher than those of first year. Addition of molybdenum increased the yield by 5.64 per cent over no molybdenum control. The treatment effects during this year were similar to those of first year *i.e.,* the main affects of Zn, B and Mo were significant but the interactions nutrient elements were not significant Zn_2B_2 gave the highest yield both in presence and absence of molybdenum.

The yield varied from 2000.00 to 2745.00 kg ha^{-1} and 2155.00 to 2940.00 kg ha^{-1} in case of without and with molybdenum respectively, during second year. In the treatments Zn_0B_0 addition of molybdenum alone increased the yield by 7.75 per cent. The main affects of Zn, B and Mo were significant and there interaction Zn × Mo and Zn × B were significant. The effect of zinc and boron levels on stover yield kg ha^{-1} without and with molybdenum of chickpea shown in Fig. 4.8(a) and 4.8(b).

Table 4.13: Effect of Zn, B and Mo levels on stover yield (kg ha^{-1}) in Chickpea

Treatments	2012-13				2013-14			
	Without Molybdenum				Without Molybdenum			
	Zn_0	Zn_1	Zn_2	Mean	Zn_0	Zn_1	Zn_2	Mean
B_0	1980.00	2407.00	2439.00	2275.33	2000.00	2427.00	2459.00	2295.33
B_1	2178.00	2565.00	2610.00	2451.00	2198.00	2585.00	2630.00	2471.00
B_2	2424.00	2702.00	2725.00	2617.00	2444.00	2722.00	2745.00	2637.00
Mean	2194.00	2558.00	2591.33	2447.78	2214.00	2578.00	2611.33	2467.78
	With Molybdenum				With Molybdenum			
B_0	2145.00	2558.00	2718.00	2473.67	2155.00	2568.00	2728.33	2483.78
B_1	2442.00	2790.00	2876.00	2702.67	2152.00	2800.00	2886.00	2612.67
B_2	2436.00	2778.00	2930.00	2714.67	2446.00	2788.00	2940.00	2724.67
Mean	2341.00	2708.67	2841.33	2630.33	2251.00	2718.67	2851.44	2607.04
	S.E.(d)		C.D.(P=0.05)		S.E.(d)		C.D.(P=0.05)	
Zn	32.149		65.353		22.063		44.850	
B	32.149		65.353		22.063		44.850	
Mo	26.250		53.360		18.014		36.620	
Zn×B	55.684		N.S.		38.214		77.682	
B×Mo	45.466		N.S.		31.202		N.S.	
Zn×Mo	45.466		N.S.		31.202		63.427	
Zn×B×Mo	78.749		N.S.		54.043		N.S.	

Table 4.14: Effect of Zn, B and Mo levels on per cent harvest index in Chickpea

Treatments	2012-13				2013-14			
	Without Molybdenum				Without Molybdenum			
	Zn_0	Zn_1	Zn_2	Mean	Zn_0	Zn_1	Zn_2	Mean
B_0	47.61	46.95	46.74	47.10	47.44	46.80	46.59	46.94
B_1	47.61	46.73	46.30	46.88	47.45	46.59	46.16	46.73
B_2	45.45	45.55	45.34	45.45	45.25	45.36	45.21	45.27
Mean	46.89	46.41	46.13	46.48	46.71	46.25	45.99	46.32
	With Molybdenum				With Molybdenum			
B_0	47.62	46.29	44.85	46.25	47.57	46.25	44.81	46.21
B_1	47.17	45.45	44.65	45.76	50.38	45.42	44.62	46.81
B_2	47.17	45.45	44.24	45.62	47.07	45.37	44.21	45.55
Mean	47.32	45.73	44.58	45.88	48.34	45.68	44.55	46.19
	S.E.(d)		C.D.(P=0.05)		S.E.(d)		C.D.(P=0.05)	
Zn	0.176		0.357		0.201		0.408	
B	0.176		0.357		0.201		0.408	
Mo	0.143		0.292		0.164		N.S.	
Zn×B	0.304		N.S.		0.348		0.707	
B×Mo	0.248		0.505		0.284		0.577	
Zn×Mo	0.248		0.505		0.284		0.577	
Zn×B×Mo	0.430		N.S.		0.492		1.000	

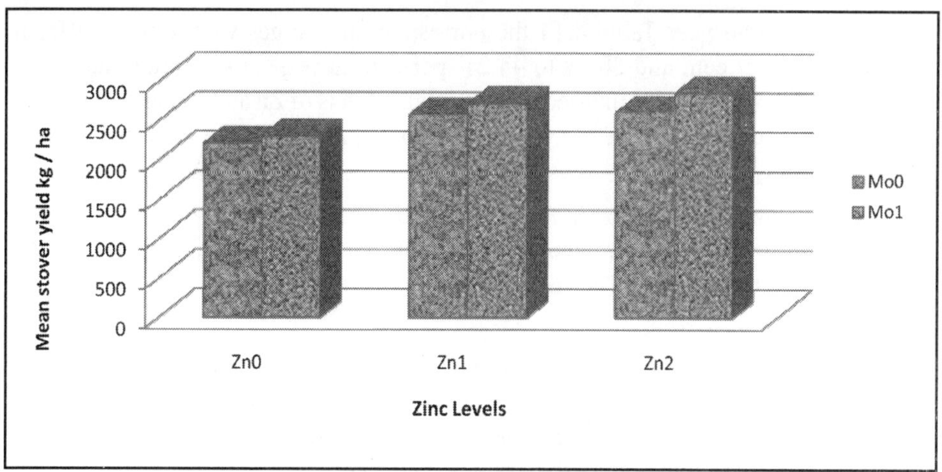

Fig. 4.8(a): The effect of zinc levels on stover yield kg ha^{-1} with and without molybdenum of Chickpea

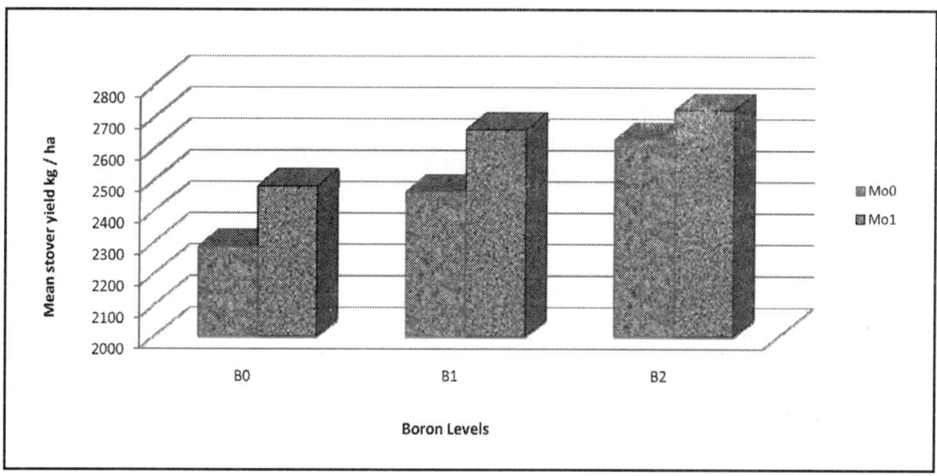

Fig. 4.8(b): The effect of boron levels on stover yield kg ha^{-1} with and without molybdenum of Chickpea

(c) Harvest Index (%)

On a count of its plant type, the vegetative part of chickpea is only slightly higher than the economic part and so also the economic yield and harvest index in general, is observed to be fairly high. It varied from 47.61 to 45.34 per cent. Due to lower yields the harvest index was control higher than the highest yielding treatment (Zn_2B_2) in case of both, without and with molybdenum. In case of the latter it ranged from 47.62 to 44.24 per cent. The main effects of Zn, B and Mo and interaction Zn × Mo and B × Mo were significant but Zn × B and Zn × B × Mo were not significant during the first year (2012-13).

During second year Table 4.14 the corresponding ranges were observed from 47.45 to 45.21 per cent and 50.38 to 44.21 per cent in respect of without and with molybdenum respectively. During second year main effects of Zn and B were significant among the interactions Zn × B, B × Mo, Zn × Mo and Zn × B × Mo were significant.

Concentration of Nutrients

For obtaining the variation in the concentration of the nutrients due to grain and stover different treatments were analyzed for N, P, K, S, Zn, B, Mo, Cu, Fe and Mn after the harvest of the crop. The results are described below:

(a) Nitrogen

Chickpea is a high protein crop and naturally the concentration of N was quite high in respect of different treatments. It varied from 2.87 in control to 3.55 per cent in Zn_2B_2 during first year (2012-13) where no molybdenum was added. In case the crop fertilized with molybdenum, the grain nitrogen content varied from 2.88 to 3.56 per cent the lowest and highest values were observed in Zn_0B_0 and Zn_2B_2. The results were significant statistically due to different levels of B and Zn wherein only the main effects of B and Zn were significant. Molybdenum application did not cause any significant variation in nitrogen content of grain and the interactions different nutrients were also not significant.

The trends of results during second year (2013-14) were similar to those of first year. In this case range of variation in grain nitrogen was from 2.89 to 3.57 and 2.92 to 3.60 per cent in without and with molybdenum respectively Table 4.15.

In stover, it varied from 1.96 to 2.24 per cent during first year (2012-13) where no molybdenum was added. In case the crop was fertilized with molybdenum the stover nitrogen content varied from 2.01 to 2.30 per cent. The highest and lowest results were obtained in Zn_0B_0 and Zn_2B_2. The results were significant statistically due to different levels of B and Zn wherein only the main effects of Zn and B were significant, and molybdenum application did not cause any significant variation in nitrogen content of stover and the interactions different nutrients were also not significant.

The trends of results during second year (2013-14) were similar to Zn, and B of first year. In this case range of variation in stover nitrogen was from 2.00 to 2.28 and 2.03 to 2.30 per cent in without and with molybdenum respectively Table 4.16.

(b) Phosphorous

As shown in Table 4.17 the phosphorous content in grain it varied from 0.30 to 0.38 per cent during first year (2012-13) where no molybdenum was added. In case the crop was fertilized with molybdenum the grain phosphorous content varied from 0.33 to 0.39 per cent. The results were significant statistically due to different levels of Zn, B and Mo wherein the main effects of Zn, B and Mo were significant and the interactions Zn × B nutrients were also significant.

Table 4.15: Effect of Zn, B and Mo levels on per cent nitrogen content in grain of Chickpea

Treatments	2012-13				2013-14			
	Without Molybdenum				Without Molybdenum			
	Zn_0	Zn_1	Zn_2	Mean	Zn_0	Zn_1	Zn_2	Mean
B_0	2.87	3.07	3.20	3.05	2.89	3.09	3.22	3.07
B_1	2.98	3.13	3.40	3.17	3.00	3.15	3.42	3.19
B_2	3.10	3.23	3.55	3.29	3.12	3.25	3.57	3.31
Mean	2.98	3.14	3.38	3.17	3.00	316	3.40	3.19
	With Molybdenum				With Molybdenum			
B_0	2.88	3.07	3.21	3.05	2.92	3.12	3.25	3.10
B_1	2.99	3.14	3.41	3.18	3.03	3.18	3.48	3.23
B_2	3.11	3.24	3.56	3.30	3.15	3.27	3.60	3.34
Mean	2.99	3.15	3.39	3.18	3.03	3.19	3.44	3.22
	S.E.(d)		C.D.(P=0.05)		S.E.(d)		C.D.(P=0.05)	
Zn	0.040		0.080		0.056		0.114	
B	0.040		0.080		0.056		0.114	
Mo	0.032		N.S.		0.046		N.S.	
Zn×B	0.069		N.S.		0.097		N.S.	
B×Mo	0.056		N.S.		0.079		N.S.	
Zn×Mo	0.056		N.S.		0.079		N.S.	
Zn×B×Mo	0.097		N.S.		0.137		N.S.	

Table 4.16: Effect of Zn, B and Mo levels on per cent nitrogen content in stover of Chickpea

Treatments	2012-13				2013-14			
	Without Molybdenum				Without Molybdenum			
	Zn_0	**Zn_1**	**Zn_2**	**Mean**	**Zn_0**	**Zn_1**	**Zn_2**	**Mean**
B_0	1.96	2.09	2.18	2.08	2.00	2.11	2.22	2.11
B_1	2.08	2.12	2.20	2.13	2.10	2.15	2.23	2.16
B_2	2.13	2.13	2.24	2.17	2.15	2.16	2.28	2.20
Mean	2.06	2.11	2.21	2.13	2.08	2.14	2.24	2.16
	With Molybdenum				**With Molybdenum**			
B_0	2.01	2.10	2.22	2.11	2.03	2.13	2.25	2.14
B_1	2.11	2.18	2.24	2.18	2.12	2.21	2.27	2.20
B_2	2.17	2.18	2.30	2.22	2.19	2.21	2.30	2.23
Mean	2.10	2.15	2.25	2.17	2.11	2.18	2.27	2.19
	S.E.(d)		C.D.(P=0.05)		S.E.(d)		C.D.(P=0.05)	
Zn	0.028		0.057		0.035		0.071	
B	0.028		0.057		0.035		0.071	
Mo	0.023		N.S.		0.028		N.S.	
Zn×B	0.049		N.S.		0.060		N.S.	
B×Mo	0.040		N.S.		0.049		N.S.	
Zn×Mo	0.040		N.S.		0.049		N.S.	
Zn×B×Mo	0.069		N.S.		0.085		N.S.	

The trends of results during second year (2013-14) were similar to those of first year. Only the main effects of Zn, B and Mo but the interaction were not significant. In this case range of variation in grain phosphorous was from 0.29 to 0.40 and 0.32 to 0.41 per cent in without and with molybdenum respectively Table 4.17.

In stover phosphorus content it varied from 0.33 to 0.40 per cent during first year (2012-13) where no molybdenum was added. In case the crop was treated with molybdenum the stover phosphorous content varied from 0.37 to 0.41 per cent. The results were significant statistically due to different levels of Zn, B and Mo where in the main effects were significant.

The trends of results during second year (2013-14) were similar to those of first year. Only the main effects Zn and B were significant for phosphorous content of stover and the interactions were also not significant. In this case range of variation in stover phosphorous was from 0.34 to 0.42 and 0.37 to 0.40 per cent in without and with molybdenum respectively Table 4.18.

(c) Potassium

Potassium content of grain it varied from 0.44 to 0.53 per cent during first year (2012-13) where no molybdenum was added. In presence of molybdenum the grain potassium content varied from 0.50 to 0.54 per cent. The results were significant statistically due to different levels of Zn, B and Mo wherein only the main effects were significant in potassium content of grain and the interactions different nutrients were not significant.

The during second year (2013-14) main effects of Zn, B and Mo and interaction Zn × B were significant. In this case range of variation in grain potassium was from 0.45 to 0.54 and 0.50 to 0.55 per cent in without and with molybdenum respectively Table 4.19.

Potassium content of stover it varied from 1.63 to 1.87 per cent during first year (2012-13) in case of without molybdenum. In case the crop was fertilized with molybdenum the stover potassium content varied from 1.75 to 1.89 per cent. The results were significant statistically due to different levels of Zn, B and Mo. The main effects of Zn, B and Mo were significant and no interactions were significant except Zn × B which was significant during first year.

The data regarding the potassium content of stover as shown in Table 4.20 revealed that the main effects of Zn and B were significant but that of Mo it was not significant. Among the interaction Zn × B was significant and the rest were not significant. In this case range of variation in stover potassium was from 1.64 to 1.88 and 1.76 to 1.89 per cent in without and with molybdenum respectively during second year.

Table 4.17: Effect of Zn, B and Mo levels on per cent phosphorus content in grain of Chickpea

Treatments	2012-13				2013-14			
	Without Molybdenum				Without Molybdenum			
	Zn_0	Zn_1	Zn_2	Mean	Zn_0	Zn_1	Zn_2	Mean
B_0	0.30	0.32	0.35	0.32	0.29	0.36	0.37	0.34
B_1	0.34	0.35	0.36	0.35	0.33	039	0.39	0.37
B_2	0.33	0.38	0.34	0.35	0.32	0.37	0.40	0.36
Mean	0.32	0.35	0.35	0.34	0.31	0.37	0.39	0.36
	With Molybdenum				With Molybdenum			
B_0	0.33	0.36	0.38	0.36	0.32	0.39	0.39	0.37
B_1	0.35	0.38	0.39	0.37	0.34	0.41	0.40	0.38
B_2	0.33	0.39	0.35	0.36	0.32	0.38	0.41	0.37
Mean	0.34	0.38	0.37	0.36	0.33	0.39	0.40	0.37
	S.E.(d)		C.D.(P=0.05)		S.E.(d)		C.D.(P=0.05)	
Zn	0.007		0.013		0.005		0.011	
B	0.007		0.013		0.005		0.011	
Mo	0.005		0.011		0.004		0.009	
Zn×B	0.011		0.023		0.009		N.S.	
B×Mo	0.009		N.S.		0.008		N.S.	
Zn×Mo	0.009		N.S.		0.008		N.S.	
Zn×B×Mo	0.016		N.S.		0.013		N.S.	

Table 4.18: Effect of Zn, B and Mo levels on per cent phosphorus content in stover of Chickpea

Treatments	2012-13				2013-14			
	Without Molybdenum				Without Molybdenum			
	Zn_0	Zn_1	Zn_2	Mean	Zn_0	Zn_1	Zn_2	Mean
B_0	0.33	0.37	0.39	0.36	0.34	0.38	0.40	0.37
B_1	0.39	0.38	0.39	0.39	0.39	0.39	0.41	0.40
B_2	0.39	0.39	0.40	0.39	0.40	0.39	0.42	0.40
Mean	0.37	0.38	0.39	0.38	0.38	0.39	0.41	0.39
	With Molybdenum				With Molybdenum			
B_0	0.37	0.39	0.41	0.39	0.37	0.39	0.40	0.39
B_1	0.39	0.40	0.40	0.40	0.39	0.40	0.41	0.40
B_2	0.40	0.40	0.41	0.40	0.41	0.40	0.40	0.40
Mean	0.39	0.40	0.41	0.40	0.39	0.40	0.40	0.40
	S.E.(d)		C.D.(P=0.05)		S.E.(d)		C.D.(P=0.05)	
Zn	0.007		0.015		0.009		0.018	
B	0.007		0.015		0.009		0.018	
Mo	0.006		0.012		0.007		N.S.	
Zn×B	0.013		N.S.		0.016		N.S.	
B×Mo	0.011		N.S.		0.013		N.S.	
Zn×Mo	0.011		N.S.		0.013		N.S.	
Zn×B×Mo	0.018		N.S.		0.022		N.S.	

Table 4.19: Effect of Zn, B and Mo levels on per cent potassium content in grain of Chickpea

Treatments	2012-13				2013-14			
	Without Molybdenum				**Without Molybdenum**			
	Zn_0	**Zn_1**	**Zn_2**	**Mean**	**Zn_0**	**Zn_1**	**Zn_2**	**Mean**
B_0	0.44	0.50	0.52	0.49	0.45	0.51	0.53	0.50
B_1	0.50	0.51	0.52	0.51	0.51	0.52	0.53	0.52
B_2	0.51	0.51	0.53	0.52	0.52	0.52	0.54	0.53
Mean	0.48	0.51	0.52	0.50	0.49	0.52	0.53	0.51
	With Molybdenum				**With Molybdenum**			
B_0	0.50	0.51	0.53	0.51	0.50	0.51	0.53	0.51
B_1	0.51	0.52	0.53	0.52	0.52	0.53	0.54	0.53
B_2	0.53	0.52	0.54	0.53	0.53	0.53	0.55	0.54
Mean	0.51	0.52	0.53	0.52	0.52	0.52	0.54	0.53
	S.E.(d)		C.D.(P=0.05)		S.E.(d)		C.D.(P=0.05)	
Zn	0.008		0.017		0.006		0.011	
B	0.008		0.017		0.006		0.011	
Mo	0.007		0.014		0.005		0.009	
Zn×B	0.014		N.S.		0.010		0.020	
B×Mo	0.012		N.S.		0.008		N.S.	
Zn×Mo	0.012		N.S.		0.008		N.S.	
Zn×B×Mo	0.020		N.S.		0.014		N.S.	

Table 4.:20: Effect of Zn, B and Mo levels on per cent potassium content in stover of Chickpea

Treatments	2012-13				2013-14			
	Without Molybdenum				Without Molybdenum			
	Zn_0	**Zn_1**	**Zn_2**	**Mean**	**Zn_0**	**Zn_1**	**Zn_2**	**Mean**
B_0	1.63	1.82	1.84	1.76	1.64	1.83	1.86	1.78
B_1	1.82	1.84	1.85	1.84	1.83	1.85	1.88	1.85
B_2	1.85	1.86	1.87	1.86	1.86	1.87	1.85	1.86
Mean	1.77	1.84	1.85	1.82	1.78	1.85	1.86	1.83
	With Molybdenum				**With Molybdenum**			
B_0	1.75	1.83	1.83	1.80	1.76	1.84	1.86	1.82
B_1	1.83	1.89	1.86	1.86	1.84	1.85	1.89	1.86
B_2	1.88	1.89	1.88	1.88	1.87	1.86	1.88	1.87
Mean	1.82	1.87	1.86	1.85	1.82	1.85	1.88	1.85
	S.E.(d)		C.D.(P=0.05)		S.E.(d)		C.D.(P=0.05)	
Zn	0.016		0.033		0.021		0.043	
B	0.016		0.033		0.021		0.043	
Mo	0.013		0.027		0.017		N.S.	
Zn×B	0.028		0.057		0.037		0.074	
B×Mo	0.023		N.S.		0.030		N.S.	
Zn×Mo	0.023		N.S.		0.030		N.S.	
Zn×B×Mo	0.040		N.S.		0.052		N.S.	

(d) Sulphur

As given in Table 4.21 chickpea is a high protein crop and naturally the concentration grain sulphur was quite high in respect of different treatments. It varied from 0.64 to 0.70 per cent during first year (2012-13) were no molybdenum was added. In case the crop was fertilized with molybdenum the grain sulphur content varied from 0.67 to 0.71 per cent. The results were significant statistically due to different levels of Zn, B and Mo wherein only the main effects had significant variation in sulphur content of grain and the interaction Zn × B were also significant.

The trends of results during second year (2013-14) were similar to those of first year. The main effects of Zn, B and Mo and all interaction effects were not significant. Table 4.21 in this case range of variation in grain sulphur were from 0.65 to 0.71 and 0.68 to 0.73 per cent in without and with molybdenum respectively.

The lowest and highest values were observed in Zn_0B_0 and Zn_2B_2. In stover sulphur content varied from 0.23 to 0.27 per cent during first year (2012-13) where no molybdenum was added. In case the crop was fertilized with molybdenum the stover sulphur content varied from 0.25 to 0.27 per cent. The results were significant statistically due to different levels of B and Zn wherein the main effect of only Zn was significant.

The trends of results during second year (2013-14) the sulphur content of stover varied from 0.23 to 0.27 and 0.25 to 0.28 per cent in without and with molybdenum respectively in (Table 4.22). The main effect of Zn was significant, rest of the variables were not significant.

(e) Zinc

The data regarding variations in content the zinc in grain and stover due to Zn, B and Mo during the both years are reported separately for the both years and is given in Table 4.23. The data revealed that application of nutrients had as increasing effect on zinc content of grain, wherein it ranged from 38.50 to 46.20 mg kg^{-1} and treatment Zn_2B_2 gave the highest value followed by Zn_2B_2. The results in increasing the zinc content were significant.

The main effects of Zn, B and Mo and interaction Zn × B were significant in grain during first year and rest of the interactions were not significant.

During second year the grain zinc content varied from 39.20 to 46.80 mg kg^{-1} and treatment combination Zn_0B_0 and Zn_2B_2 gave the lowest and highest values in case of without molybdenum. In case of with molybdenum, during second year the zinc content ranged from 40.00 to 47.69 mg kg^{-1} and minimum and maximum values in grain zinc content were observed in Zn_0B_0 and Zn_2B_2, respectively. The main effects were significant for Zn, B and Mo. However, among the interactions Zn × B was also significant but rest of the interactions were not significant.

Table 4.21: Effect of Zn, B and Mo levels on per cent sulphur content in grain of Chickpea

Treatments	2012-13				2013-14			
	Without Molybdenum				Without Molybdenum			
	Zn_0	Zn_1	Zn_2	Mean	Zn_0	Zn_1	Zn_2	Mean
B_0	0.64	0.68	0.69	0.67	0.65	0.68	0.70	0.68
B_1	0.68	0.69	0.70	0.69	0.69	0.71	0.70	0.70
B_2	0.69	0.68	0.69	0.69	0.70	0.69	0.71	0.70
Mean	0.67	0.68	0.69	0.68	0.68	0.69	0.70	0.69
	With Molybdenum				With Molybdenum			
B_0	0.67	0.68	0.70	0.68	0.68	0.69	0.72	0.70
B_1	0.70	0.71	0.71	0.71	0.71	0.72	0.72	0.72
B_2	0.71	0.69	0.69	0.70	0.72	0.71	0.73	0.72
Mean	0.69	0.69	0.70	0.70	0.70	0.71	0.72	0.71
	S.E.(d)		C.D.(P=0.05)		S.E.(d)		C.D.(P=0.05)	
Zn	0.005		0.011		0.008		0.017	
B	0.005		0.011		0.008		0.017	
Mo	0.004		0.009		0.007		0.014	
Zn×B	0.009		0.019		0.014		N.S.	
B×Mo	0.007		N.S.		0.012		N.S.	
Zn×Mo	0.007		N.S.		0.012		N.S.	
Zn×B×Mo	0.013		N.S.		0.020		N.S.	

Table 4.22: Effect of Zn, B and Mo levels on per cent sulphur content in stover of Chickpea

Treatments	2012-13				2013-14			
	Without Molybdenum				**Without Molybdenum**			
	Zn_0	**Zn_1**	**Zn_2**	**Mean**	**Zn_0**	**Zn_1**	**Zn_2**	**Mean**
B_0	0.23	0.25	0.27	0.25	0.23	0.26	0.27	0.25
B_1	0.25	0.26	0.27	0.26	0.26	0.26	0.27	0.26
B_2	0.26	0.26	0.27	0.26	0.26	0.26	0.27	0.26
Mean	0.25	0.26	0.27	0.26	0.25	0.26	0.27	0.26
	With Molybdenum				**With Molybdenum**			
B_0	0.25	0.26	0.27	0.26	0.25	0.26	0.27	0.26
B_1	0.26	0.26	0.27	0.26	0.26	0.26	0.27	0.26
B_2	0.26	0.26	0.27	0.26	0.26	0.27	0.28	0.27
Mean	0.26	0.26	0.27	0.26	0.26	0.26	0.27	0.26
	S.E.(d)		C.D.(P=0.05)		S.E.(d)		C.D.(P=0.05)	
Zn	0.005		0.010		0.005		0.010	
B	0.005		N.S.		0.005		N.S.	
Mo	0.004		N.S.		0.004		N.S.	
Zn×B	0.008		N.S.		0.009		N.S.	
B×Mo	0.007		N.S.		0.007		N.S.	
Zn×Mo	0.007		N.S.		0.007		N.S.	
Zn×B×Mo	0.012		N.S.		0.012		N.S.	

Table 4.23: Effect of Zn, B and Mo levels on zinc content (mg kg^{-1}) in grain of Chickpea

Treatments	2012-13				2013-14			
	Without Molybdenum				Without Molybdenum			
	Zn_0	**Zn_1**	**Zn_2**	**Mean**	**Zn_0**	**Zn_1**	**Zn_2**	**Mean**
B_0	38.50	39.30	43.30	40.37	39.20	40.08	44.00	41.09
B_1	40.10	42.40	44.60	42.37	40.80	43.20	45.35	43.12
B_2	39.40	43.80	46.20	43.13	40.43	44.50	46.80	43.91
Mean	39.33	41.83	44.70	41.96	40.14	42.59	45.38	42.71
	With Molybdenum				**With Molybdenum**			
B_0	39.30	40.10	44.00	41.13	40.00	40.80	44.80	41.87
B_1	41.00	43.60	45.40	43.33	41.70	43.90	46.15	43.92
B_2	40.20	44.70	47.00	43.97	40.90	45.30	47.69	44.63
Mean	40.17	42.80	45.47	42.81	40.87	43.33	46.21	43.47
	S.E.(d)		C.D.(P=0.05)		S.E.(d)		C.D.(P=0.05)	
Zn	0.319		0.648		0.313		0.637	
B	0.319		0.648		0.313		0.637	
Mo	0.260		0.529		0.256		0.520	
Zn×B	0.552		1.122		0.542		1.103	
B×Mo	0.451		N.S.		0.443		N.S.	
Zn×Mo	0.451		N.S.		0.443		N.S.	
Zn×B×Mo	0.781		N.S.		0.767		N.S.	

Table 4.24: Effect of Zn, B and Mo levels on zinc content (mg kg^{-1}) in stover of Chickpea

Treatments	2012-13				2013-14			
	Without Molybdenum				Without Molybdenum			
	Zn_0	Zn_1	Zn_2	Mean	Zn_0	Zn_1	Zn_2	Mean
B_0	17.20	19.00	24.90	20.37	17.50	19.20	25.15	20.62
B_1	19.50	23.70	26.80	23.33	19.70	23.90	27.00	23.53
B_2	21.70	26.40	30.00	26.03	21.90	26.55	30.00	26.22
Mean	19.47	23.03	27.23	23.24	19.70	23.22	27.45	23.46
	With Molybdenum				With Molybdenum			
B_0	18.30	20.50	26.80	21.87	18.50	20.60	26.85	21.98
B_1	20.40	24.80	27.90	24.37	20.60	24.95	28.10	24.55
B_2	22.80	27.70	31.30	27.27	22.95	27.90	31.45	27.43
Mean	20.50	24.33	28.67	24.50	20.68	24.48	28.80	24.66
	S.E.(d)		C.D.(P=0.05)		S.E.(d)		C.D.(P=0.05)	
Zn	0.227		0.461		0.225		0.458	
B	0.227		0.461		0.225		0.458	
Mo	0.185		0.376		0.184		0.374	
Zn×B	0.392		0.798		0.390		0.793	
B×Mo	0.320		N.S.		0.319		N.S.	
Zn×Mo	0.320		N.S.		0.319		N.S.	
Zn×B×Mo	0.555		N.S.		0.552		N.S.	

Table 4.24 describe the variation in zinc concentration due to Zn, B and Mo levels in stover. The results revealed that Zn_0B_0 and Zn_2B_2 gave the highest values of 17.20 to 30.00 mg kg^{-1} respectively. In case of without molybdenum during first year. In case of with molybdenum during the same year it ranged from 18.30 to 31.30 mg kg^{-1} and these values were given by Zn_0B_0 and Zn_2B_2 respectively. The main effects of Zn, B and Mo and interaction Zn × B resulted in significant increase in stover zinc content.

During second year the stover zinc content varied from 17.50 to 30.00 mg kg^{-1} respectively without Mo. In case of with Mo during the same year it ranged from 18.50 to 31.45 mg kg^{-1} and these values were given by Zn_0B_0 and $Zn_2B_{2.}$ Zn × B interaction was also significant but rest of interactions were not significant.

(f) Boron

The data regarding variations in content of boron in grain and stover due to Zn, B and Mo during both the years are reported separately for the both years is given in Table 4.25. The data revealed that application of nutrients had as increasing effects on boron content of grain. Wherein it ranged from 48.00 to 56.00 mg kg^{-1} and treatment Zn_0B_0 and Zn_2B_2 gave the lowest and highest value the results were significant. The main effects of Zn, B and Mo and interaction Zn × B were significant in grain during first year. Rests of the interactions were not significant.

During second year the grain boron content varied from 49.00 to 57.39 mg kg^{-1} and treatment combination Zn_0B_0 and Zn_2B_2 gave the lowest and highest values in case of without molybdenum. In case of with molybdenum (during second year) the boron content ranged from 52.10 to 58.00 mg kg^{-1} and minimum and maximum values in grain boron content were observed in Zn_0B_0 and Zn_2B_2 respectively. The main effects were significant for Zn, B and Mo and interactions Zn × B and Zn × B × Mo were also significant.

Table 4.26 describe the variation due to Zn, B and Mo levels in stover boron content of chickpea. The results revealed that Zn_0B_0 and Zn_2B_2 gave the highest values of 36.00 to 42.00 mg kg^{-1} respectively. In case of without molybdenum during first year. In case of with molybdenum during the same year it ranged from 39.00 to 43.00 mg kg^{-1} and these values were given by Zn_0B_0 and Zn_2B_2 respectively. The main effects of Zn, B and Mo were significant and interactions were not significant in stover boron content.

During second year the stover boron content varied from 36.00 to 43.00 and 40.00 to 44.00 mg kg^{-1} without and with molybdenum values were given by Zn_0B_0 and $Zn_2B_{2.}$ The main effects Zn, B and Mo and Zn × Mo interaction were also significant but rest of interactions was not significant.

(g) Molybdenum

The data regarding variations in content of the molybdenum in grain and stover due to Zn, B and Mo during both the years are reported for the both years in Table 4.27. The data revealed that application of nutrients had as increasing effect on

Table 4.25: Effect of Zn, B and Mo levels on boron content (mg kg^{-1}) in grain of Chickpea

Treatments	2012-13				2013-14			
	Without Molybdenum				Without Molybdenum			
	Zn_0	Zn_1	Zn_2	Mean	Zn_0	Zn_1	Zn_2	Mean
B_0	48.00	53.00	54.00	51.67	49.00	53.50	55.82	52.77
B_1	54.00	54.00	55.00	54.33	54.00	55.25	56.35	55.20
B_2	55.00	54.48	56.00	55.16	55.00	55.00	57.39	55.80
Mean	52.33	53.83	55.00	53.72	52.67	54.58	56.52	54.59
	With Molybdenum				With Molybdenum			
B_0	52.00	54.00	55.63	53.88	52.10	54.00	56.26	54.12
B_1	54.00	55.00	56.00	55.00	55.00	57.70	57.00	56.57
B_2	56.00	55.90	57.00	56.30	56.00	56.80	58.00	56.93
Mean	54.00	54.97	56.21	55.06	54.37	56.17	57.09	55.87
	S.E.(d)		C.D.(P=0.05)		S.E.(d)		C.D.(P=0.05)	
Zn	0.446		0.907		0.273		0.555	
B	0.446		0.907		0.273		0.555	
Mo	0.364		0.740		0.223		0.453	
Zn×B	0.772		1.570		0.473		0.961	
B×Mo	0.631		N.S.		0.386		N.S.	
Zn×Mo	0.631		N.S.		0.386		N.S.	
Zn×B×Mo	1.092		N.S.		0.669		1.360	

Table 4.26: Effect of Zn, B and Mo levels on boron content (mg kg^{-1}) in stover of Chickpea

Treatments	2012-13				2013-14			
	Without Molybdenum				Without Molybdenum			
	Zn_0	Zn_1	Zn_2	Mean	Zn_0	Zn_1	Zn_2	Mean
B_0	36.00	39.53	40.00	38.51	36.00	41.19	41.00	39.40
B_1	38.00	40.00	41.00	39.67	39.00	41.50	42.00	40.83
B_2	39.00	41.00	42.00	40.67	40.00	42.00	43.00	41.67
Mean	37.67	40.18	41.00	39.61	38.33	41.56	42.00	40.63
	With Molybdenum				With Molybdenum			
B_0	39.00	40.20	41.00	40.07	40.00	41.30	42.00	41.10
B_1	40.00	41.00	42.00	41.00	41.00	42.50	43.00	42.17
B_2	41.00	42.00	43.00	42.00	42.00	43.00	44.00	43.00
Mean	40.00	41.07	42.00	41.02	41.00	42.27	43.00	42.09
	S.E.(d)		C.D.(P=0.05)		S.E.(d)		C.D.(P=0.05)	
Zn	0.412		0.837		0.283		0.576	
B	0.412		0.837		0.283		0.576	
Mo	0.336		0.684		0.231		0.470	
Zn×B	0.713		N.S.		0.491		N.S.	
B×Mo	0.582		N.S.		0.401		N.S.	
Zn×Mo	0.582		N.S.		0.401		0.814	
Zn×B×Mo	1.009		N.S.		0.694		N.S.	

molybdenum content of grain. Wherein it ranged from 3.04 to 4.16 and 3.20 to 4.40 mg kg^{-1} without and with molybdenum and treatment Zn_0B_0 and Zn_2B_2 gave the lowest and highest value the results were significant. The main effects of Zn, B and Mo and interaction Zn x B were significant in grain during first year rest of the interactions were not significant.

During second year the grain molybdenum content varied from 3.12 to 4.24 mg kg^{-1} and treatment combination Zn_0B_0 and Zn_2B_2 gave the lowest and highest values in case of without molybdenum. In case of with molybdenum (during second year) the molybdenum content ranged from 3.28 to 4.56 mg kg^{-1} and minimum and maximum values in grain molybdenum content were observed in Zn_0B_0 and Zn_2B_2 respectively. The main effects were significant for Zn, B and Mo. However, among the interactions Zn × B was also significant rest of the interactions were not significant.

As described in Table 4.28 the variation due to Zn, B and Mo levels in stover molybdenum content of chickpea showed significant increasing effect on molybdenum content. The results revealed that Zn_0B_0 and Zn_2B_2 gave the lowest and highest values of 0.62 to 0.70 mg kg^{-1} respectively in case of without molybdenum during first year. In case of with molybdenum during the same year it ranged from 0.64 to 0.76 mg kg^{-1} and these values were given by Zn_0B_0 and Zn_2B_2 respectively. The main effects of Zn, B and Mo were significant and interaction did not significant in stover molybdenum content.

During second year the stover molybdenum content varied from 0.62 to 0.70 and 0.64 to 0.77 mg kg^{-1} without and with molybdenum values were given by Zn_0B_0 and Zn_2B_2. The main effects of Zn, B and Mo were significant and interaction did not significant in stover molybdenum content.

(h) Copper

The data regarding the effect of zinc and boron levels in presence and absence of molybdenum on the copper content in grain of chickpea for the year 2012-13 and 2013-14 in are presented in Table 4.29 the results were statistically significant throughout during both the years wherein the nutrient levels tended to increase the copper content. It was observed that zinc levels increased the copper content linearly and significantly. In case of boron B_1 increased the copper content significantly but at B_2 the content decreased significantly during both the years in presence and absence of molybdenum. Molybdenum addition increased the copper content significantly as compared to no molybdenum. The main effects of Zn, B and Mo and Zn × B interaction were significant the rest of variables were not significant.

Copper content in grain ranged from 22.90 to 35.30 and 29.00 to 41.30 mg kg^{-1} in without and with molybdenum, respectively during first year.

Whereas during second year without molybdenum showed a range from 23.40 and 35.80 mg kg^{-1} and with molybdenum, it ranged from 29.50 to 41.80 mg kg^{-1} respectively.

The data regarding the effect of zinc and boron levels in presence and absence of molybdenum on the copper content in stover of chickpea for the year 2012-13 and

Table 4.27: Effect of Zn, B and Mo levels on molybdenum content (mg kg^{-1}) in grain of Chickpea

Treatments	2012-13				2013-14			
	Without Molybdenum				Without Molybdenum			
	Zn_0	Zn_1	Zn_2	Mean	Zn_0	Zn_1	Zn_2	Mean
B_0	3.04	3.24	3.45	3.24	3.12	3.32	3.53	3.32
B_1	3.24	3.50	3.76	3.50	3.32	3.58	3.84	3.58
B_2	3.30	3.56	4.16	3.67	3.38	3.64	4.24	3.75
Mean	3.19	3.43	3.79	3.47	3.27	3.51	3.87	3.55
	With Molybdenum				With Molybdenum			
B_0	3.20	3.54	3.77	3.50	3.28	3.62	3.85	3.58
B_1	3.46	3.76	4.05	3.76	3.54	3.84	4.13	3.84
B_2	3.60	3.85	4.40	3.95	3.68	3.93	4.56	4.06
Mean	3.42	3.72	4.07	3.74	3.50	3.80	4.18	3.83
	S.E.(d)		C.D.(P=0.05)		S.E.(d)		C.D.(P=0.05)	
Zn	0.040		0.082		0.029		0.058	
B	0.040		0.082		0.029		0.058	
Mo	0.033		0.067		0.023		0.048	
Zn×B	0.070		0.142		0.050		0.101	
B×Mo	0.057		N.S.		0.041		N.S.	
Zn×Mo	0.057		N.S.		0.041		N.S.	
Zn×B×Mo	0.099		N.S.		0.070		N.S.	

Table 4.28: Effect of Zn, B and Mo levels on molybdenum content (mg kg^{-1}) in stover of Chickpea

Treatments	2012-13				2013-14			
	Without Molybdenum				Without Molybdenum			
	Zn_0	Zn_1	Zn_2	Mean	Zn_0	Zn_1	Zn_2	Mean
B_0	0.62	0.64	0.66	0.64	0.62	0.64	0.66	0.64
B_1	0.64	0.67	0.69	0.67	0.64	0.67	0.70	0.67
B_2	0.65	0.67	0.70	0.67	0.65	0.68	0.70	0.67
Mean	0.64	0.66	0.68	0.66	0.64	0.66	0.69	0.66
	With Molybdenum				With Molybdenum			
B_0	0.64	0.67	0.69	0.67	0.64	0.67	0.70	0.67
B_1	0.66	0.69	0.72	0.69	0.66	0.69	0.72	0.69
B_2	0.67	0.70	0.76	0.71	0.68	0.70	0.77	0.72
Mean	0.66	0.69	0.72	0.69	0.66	0.69	0.73	0.69
	S.E.(d)		C.D.(P=0.05)		S.E.(d)		C.D.(P=0.05)	
Zn	0.012		0.025		0.015		0.031	
B	0.012		0.025		0.015		0.031	
Mo	0.010		0.020		0.013		0.026	
Zn×B	0.021		N.S.		0.027		N.S.	
B×Mo	0.017		N.S.		0.022		N.S.	
Zn×Mo	0.017		N.S.		0.022		N.S.	
Zn×B×Mo	0.030		N.S.		0.038		N.S.	

Table 4.29: Effect of Zn, B and Mo levels on copper content (mg kg^{-1}) in grain of Chickpea

Treatments	2012-13				2013-14			
	Without Molybdenum				Without Molybdenum			
	Zn_0	**Zn_1**	**Zn_2**	**Mean**	**Zn_0**	**Zn_1**	**Zn_2**	**Mean**
B_0	22.90	24.90	33.70	27.17	23.40	25.40	34.20	27.67
B_1	25.50	28.70	35.30	29.83	26.00	29.20	35.80	30.33
B_2	25.30	23.90	32.40	27.20	25.70	24.90	32.80	27.80
Mean	24.57	25.83	33.80	28.07	25.03	26.50	34.27	28.60
	With Molybdenum				**With Molybdenum**			
B_0	29.00	30.80	38.70	32.83	29.50	31.30	39.20	33.33
B_1	31.70	34.90	41.30	35.97	32.20	35.40	41.80	36.47
B_2	31.30	30.00	38.40	33.23	31.80	30.40	38.80	33.67
Mean	30.67	31.90	39.47	34.01	31.17	32.37	39.93	34.49
	S.E.(d)		C.D.(P=0.05)		S.E.(d)		C.D.(P=0.05)	
Zn	0.280		0.568		0.479		0.974	
B	0.280		0.568		0.479		0.974	
Mo	0.228		0.464		0.391		0.795	
Zn×B	0.484		0.984		0.830		1.687	
B×Mo	0.395		N.S.		0.678		N.S.	
Zn×Mo	0.395		N.S.		0.678		N.S.	
Zn×B×Mo	0.685		N.S.		1.174		N.S.	

Table 4.30: Effect of Zn, B and Mo levels on copper content (mg kg^{-1}) in stover of Chickpea

Treatments	2012-13				2013-14			
	Without Molybdenum				Without Molybdenum			
	Zn_0	Zn_1	Zn_2	Mean	Zn_0	Zn_1	Zn_2	Mean
B_0	17.00	18.00	18.80	17.93	17.20	18.20	19.00	18.13
B_1	18.30	19.50	20.30	19.37	18.50	19.70	20.50	19.57
B_2	18.50	20.00	20.40	19.63	18.70	20.20	20.60	19.83
Mean	17.93	19.17	19.83	18.98	18.13	19.37	20.03	19.18
	With Molybdenum				With Molybdenum			
B_0	18.20	19.15	20.95	19.43	18.40	19.35	21.15	19.63
B_1	19.07	21.35	22.40	20.94	19.27	21.55	22.60	21.14
B_2	19.65	21.85	22.65	21.38	19.85	22.05	22.85	21.58
Mean	18.97	20.78	22.00	20.59	19.17	20.98	22.20	20.79
	S.E.(d)		C.D.(P=0.05)		S.E.(d)		C.D.(P=0.05)	
Zn	0.186		0.378		0.216		0.439	
B	0.186		0.378		0.216		0.439	
Mo	0.152		0.309		0.176		0.359	
Zn×B	0.322		N.S.		0.374		N.S.	
B×Mo	0.263		N.S.		0.306		N.S.	
Zn×Mo	0.263		0.535		0.306		0.621	
Zn×B×Mo	0.456		N.S.		0.529		N.S.	

2013-14 in Table 4.30 the results were statistically significant throughout during both the years wherein the nutrient levels tended to increase the copper content. It was observed that zinc levels increased the copper content linearly and significantly. Molybdenum addition increased the copper content significantly as compared to no molybdenum. The main effects of Zn, B and Mo were significant and Zn × Mo was significant.

Copper content in stover ranged from 17.00 to 20.40 and 18.20 to 22.65 mg kg^{-1} in without and with molybdenum, respectively during first year. Whereas during second year without molybdenum showed a ranged from 17.20 and 20.60 mg kg^{-1} and with molybdenum it ranged from 18.40 to 22.85 mg kg^{-1} respectively. The main effects and interactions was significant similar to during first year.

(i) Iron

The data regarding the effect of zinc and boron levels in presence and absence of molybdenum on the iron content in grain of chickpea for the year 2012-13 and 2013-14 are given in Table 4.31 the results were statistically significant throughout during both the years wherein the nutrient levels tended to increase the iron content. It was observed that zinc levels increased the iron content linearly and significantly. In case of boron, B_1 and B_2 increased the iron content significantly during both the years in presence and absence of molybdenum. Molybdenum addition increased the iron content significantly as compare to no molybdenum. The main effects of Zn, B and Mo and Zn x B interaction were significant the rest of variables were not significant.

Iron content in grain ranged from 62.30 to 74.80 and 69.30 to 81.80 mg kg^{-1} in without and with molybdenum respectively during first year. Whereas during second year without molybdenum showed a ranged from 62.50 and 74.99 mg kg^{-1} and with molybdenum it ranged from 69.49 to 81.99 mg kg^{-1} respectively.

On the iron content in stover of chickpea for the year 2012-13 and 2013-14 shown in Table 4.32. The results were statistically significant during both the years. Treatments tended to increase the iron content. It was observed that zinc levels increased the iron content linearly and significantly. Molybdenum addition increased the iron content significantly as compared to no molybdenum. In case of boron B_1 increased the iron content significantly but at $B_{2,}$ the content decreased significantly during both the years in presence and absence of molybdenum. The main effects of Zn, B and Mo and Zn × B interaction were significant the rest of variables were not significant during both the years.

Iron content in stover ranged from 503.00 to 655.00 and 539.00 to 705.00 mg kg^{-1} in without and with molybdenum respectively during first year. Whereas during second year without molybdenum showed a ranged from 508.00 and 660.00 mg kg^{-1} and with molybdenum it ranged from 545.00 to 711.00 mg kg^{-1} respectively.

(j) Manganese

The data regarding the effect of zinc and boron levels in presence and absence of molybdenum on the manganese content in grain of chickpea for the year 2012-13

Table 4.31: Effect of Zn, B and Mo levels on iron content (mg kg^{-1}) in grain of Chickpea

Treatments	2012-13				2013-14			
	Without Molybdenum				Without Molybdenum			
	Zn_0	Zn_1	Zn_2	Mean	Zn_0	Zn_1	Zn_2	Mean
B_0	62.30	66.40	69.90	66.20	62.50	66.60	70.10	66.40
B_1	66.60	70.80	74.40	70.60	66.80	71.01	74.61	70.81
B_2	70.70	74.80	74.20	73.23	70.89	74.99	74.39	73.42
Mean	66.53	70.67	72.83	70.01	66.73	70.87	73.03	70.21
	With Molybdenum				With Molybdenum			
B_0	69.30	73.40	77.00	73.23	69.49	73.59	77.20	73.43
B_1	73.70	78.00	81.60	77.77	73.90	78.21	81.81	77.97
B_2	76.50	81.80	81.20	79.83	76.69	81.99	81.39	80.02
Mean	73.17	77.73	79.93	76.94	73.36	77.93	80.13	77.14
	S.E.(d)		C.D.(P=0.05)		S.E.(d)		C.D.(P=0.05)	
Zn	0.400		0.813		0.414		0.841	
B	0.400		0.813		0.414		0.841	
Mo	0.326		0.664		0.338		0.686	
Zn×B	0.692		1.408		0.716		1.456	
B×Mo	0.565		N.S.		0.585		N.S.	
Zn×Mo	0.565		N.S.		0.585		N.S.	
Zn×B×Mo	0.979		N.S.		1.013		N.S.	

Table 4.32: Effect of Zn, B and Mo levels on iron content (mg kg^{-1}) in stover of Chickpea

Treatments	2012-13				2013-14			
	Without Molybdenum				Without Molybdenum			
	Zn_0	Zn_1	Zn_2	Mean	Zn_0	Zn_1	Zn_2	Mean
B_0	503.00	639.00	624.00	588.67	508.00	644.00	630.00	594.00
B_1	573.00	623.00	655.00	617.00	578.00	628.00	660.00	622.00
B_2	580.00	604.00	650.00	611.33	585.00	609.00	655.00	616.33
Mean	552.00	622.00	643.00	605.67	557.00	627.00	648.33	610.78
	With Molybdenum				With Molybdenum			
B_0	539.00	694.00	630.00	621.00	545.00	700.00	636.00	627.00
B_1	594.00	670.00	705.00	656.33	600.00	676.00	711.00	662.33
B_2	625.00	659.00	700.00	661.33	631.00	665.00	706.00	667.33
Mean	586.00	674.33	678.33	646.22	592.00	680.33	684.33	652.22
	S.E.(d)		C.D.(P=0.05)		S.E.(d)		C.D.(P=0.05)	
Zn	6.146		12.494		5.214		10.599	
B	6.146		12.494		5.214		10.599	
Mo	5.018		10.201		4.247		8.654	
Zn×B	10.645		21.639		9.031		18.358	
B×Mo	8.692		N.S.		7.374		N.S.	
Zn×Mo	8.692		N.S.		7.374		N.S.	
Zn×B×Mo	15.055		N.S.		12.772		N.S.	

and 2013-14 as shown in Table 4.33. The nutrient levels tended to increase the manganese content significantly. It was observed the increase in manganese content due to zinc levels was linear and significant. Molybdenum addition increased the manganese content significantly as compared to no molybdenum. The main effects of Zn, B and Mo were significant and interaction of the variables was not significant.

Manganese content in grain ranged from 44.43 to 57.10 and 46.25 to 58.65 mg kg^{-1} in without and with molybdenum, respectively, during first year. Whereas during second year without molybdenum it showed a ranged from 44.15 and 57.20 mg kg^{-1} and with molybdenum it ranged from 46.30 to 58.80 mg kg^{-1} respectively.

Table 4.34 show the data on manganese content stover under different treatments. The results were statistically significant during both the years wherein the nutrient levels tended to increase the manganese content. It was observed that zinc levels increased the manganese content linearly and significantly. Molybdenum addition increased the manganese content significantly as compared to no molybdenum. The main effects of Zn, B and Mo and Zn × B interaction were significant the rest of variables were not significant.

Manganese content in stover ranged from 35.23 to 46.50 and 46.00 to 57.20 mg kg^{-1} in without and with molybdenum respectively during first year. Whereas during second year without molybdenum showed a ranged from 32.00 and 46.60 mg kg^{-1} and with molybdenum it ranged from 46.10 to 57.30 mg kg^{-1} respectively.

Nutrient Uptakes

The nutrient uptake values in grain, stover and grain + stover were computed from the concentrations and respective yields treatment wise on the data are presented wherein as under:

(a) Nitrogen

The data in Table 4.35 revealed the grain uptake values of nitrogen under the effect of Zn and B levels in absence and presence of molybdenum. It was clearly demonstrated that addition of molybdenum increased the nitrogen uptake significantly during both the years. There was linear and significant enhancement in uptake values with increasing levels of zinc and boron during both the years. The main effects of Zn, B and Mo were significant and interactions Zn × B and Zn × Mo were significant during both the years.

The grain nitrogen uptake was observed in appreciable amounts in chickpea crop. It ranged from 51.66 to 80.23 and 56.16 to 82.77 kg ha^{-1} in without and with molybdenum during the first year. Parallel to this the ranges of variation during second year were 52.16 to 80.86 kg ha^{-1} in without molybdenum and from 57.09 to 83.88 kg ha^{-1} in with molybdenum respectively.

The data in Table 4.36 revealed the stover uptake values of nitrogen under the effect of Zn and B levels in absence and presence of molybdenum. It was clearly demonstrated that addition of molybdenum increased the nitrogen uptake significantly during both the years. There was linear and significant enhancement in uptake values

Table 4.33: Effect of Zn, B and Mo levels on manganese content (mg kg^{-1}) in grain of Chickpea

Treatments	2012-13				2013-14			
	Without Molybdenum				Without Molybdenum			
	Zn_0	Zn_1	Zn_2	Mean	Zn_0	Zn_1	Zn_2	Mean
B_0	44.43	48.00	51.74	48.06	44.15	48.10	51.79	48.01
B_1	48.15	51.15	54.65	51.32	48.20	51.25	54.70	51.38
B_2	50.65	53.45	57.10	53.73	50.70	53.50	57.20	53.80
Mean	47.74	50.87	54.50	51.04	47.68	50.95	54.56	51.07
	With Molybdenum				With Molybdenum			
B_0	46.25	50.15	53.90	50.10	46.30	50.25	54.00	50.18
B_1	50.30	53.30	56.65	53.42	50.35	53.40	56.75	53.50
B_2	52.00	54.80	58.65	55.15	52.10	54.90	58.80	55.27
Mean	49.52	52.75	56.40	52.89	49.58	52.85	56.52	52.98
	S.E.(d)		C.D.(P=0.05)		S.E.(d)		C.D.(P=0.05)	
Zn	0.415		0.844		0.407		0.828	
B	0.415		0.844		0.407		0.828	
Mo	0.339		0.689		0.333		0.676	
Zn×B	0.719		N.S.		0.706		N.S.	
B×Mo	0.587		N.S.		0.576		N.S.	
Zn×Mo	0.587		N.S.		0.576		N.S.	
Zn×B×Mo	1.017		N.S.		0.998		N.S.	

Table 4.34: Effect of Zn, B and Mo levels on manganese content (mg kg^{-1}) in stover of Chickpea

Treatments	2012-13				2013-14			
	Without Molybdenum				Without Molybdenum			
	Zn_0	Zn_1	Zn_2	Mean	Zn_0	Zn_1	Zn_2	Mean
B_0	35.23	38.80	42.60	38.88	32.00	38.90	42.70	37.87
B_1	37.70	39.20	46.50	41.13	37.80	39.30	46.60	41.23
B_2	38.60	41.51	45.50	41.87	38.70	41.61	45.60	41.97
Mean	37.18	39.84	44.87	40.63	36.17	39.94	44.97	40.36
	With Molybdenum				With Molybdenum			
B_0	46.00	49.80	53.30	49.70	46.10	49.90	53.40	49.80
B_1	48.20	49.90	57.20	51.77	48.30	50.00	57.30	51.87
B_2	49.30	51.30	56.20	52.27	49.40	51.40	56.31	52.37
Mean	47.83	50.33	55.57	51.24	47.93	50.43	55.67	51.35
	S.E.(d)		C.D.(P=0.05)		S.E.(d)		C.D.(P=0.05)	
Zn	0.359		0.729		0.455		0.925	
B	0.359		0.729		0.455		0.925	
Mo	0.293		0.595		0.372		0.755	
Zn×B	0.621		1.263		0.788		1.602	
B×Mo	0.507		N.S.		0.643		N.S.	
Zn×Mo	0.507		N.S.		0.643		N.S.	
Zn×B×Mo	0.878		N.S.		1.115		N.S.	

with increasing levels of zinc and boron during both the years. The main effects of Zn, B and Mo were significant.

The stover nitrogen uptake was observed in appreciable amounts in chickpea crop. It ranged from 38.81 to 61.04 kg ha^{-1} without molybdenum and 43.11 to 67.39 kg ha^{-1} with molybdenum during the first year. Parallel to this the ranges of variation during second year were 40.00 to 62.59 and 43.75 to 67.62 kg ha^{-1} in without and with molybdenum respectively. The main effects of Zn, B and Mo were significant and interactions Zn × B and Zn × Mo were significant during second year.

(b) Phosphorous

The data in Table 4.37 revealed the grain uptake values of phosphorous under the effect of Zn and B levels in absence and presence of molybdenum. It was revealed that addition of molybdenum increased the phosphorous uptake significantly during both the years. The main effects of Zn, B and Mo were significant and interactions were not significant during both the years.

The grain phosphorous uptake was observed in appreciable amounts in chickpea crop it ranged from 5.40 to 8.59 and 6.44 to 9.05 kg ha^{-1} in without and with molybdenum during the first year. During second year was 5.23 to 9.06 kg ha^{-1} in without molybdenum and from 6.26 to 9.55 kg ha^{-1} in with molybdenum respectively.

The data in Table 4.38 revealed the stover uptake values of phosphorous under the effect of Zn and B levels in absence and presence of molybdenum. It was observed that addition of molybdenum increased the phosphorous uptake significantly during both the years. There was linear and significant enhancement in uptake values with increasing levels of zinc and boron during both the years. The main effects of Zn, B and Mo were significant and interaction Z × B were significant during first year. During second year the main effects of Zn and B and interactions Zn × B, Zn × Mo and Zn × B × Mo were significant.

The stover phosphorous uptake was observed in appreciable amounts in chickpea crop. It ranged from 6.53 to 10.90 kg ha^{-1} without molybdenum and 7.94 to 12.01 kg ha^{-1} with molybdenum during the first year. Parallel to this the ranges of variation during second year were 6.80 to 10.91 and 8.04 to 12.05 kg ha^{-1} in without and with molybdenum respectively.

(c) Potassium

The data in Table 4.39 revealed the grain uptake values of potassium under the effect of Zn and B levels in absence and presence of molybdenum. It was demonstrated that addition of molybdenum increased the potassium uptake significantly during both the years. There was linear and significant enhancement in uptake values with increasing levels of zinc and boron during both the years. The main effects of Zn, B and Mo and interactions Zn × B and Zn × Mo were significant during first year. During second year the main effects of Zn, B and Mo were significant.

Table 4.35: Effect of Zn, B and Mo levels on nitrogen uptake (kg ha[-1]) in grain of Chickpea

Treatments	2012-13				2013-14			
	Without Molybdenum				Without Molybdenum			
	Zn_0	Zn_1	Zn_2	Mean	Zn_0	Zn_1	Zn_2	Mean
B_0	51.66	65.39	68.48	61.84	52.16	65.97	69.07	62.40
B_1	59.00	70.45	76.50	68.65	59.55	71.03	77.12	69.23
B_2	62.62	73.00	80.23	71.95	63.02	73.45	80.86	72.44
Mean	57.76	69.61	75.07	67.48	58.24	70.15	75.68	68.03
	With Molybdenum				With Molybdenum			
B_0	56.16	67.69	70.94	64.93	57.09	68.95	71.99	66.01
B_1	65.18	73.00	79.11	72.43	66.21	74.09	80.91	73.74
B_2	67.64	75.01	82.77	75.14	68.51	75.70	83.88	76.03
Mean	62.99	71.90	77.61	70.83	63.94	72.91	78.93	71.93
	S.E.(d)		C.D.(P=0.05)		S.E.(d)		C.D.(P=0.05)	
Zn	0.500		1.017		0.472		0.960	
B	0.500		1.017		0.472		0.960	
Mo	0.409		0.831		0.386		0.784	
Zn×B	0.867		1.762		0.818		1.663	
B×Mo	0.708		N.S.		0.668		N.S.	
Zn×Mo	0.708		1.439		0.668		1.358	
Zn×B×Mo	1.226		N.S.		1.157		N.S.	

Table 4.36: Effect of Zn, B and Mo levels on nitrogen uptake (kg ha^{-1}) in stover of Chickpea

Treatments	2012-13				2013-14			
	Without Molybdenum				Without Molybdenum			
	Zn_0	Zn_1	Zn_2	Mean	Zn_0	Zn_1	Zn_2	Mean
B_0	38.81	50.31	53.17	47.43	40.00	51.21	54.59	48.60
B_1	45.30	54.38	57.42	52.37	46.16	55.58	58.65	53.46
B_2	51.63	57.55	61.04	56.74	52.55	58.80	62.59	57.98
Mean	45.25	54.08	57.21	52.18	46.24	55.20	58.61	53.35
	With Molybdenum				With Molybdenum			
B_0	43.11	53.72	60.34	52.39	43.75	54.70	61.39	53.28
B_1	51.53	60.82	64.42	58.92	45.62	61.88	65.51	57.67
B_2	52.86	60.56	67.39	60.27	53.57	61.61	67.62	60.93
Mean	49.17	58.37	64.05	57.19	47.65	59.40	64.84	57.29
	S.E.(d)		C.D.(P=0.05)		S.E.(d)		C.D.(P=0.05)	
Zn	0.649		1.320		0.464		0.943	
B	0.649		1.320		0.464		0.943	
Mo	0.530		1.077		0.379		0.770	
Zn×B	1.124		N.S.		0.803		1.633	
B×Mo	0.918		N.S.		0.656		N.S.	
Zn×Mo	0.918		N.S.		0.656		1.334	
Zn×B×Mo	1.590		N.S.		1.136		N.S.	

Table 4.37: Effect of Zn, B and Mo levels on phosphorus uptake (kg ha^{-1}) in grain of Chickpea

Treatments	2012-13				2013-14			
	Without Molybdenum				Without Molybdenum			
	Zn_0	**Zn_1**	**Zn_2**	**Mean**	**Zn_0**	**Zn_1**	**Zn_2**	**Mean**
B_0	5.40	6.82	7.49	6.57	5.23	7.69	7.94	6.95
B_1	6.73	7.88	8.10	7.57	6.55	8.79	8.79	8.04
B_2	6.67	8.59	7.68	7.65	6.46	8.36	9.06	7.96
Mean	6.27	7.76	7.76	7.26	6.08	8.28	8.60	7.65
	With Molybdenum				**With Molybdenum**			
B_0	6.44	7.94	8.40	7.59	6.26	8.62	8.64	7.84
B_1	7.63	8.84	9.03	8.50	7.43	9.55	9.30	8.76
B_2	7.18	9.05	8.14	8.12	6.96	8.80	9.55	8.44
Mean	7.08	8.61	8.52	8.07	6.88	8.99	9.16	8.35
	S.E.(d)		C.D.(P=0.05)		S.E.(d)		C.D.(P=0.05)	
Zn	0.263		0.534		0.185		0.376	
B	0.263		0.534		0.185		0.376	
Mo	0.215		0.436		0.151		0.307	
Zn×B	0.455		N.S.		0.321		N.S.	
B×Mo	0.372		N.S.		0.262		N.S.	
Zn×Mo	0.372		N.S.		0.262		N.S.	
Zn×B×Mo	0.644		N.S.		0.454		N.S.	

Table 4.38: Effect of Zn, B and Mo levels on phosphorus uptake (kg ha^{-1}) in stover of Chickpea

Treatments	2012-13				2013-14			
	Without Molybdenum				Without Molybdenum			
	Zn_0	Zn_1	Zn_2	Mean	Zn_0	Zn_1	Zn_2	Mean
B_0	6.53	8.91	9.51	8.32	6.80	10.03	11.20	9.34
B_1	8.49	9.75	10.18	9.47	8.45	10.03	11.15	9.88
B_2	9.45	10.54	10.90	10.30	10.03	10.02	10.91	10.32
Mean	8.16	9.73	10.20	9.36	8.43	10.03	11.09	9.85
	With Molybdenum				With Molybdenum			
B_0	7.94	9,98	11.14	9.69	8.04	9.78	10.62	9.48
B_1	9.52	11.16	11.50	10.73	9.78	9.22	10.84	9.95
B_2	9.74	11.11	12.01	10.95	9.78	10.08	12.05	10.64
Mean	9.07	10.75	11.55	10.46	9.20	9.69	11.17	10.02
	S.E.(d)		C.D.(P=0.05)		S.E.(d)		C.D.(P=0.05)	
Zn	0.163		0.332		0.178		0.362	
B	0.163		0.332		0.178		0.362	
Mo	0.133		0.271		0.146		N.S.	
Zn×B	0.283		0.575		0.309		0.628	
B×Mo	0.231		N.S.		0.252		N.S.	
Zn×Mo	0.231		N.S.		0.252		0.513	
Zn×B×Mo	0.400		N.S.		0.437		0.888	

The grain potassium uptake was observed in appreciable amounts in chickpea crop it ranged from 7.92 to 11.98 and 9.75 to 12.56 kg ha^{-1} in without and with molybdenum during the first year. Parallel to this the ranges of variation during second year were 8.12 to 12.23 kg ha^{-1} in without molybdenum and from 9.78 to 12.82 kg ha^{-1} in with molybdenum respectively.

The data in Table 4.40 revealed the stover uptake values of potassium under the effect of Zn and B levels in absence and presence of molybdenum. Addition of molybdenum increased the potassium uptake significantly during both the years. There was linear and significant enhancement in potassium uptake values with increasing levels of zinc and boron during both the years. The main effects of Zn, B and Mo and interactions Zn × B and B × Mo were significant during first year. During second year the main effects of Zn and B and Mo and interactions Zn × B, B × Mo, Zn × Mo and Zn × B × Mo were significant.

The stover potassium uptake was observed in appreciable amounts in chickpea crop it ranged from 32.27 to 50.26 kg ha^{-1} without molybdenum and 37.54 to 55.08 kg ha^{-1} with molybdenum during the first year. Parallel to this the ranges of variation during second year were 32.80 to 50.90 and 37.93 to 55.27 kg ha^{-1} in without and with molybdenum respectively. Remarkably potassium uptake in stover was roughly three times higher than that of grain.

(d) Sulphur

The data in Table 4.41 revealed the grain uptake values of sulphur under the effect of Zn and B levels in absence and presence of molybdenum. It was clearly demonstrated that addition of molybdenum increased the sulphur uptake significantly during both the years. There was linear and significant enhancement in sulphur uptake values with increasing levels of zinc and boron during both the years. The main effects of Zn, B and Mo were significant and interactions were not significant during both the years.

The grain sulphur uptake was observed in appreciable amounts in chickpea crop it ranged from 11.52 to 15.75 and 13.07 to 16.51 kg ha^{-1} in without and with molybdenum during the first year. Parallel to this the ranges of variation during second year were 11.73 to 16.08 kg ha^{-1} in without molybdenum and from 13.26 to 17.01 kg ha^{-1} in with molybdenum respectively.

The data in Table 4.42 revealed the stover uptake values of sulphur under the effect of Zn and B levels in absence and presence of molybdenum. It was clearly demonstrated that addition of molybdenum increased the sulphur uptake significantly during both the years. There was linear and significant enhancement in sulphur uptake values with increasing levels of zinc and boron during both the years. The main effects of Zn, B and Mo were significant and interactions were not significant during both the years.

The stover sulphur uptake was observed in appreciable amounts in chickpea crop, it ranged from 4.55 to 7.36 kg ha^{-1} without molybdenum and 5.36 to 7.91 kg ha^{-1} with molybdenum during the first year. Parallel to this the ranges of variation during second year were 4.60 to 7.41 and 5.39 to 8.23 kg ha^{-1} in without and with molybdenum respectively.

Table 4.39: Effect of Zn, B and Mo levels on potassium uptake (kg ha^{-1}) in grain of Chickpea

Treatments	2012-13				2013-14			
	Without Molybdenum				Without Molybdenum			
	Zn_0	Zn_1	Zn_2	Mean	Zn_0	Zn_1	Zn_2	Mean
B_0	7.92	10.65	11.13	9.90	8.12	10.89	11.37	10.13
B_1	9.90	11.48	11.70	11.03	10.12	11.73	11.95	11.27
B_2	10.30	11.53	11.98	11.27	10.50	11.75	12.23	11.49
Mean	9.37	11.22	11.60	10.73	9.58	11.46	11.85	10.96
	With Molybdenum				With Molybdenum			
B_0	9.75	11.25	11.71	10.90	9.78	11.27	11.74	10.93
B_1	11.12	12.09	12.30	11.84	11.36	12.35	12.56	12.09
B_2	11.53	12.04	12.56	12.04	11.53	12.27	12.82	12.21
Mean	10.80	11.79	12.19	11.59	10.89	11.96	12.37	11.74
	S.E.(d)		C.D.(P=0.05)		S.E.(d)		C.D.(P=0.05)	
Zn	0.167		0.340		0.196		0.398	
B	0.167		0.340		0.196		0.398	
Mo	0.137		0.278		0.160		0.325	
Zn×B	0.290		0.589		0.339		N.S.	
B×Mo	0.237		N.S.		0.277		N.S.	
Zn×Mo	0.237		0.481		0.277		N.S.	
Zn×B×Mo	0.410		N.S.		0.480		N.S.	

Table 4.40: Effect of Zn, B and Mo levels on potassium uptake (kg ha^{-1}) in stover of Chickpea

Treatments	2012-13				2013-14			
	Without Molybdenum				Without Molybdenum			
	Zn_0	Zn_1	Zn_2	Mean	Zn_0	Zn_1	Zn_2	Mean
B_0	32.27	43.81	44.63	40.24	32.80	44.41	45.74	40.98
B_1	39.64	47.20	48.29	45.04	40.22	47.82	49.44	45.83
B_2	44.84	50.26	50.26	48.45	45.46	50.90	50.78	49.05
Mean	38.92	47.09	47.73	44.58	39.49	47.71	48.65	45.29
	With Molybdenum				With Molybdenum			
B_0	37.54	46.81	49.74	44.70	37.93	47.25	50.75	45.31
B_1	44.69	52.73	53.49	50.30	39.60	51.80	54.55	48.65
B_2	45.80	52.50	55.08	51.13	45.74	51.86	55.27	50.96
Mean	42.68	50.68	52.77	48.71	41.09	50.30	53.52	48.31
	S.E.(d)		C.D.(P=0.05)		S.E.(d)		C.D.(P=0.05)	
Zn	0.394		0.800		0.453		0.921	
B	0.394		0.800		0.453		0.921	
Mo	0.322		0.654		0.370		0.752	
Zn×B	0.682		1.386		0.785		1.595	
B×Mo	0.557		1.132		0.641		1.303	
Zn×Mo	0.557		N.S.		0.641		1.303	
Zn×B×Mo	0.965		N.S.		1.110		2.256	

Uptake of Micronutrients

The uptake data regarding the micronutrients showed that the requirement of these micronutrients in chickpea was appreciably high and that for the good harvest micronutrient management in this crop is essential. Uptake values of different micronutrients values were computed and described as below:

(e) Zinc

Table 4.43 showed the data regarding the grain uptake of zinc for both the years (2012-13 and 2013-14) in absence and presence of molybdenum. The uptake of zinc varied from 69.30 to 104.41 g ha^{-1} in case of without molybdenum. Like-wise, in case of molybdenum treatment it ranged from 76.64 to 109.28 g ha^{-1} during first year. Molybdenum application increased the zinc uptake by 6.82 per cent. The increase in zinc uptake under different treatment was significant in which only the main effects of Zn, B and Mo were significant but the interaction were not significant during first year.

During second year also the treatment effects were more or less similar to those of first year but in general the values were somewhat higher during this year as compared to the first year. In absence of molybdenum the minimum and maximum values observed 70.76 and 106.00 g ha^{-1} the increase in zinc uptake due to addition of molybdenum was about 6.5 per cent.

Table 4.44 showed the data regarding the stover uptake of zinc for both the years (2012-13 and 2013-14) in absence and presence of molybdenum. The uptake of zinc varied from 34.06 to 81.75 g ha^{-1} in case of without molybdenum. Like-wise incase of molybdenum treatment it ranged from 39.25 to 91.71 g ha^{-1} during first year. Molybdenum application increased the zinc uptake by 13.20 per cent. The increase in zinc uptake under different treatment was significant in which only the main effects of Zn, B and Mo were significant and the interactions Zn × B, Zn × Mo were significant during both the years.

During second year also the treatment effects were similar to those of first year but in general the values were somewhat higher during this year as compared to the first year in absence of molybdenum the minimum and maximum values observed that 35.00 and 82.90 g ha^{-1} the increase in zinc uptake due to addition of molybdenum was about 11.26 per cent.

(f) Boron

It was observed Table 4.45 that the uptake of boron in grain varied from 86.40 to 126.56 g ha^{-1} in case of without molybdenum. Likewise incase of molybdenum treatment it ranged from 101.40 to 132.53 g ha^{-1} during first year. Molybdenum application increased the boron uptake by 7.29 per cent. The increase in boron uptake under different treatment was significant in which only the main effects of Zn, B and Mo and interaction Zn × B and Zn × Mo were significant during first year.

During second year also the treatment effects were similar to those of first year in grain but in general the values were somewhat higher during this year as compared to the first year in absence of molybdenum the minimum and maximum values observed

Table 4.41: Effect of Zn, B and Mo levels on sulphur uptake (kg ha^{-1}) in grain of Chickpea

Treatments	2012-13				2013-14			
	Without Molybdenum				Without Molybdenum			
	Zn_0	**Zn_1**	**Zn_2**	**Mean**	**Zn_0**	**Zn_1**	**Zn_2**	**Mean**
B_0	11.52	14.48	14.77	13.59	11.73	14.52	15.02	13.76
B_1	13.46	15.53	15.75	14.91	13.70	16.01	16.08	15.26
B_2	13.94	15.37	15.59	14.97	14.14	15.59	15.79	15.17
Mean	12.97	15.13	15.37	14.49	13.19	15.37	15.63	14.73
	With Molybdenum				**With Molybdenum**			
B_0	13.07	14.99	15.47	14.51	13.26	15.25	15.95	14.82
B_1	15.26	16.47	16.51	16.08	15.31	16.78	17.01	16.37
B_2	15.44	15.97	16.04	15.82	15.66	16.44	16.74	16.28
Mean	14.59	15.81	16.00	15.47	14.74	16.16	16.57	15.82
	S.E.(d)		C.D.(P=0.05)		S.E.(d)		C.D.(P=0.05)	
Zn	0.268		0.545		0.219		0.445	
B	0.268		0.545		0.219		0.445	
Mo	0.219		0.445		0.179		0.363	
Zn×B	0.464		N.S.		0.379		N.S.	
B×Mo	0.379		N.S.		0.309		N.S.	
Zn×Mo	0.379		N.S.		0.309		N.S.	
Zn×B×Mo	0.656		N.S.		0.536		N.S.	

Table 4.42: Effect of Zn, B and Mo levels on sulphur uptake (kg ha^{-1}) in stover of Chickpea

Treatments	2012-13				2013-14			
	Without Molybdenum				Without Molybdenum			
	Zn_0	Zn_1	Zn_2	Mean	Zn_0	Zn_1	Zn_2	Mean
B_0	4.55	6.02	6.59	5.72	4.60	6.31	6.64	5.85
B_1	5.45	6.67	7.05	6.39	5.71	6.72	7.10	6.51
B_2	6.30	7.03	7.36	6.90	6.35	7.08	7.41	6.95
Mean	5.43	6.57	7.00	6.34	5.55	6.70	7.05	6.44
	With Molybdenum				With Molybdenum			
B_0	5.36	6.65	7.34	6.45	5.39	6.68	7.37	6.48
B_1	6.35	7.25	7.77	7.12	5.60	7.28	7.79	6.89
B_2	6.33	7.22	7.91	7.15	6.36	7.53	8.23	7.37
Mean	6.01	7.04	7.67	6.91	5.78	7.16	7.80	6.91
	S.E.(d)		C.D.(P=0.05)		S.E.(d)		C.D.(P=0.05)	
Zn	0.159		0.323		0.120		0.244	
B	0.159		0.323		0.120		0.244	
Mo	0.130		0.264		0.098		0.199	
Zn×B	0.276		N.S.		0.208		N.S.	
B×Mo	0.225		N.S.		0.169		N.S.	
Zn×Mo	0.225		N.S.		0.169		N.S.	
Zn×B×Mo	0.390		N.S.		0.293		N.S.	

Table 4.43: Effect of Zn, B and Mo levels on zinc uptake (g ha^{-1}) in grain of Chickpea

Treatments	2012-13				2013-14			
	Without Molybdenum				Without Molybdenum			
	Zn_0	Zn_1	Zn_2	Mean	Zn_0	Zn_1	Zn_2	Mean
B_0	69.30	83.71	92.66	81.89	70.76	85.57	94.38	83.57
B_1	79.40	95.40	100.35	91.72	80.99	97.42	102.26	93.56
B_2	79.59	98.99	104.41	94.33	81.67	100.57	106.00	96.08
Mean	76.10	92.70	99.14	89.31	77.81	94.52	100.88	91.07
	With Molybdenum				With Molybdenum			
B_0	76.64	88.42	97.24	87.43	78.20	90.17	99.23	89.20
B_1	89.38	101.37	105.33	98.69	91.11	102.29	107.30	100.23
B_2	87.44	103.48	109.28	100.07	88.96	104.87	111.12	101.65
Mean	84.49	97.76	103.95	95.40	86.09	99.11	105.88	97.03
	S.E.(d)		C.D.(P=0.05)		S.E.(d)		C.D.(P=0.05)	
Zn	1.183		2.405		1.257		2.555	
B	1.183		2.405		1.257		2.555	
Mo	0.966		1.963		1.026		2.086	
Zn×B	2.049		N.S.		2.177		N.S.	
B×Mo	1.673		N.S.		1.778		N.S.	
Zn×Mo	1.673		N.S.		1.778		N.S.	
Zn×B×Mo	2.897		N.S.		3.079		N.S.	

Table 4.44: Effect of Zn, B and Mo levels on zinc uptake (g ha^{-1}) in stover of Chickpea

Treatments	2012-13				2013-14			
	Without Molybdenum				Without Molybdenum			
	Zn_0	Zn_1	Zn_2	Mean	Zn_0	Zn_1	Zn_2	Mean
B_0	34.06	45.73	60.73	46.84	35.00	46.60	61.84	47.81
B_1	42.47	60.79	69.95	57.74	43.30	61.78	71.01	58.70
B_2	52.60	71.33	81.75	68.56	53.52	72.27	82.90	69.56
Mean	43.04	59.28	70.81	57.71	43.94	60.22	71.92	58.69
	With Molybdenum				With Molybdenum			
B_0	39.25	52.44	72.84	54.84	39.87	52.90	73.26	55.34
B_1	49.82	69.19	80.24	66.42	44.33	69.86	81.10	65.10
B_2	55.54	76.95	91.71	74.73	56.14	77.79	92.46	75.46
Mean	48.20	66.19	81.60	65.33	46.78	66.85	82.27	65.30
	S.E.(d)		C.D.(P=0.05)		S.E.(d)		C.D.(P=0.05)	
Zn	0.517		1.050		0.854		1.735	
B	0.517		1.050		0.854		1.735	
Mo	0.422		0.857		0.697		1.417	
Zn×B	0.895		1.819		1.479		3.006	
B×Mo	0.730		N.S.		1.207		N.S.	
Zn×Mo	0.730		1.485		1.207		2.454	
Zn×B×Mo	1.265		N.S.		2.091		N.S.	

that 88.45 and 129.99 g ha^{-1} the increase in boron uptake due to addition of molybdenum was about 7.15 per cent. The main effects of Zn, B and Mo and interaction Zn × B were significant during second year.

Table 4.46 showed the data regarding the stover uptake of boron for both the years (2012-13 and 2013-14) in absence and presence of molybdenum. The uptake of boron varied from 71.28 to 114.45 g ha^{-1} in case of without molybdenum. Likewise incase of molybdenum treatment it ranged from 83.66 to 125.99 g ha^{-1} during first year. Molybdenum application increased the boron uptake by 11.09 per cent. The increase in boron uptake under different treatment was significant in which main effects of Zn, B and Mo were significant and also interactions B × Mo and Zn × Mo were significant during first year.

During second year also the treatment effects like those of first year but in general the values were somewhat higher during this year as compared to the first year in absence of molybdenum the minimum and maximum values observed that 72.00 and 118.04 g ha^{-1} the increase in boron uptake due to addition of molybdenum was about 9.24 per cent. The main effects of Zn, B and Mo were significant but the interactions were not significant.

(g) Molybdenum

Table 4.47 showed the data regarding the grain uptake of molybdenum for both the years (2012-13 and 2013-14) in absence and presence of molybdenum. The uptake of molybdenum varied from 5.47 to 9.40 g ha^{-1} in case of without molybdenum. Likewise incase of molybdenum treatment it ranged from 6.24 to 10.23 g ha^{-1} during first year. Molybdenum application increased the molybdenum uptake by 12.70 per cent. The increase in molybdenum uptake under different treatment was significant in which only the main effects of Zn, B and Mo were significant but the interactions were not significant during first year.

During second year also the treatment effects were similar to those of first year but in general the values were somewhat higher during this year as compared to the first year in absence of molybdenum the minimum and maximum values observed that 5.63 and 9.60 g ha^{-1} the increase in molybdenum uptake due to addition of molybdenum was about 12.65 per cent.

Table 4.48 showed the data regarding the stover uptake of molybdenum for both the years (2012-13 and 2013-14) in absence and presence of molybdenum. The uptake of molybdenum varied from 1.23 to 1.90 g ha^{-1} in case of without molybdenum. Likewise incase of molybdenum treatment it ranged from 1.36 to 2.24 g ha^{-1} during first year. Molybdenum application increased the molybdenum uptake by 12.35 per cent. The increase in molybdenum uptake under different treatment was significant in which only the main effects of Zn, B and Mo were significant, interaction Zn × Mo was significant during first year.

During second year also the treatment effects were similar to those of first year but in general the values were somewhat higher during this year as compared to the

Table 4.45: Effect of Zn, B and Mo levels on boron uptake (g ha^{-1}) in grain of Chickpea

Treatments	2012-13				2013-14			
	Without Molybdenum				Without Molybdenum			
	Zn_0	Zn_1	Zn_2	Mean	Zn_0	Zn_1	Zn_2	Mean
B_0	86.40	112.89	115.56	104.95	88.45	114.22	119.73	107.47
B_1	106.92	121.50	123.75	117.39	107.19	124.59	127.07	119.62
B_2	111.10	123.12	126.56	120.26	111.10	124.30	129.99	121.80
Mean	101.47	119.17	121.96	114.20	102.25	121.04	125.60	116.29
	With Molybdenum				With Molybdenum			
B_0	101.40	119.07	122.94	114.47	101.86	119.34	124.62	115.27
B_1	117.72	127.88	129.92	125.17	120.18	134.44	132.53	129.05
B_2	121.80	129.41	132.53	127.91	121.80	131.49	135.14	129.48
Mean	113.64	125.45	128.46	122.52	114.61	128.42	130.76	124.60
	S.E.(d)		C.D.(P=0.05)		S.E.(d)		C.D.(P=0.05)	
Zn	1.036		2.107		1.566		3.184	
B	1.036		2.107		1.566		3.184	
Mo	0.846		1.720		1.279		2.600	
Zn×B	1.795		3.649		2.713		5.515	
B×Mo	1.466		N.S.		2.215		N.S.	
Zn×Mo	1.466		2.980		2.215		N.S.	
Zn×B×Mo	2.539		N.S.		3.837		N.S.	

Table 4.46: Effect of Zn, B and Mo levels on boron uptake (g ha^{-1}) in stover of Chickpea

Treatments	2012-13				2013-14			
	Without Molybdenum				Without Molybdenum			
	Zn_0	Zn_1	Zn_2	Mean	Zn_0	Zn_1	Zn_2	Mean
B_0	71.28	95.15	97.56	88.00	72.00	99.97	100.82	90.93
B_1	82.76	102.60	107.01	97.46	85.72	107.28	110.46	101.15
B_2	94.54	110.78	114.45	106.59	97.76	111.32	118.04	109.04
Mean	82.86	102.84	106.34	97.35	85.16	106.19	109.77	100.37
	With Molybdenum				With Molybdenum			
B_0	83.66	102.83	111.44	99.31	86.20	106.06	114.59	102.28
B_1	97.68	114.39	120.79	110.95	88.23	119.00	124.10	110.44
B_2	99.88	116.68	125.99	114.18	102.73	119.88	129.36	117.32
Mean	93.74	111.30	119.41	108.15	92.39	114.98	122.68	110.02
	S.E.(d)		C.D.(P=0.05)		S.E.(d)		C.D.(P=0.05)	
Zn	0.895		1.819		2.234		4.542	
B	0.895		1.819		2.234		4.542	
Mo	0.731		1.485		1.824		3.709	
Zn×B	1.550		N.S.		3.870		N.S.	
B×Mo	1.266		2.573		3.160		N.S.	
Zn×Mo	1.266		2.573		3.160		N.S.	
Zn×B×Mo	2.192		N.S.		5.473		N.S.	

first year in absence of molybdenum the minimum and maximum values observed that 1.24 and 1.92 g ha^{-1} the increase in molybdenum uptake due to addition of molybdenum was about 8.54 per cent. Main effects of Zn, B and Mo and interactions Zn × B, B × Mo and Zn × B × Mo were significant during second year.

(h) Copper

The variation in grain copper uptake under different level of zinc and boron in absence and presence of molybdenum is presented in Table 4.49. Large variations were observed under different treatment and results were highly significant. Zn_2B_1 gave the highest copper uptake and B_2 registered a significant a decline with Zn_1 and Zn_2 both absence and presence of molybdenum. The ranges of variation were from 41.22 to 79.43 g ha^{-1} and 56.55 to 95.82 g ha^{-1} in without and with molybdenum respectively. Addition of molybdenum increased the uptake about by 26.41 per cent over without molybdenum control. Zn, B, Mo main effects and Zn × B interaction were also to be significant, during both the years.

During second year also the trends of results were similar to that of year. In general the uptake values were somewhat higher during second year as compare to first year. In this case also Zn_2B_1 gave the higher uptake than Zn_2B_2. There was about 26 per cent increase in uptake values in presence of molybdenum over absence of molybdenum. The minimum and maximum values in this case were 42.24 and 80.73 in without molybdenum, whereas with molybdenum these values were 57.67 and 97.19 g ha^{-1} respectively.

The variation in stover copper uptake under different level of zinc and boron in absence and presence of molybdenum is presented in Table 4.50, treatment variations in uptake values were large and results were highly significant. Zn_2B_2 gave the highest copper uptake. The ranges of variation were from 33.66 to 55.59 g ha^{-1} and 39.04 to 66.36 g ha^{-1} in without and with molybdenum, respectively. Addition of molybdenum increased the uptake about by 16.73 per cent over without molybdenum control during first year. Main effects of Zn, B and Mo and the interactions B × Mo and Zn × Mo were significant during first year.

During second year copper uptake in stover showed that the main effects Zn, B and Mo and interactions Zn × B and Zn × Mo were significant during second year. In general the uptake values were somewhat higher during second year as compared to first year. In this case also Zn_2B_2 gave the higher uptake than Zn_2B_1. There was about 14.78 per cent increase in uptake values in due molybdenum over its control. The minimum and maximum values in this case were 34.40 and 56.55 in without molybdenum whereas with molybdenum these values were 39.65 and 67.18 g ha^{-1} respectively.

(i) Iron

Table 4.51 shows the variation in grain iron uptake under different level of zinc and boron in absence and presence of molybdenum. Effects of different treatments were highly significant. The ranges of variation were from 112.14 to 169.05 g ha^{-1} and

Table 4.47: Effect of Zn, B and Mo levels on molybdenum uptake (g ha^{-1}) in grain of Chickpea

Treatments	2012-13				2013-14			
	Without Molybdenum				Without Molybdenum			
	Zn_0	Zn_1	Zn_2	Mean	Zn_0	Zn_1	Zn_2	Mean
B_0	5.47	6.90	7.38	6.58	5.63	7.09	7.57	6.76
B_1	6.42	7.88	8.46	7.59	6.59	8.07	8.66	7.77
B_2	6.67	8.05	9.40	8.04	6.83	8.23	9.60	8.22
Mean	6.19	7.61	8.41	7.40	6.35	7.80	8.61	7.59
	With Molybdenum				With Molybdenum			
B_0	6.24	7.81	8.33	7.46	6.41	8.00	8.53	7.65
B_1	7.54	8.74	9.40	8.56	7.73	8.95	9.60	8.76
B_2	7.83	8.91	10.23	8.99	8.00	9.10	10.62	9.24
Mean	7.20	8.49	9.32	8.34	7.38	8.68	9.58	8.55
	S.E.(d)		C.D.(P=0.05)		S.E.(d)		C.D.(P=0.05)	
Zn	0.180		0.365		0.187		0.380	
B	0.180		0.365		0.187		0.380	
Mo	0.147		0.298		0.153		0.310	
Zn×B	0.311		N.S.		0.324		N.S.	
B×Mo	0.254		N.S.		0.264		N.S.	
Zn×Mo	0.254		N.S.		0.264		N.S.	
Zn×B×Mo	0.440		N.S.		0.458		N.S.	

Table 4.48: Effect of Zn, B and Mo levels on molybdenum uptake (g ha^{-1}) in stover of Chickpea

Treatments	2012-13				2013-14			
	Without Molybdenum				Without Molybdenum			
	Zn_0	Zn_1	Zn_2	Mean	Zn_0	Zn_1	Zn_2	Mean
B_0	1.23	1.54	1.61	1.46	1.24	1.56	1.63	1.48
B_1	1.40	1.71	1.81	1.64	1.41	1.73	1.83	1.66
B_2	1.57	1.82	1.90	1.76	1.59	1.84	1.92	1.78
Mean	1.40	1.69	1.77	1.62	1.41	1.71	1.79	1.64
	With Molybdenum				With Molybdenum			
B_0	1.36	1.71	1.88	1.65	1.37	1.73	1.90	1.67
B_1	1.62	1.93	2.07	1.87	1.43	1.94	1.76	1.71
B_2	1.64	1.95	2.24	1.94	1.65	1.96	2.25	1.95
Mean	1.54	1.86	2.06	1.82	1.48	1.88	1.97	1.78
	S.E.(d)		C.D.(P=0.05)		S.E.(d)		C.D.(P=0.05)	
Zn	0.019		0.039		0.028		0.057	
B	0.019		0.039		0.028		0.057	
Mo	0.016		0.032		0.023		0.047	
Zn×B	0.033		N.S.		0.049		0.099	
B×Mo	0.027		N.S.		0.040		0.081	
Zn×Mo	0.027		0.055		0.040		N.S.	
Zn×B×Mo	0.047		N.S.		0.069		0.141	

Table 4.49: Effect of Zn, B and Mo levels on copper uptake (g ha^{-1}) in grain of Chickpea

Treatments	2012-13				2013-14			
	Without Molybdenum				Without Molybdenum			
	Zn_0	Zn_1	Zn_2	Mean	Zn_0	Zn_1	Zn_2	Mean
B_0	41.22	53.04	72.12	55.46	42.24	54.23	73.36	56.61
B_1	50.49	65.58	79.43	65.17	51.61	65.85	80.73	66.06
B_2	51.11	54.01	73.22	59.45	51.91	56.27	74.29	60.82
Mean	47.61	57.54	74.92	60.02	48.59	58.78	76.13	61.17
	With Molybdenum				With Molybdenum			
B_0	56.55	67.91	85.53	70.00	57.67	69.17	86.83	71.22
B_1	69.11	81.14	95.82	82.02	70.36	82.48	97.19	83.34
B_2	68.08	69.45	89.28	75.60	69.17	70.38	90.40	76.65
Mean	64.58	72.83	90.21	75.87	65.73	74.01	91.47	77.07
	S.E.(d)		C.D.(P=0.05)		S.E.(d)		C.D.(P=0.05)	
Zn	0.489		0.994		0.757		1.538	
B	0.489		0.994		0.757		1.538	
Mo	0.399		0.811		0.618		1.256	
Zn×B	0.847		1.721		1.310		2.664	
B×Mo	0.691		N.S.		1.070		N.S.	
Zn×Mo	0.691		N.S.		1.070		N.S.	
Zn×B×Mo	1.197		N.S.		1.853		N.S.	

Table 4.50: Effect of Zn, B and Mo levels on copper uptake (g ha^{-1}) in stover of Chickpea

Treatments	2012-13				2013-14			
	Without Molybdenum				Without Molybdenum			
	Zn_0	Zn_1	Zn_2	Mean	Zn_0	Zn_1	Zn_2	Mean
B_0	33.66	43.33	45.85	40.95	34.40	44.17	46.72	41.76
B_1	39.86	50.02	52.98	47.62	40.66	50.92	53.92	48.50
B_2	44.84	54.04	55.59	51.49	45.70	54.98	56.55	52.41
Mean	39.45	49.13	51.47	46.69	40.25	50.02	52.40	47.56
	With Molybdenum				With Molybdenum			
B_0	39.04	48.99	56.94	48.32	39.65	49.69	57.70	49.01
B_1	46.57	59.57	64.42	56.85	41.47	60.34	65.22	55.68
B_2	47.87	60.70	66.36	58.31	48.55	61.48	67.18	59.07
Mean	44.49	56.42	62.57	54.50	43.22	57.17	63.37	54.59
	S.E.(d)		C.D.(P=0.05)		S.E.(d)		C.D.(P=0.05)	
Zn	0.364		0.741		0.632		1.285	
B	0.364		0.741		0.632		1.285	
Mo	0.297		0.605		0.516		1.049	
Zn×B	0.631		N.S.		1.095		2.225	
B×Mo	0.515		1.047		0.894		N.S.	
Zn×Mo	0.515		1.047		0.894		1.817	
Zn×B×Mo	0.892		N.S.		1.548		N.S.	

135.14 to 189.37 g ha^{-1} in without and with molybdenum respectively. Addition of molybdenum increased the iron uptake about 14.98 per cent over without molybdenum control during first year. The main effects of Zn, B and Mo were significant. Additionally the interactions Zn × B, B × Mo and Zn × Mo were also significant during first year.

During second year, the main effects of Zn, B and Mo and the interaction Zn × B were significant. In general, the uptake values were somewhat higher during second year as compared to first year. The uptake values were somewhat higher during second year as compare to first year. There was about 15.00 per cent increase in iron uptake values in presence of molybdenum over absence of molybdenum. The minimum and maximum values in this case were 112.81 and 169.48 in without molybdenum whereas with molybdenum these values were 135.85 and 190.21 g ha^{-1} respectively.

The variation in stover iron uptake under different level of zinc and boron in absence and presence of molybdenum is presented in Table 4.52. Large variations were observed under different treatments and results were highly significant. Zn_2B_2 gave the highest iron uptake. The ranges of variation were from 995.94 to 1771.25 g ha^{-1} and 1156.16 to 2051.00 g ha^{-1} in without and with molybdenum, respectively. Addition of molybdenum increased the iron uptake about 14.72 per cent over without molybdenum control during first year. Zn, B, Mo main effects and interactions Zn × B, B × Mo and Zn × Mo were also significant.

During second year also the trends of results were similar to first year wherein Zn, B, Mo, Zn × B main effects and interaction were found to be significant. Table 4.51 regardless of treatments the uptake values were somewhat higher during second year as compared to first year. Zn_2B_2 gave the highest iron uptake a significant. There was about 13.00 per cent increase in uptake values in presence of molybdenum over absence of molybdenum. The minimum and maximum values in this case were 1016.00 and 1797.98 g ha^{-1} in without molybdenum whereas with molybdenum these values were 1174.48 and 2075.64 g ha^{-1} respectively.

(j) Manganese

As shown in Table 4.53 the variation in grain manganese uptake under different level of zinc and boron in absence and presence of molybdenum were significant. Large variations were observed under different treatments. The ranges of variation were from 79.98 to 129.05 g ha^{-1} and 90.19 to 136.36 g ha^{-1} in without and with molybdenum respectively. Addition of molybdenum increased the manganese uptake about 8.45 per cent over without molybdenum control during first year. Zn, B and Mo main effect were found to be significant.

During second year also the trends of results were similar to data first year in general the uptake values were somewhat higher during second year as compare to first year. In general the uptake values were somewhat higher during second year as compare to first year. There was about 8.57 per cent increase in manganese uptake values in presence of molybdenum over absence of molybdenum. The minimum and

Table 4.51: Effect of Zn, B and Mo levels on iron uptake (g ha^{-1}) in grain of Chickpea

Treatments	2012-13				2013-14			
	Without Molybdenum				Without Molybdenum			
	Zn_0	Zn_1	Zn_2	Mean	Zn_0	Zn_1	Zn_2	Mean
B_0	112.14	141.43	149.59	134.39	112.81	142.19	150.36	135.12
B_1	131.87	159.30	167.40	152.86	132.60	160.63	168.25	153.83
B_2	142.81	169.05	168.36	160.07	143.20	169.48	168.49	160.39
Mean	128.94	156.59	161.78	149.11	129.54	157.43	162.37	149.78
	With Molybdenum				With Molybdenum			
B_0	135.14	161.85	170.17	155.72	135.85	162.63	171.00	156.49
B_1	160.67	181.35	189.31	177.11	161.47	182.23	189.81	177.84
B_2	166.39	189.37	188.79	181.52	166.80	190.21	189.64	182.22
Mean	154.07	177.52	182.76	171.45	154.71	178.36	183.48	172.18
	S.E.(d)		C.D.(P=0.05)		S.E.(d)		C.D.(P=0.05)	
Zn	0.459		0.934		1.379		2.803	
B	0.459		0.934		1.379		2.803	
Mo	0.375		0.762		1.126		2.288	
Zn×B	0.796		1.617		2.388		4.854	
B×Mo	0.650		1.321		1.950		N.S.	
Zn×Mo	0.650		1.321		1.950		N.S.	
Zn×B×Mo	1.125		N.S.		3.377		N.S.	

Table 4.52: Effect of Zn, B and Mo levels on iron uptake (g ha^{-1}) in stover of Chickpea

Treatments	2012-13				2013-14			
	Without Molybdenum				Without Molybdenum			
	Zn_0	Zn_1	Zn_2	Mean	Zn_0	Zn_1	Zn_2	Mean
B_0	995.94	1538.07	1521.94	1351.98	1016.00	1562.99	1549.17	1376.05
B_1	1247.99	1598.00	1709.55	1518.51	1270.44	1623.38	1735.80	1543.21
B_2	1405.92	1632.00	1771.25	1603.06	1429.74	1657.70	1797.98	1628.47
Mean	1216.62	1589.36	1667.58	1491.18	1238.73	1614.69	1694.32	1515.91
	With Molybdenum				With Molybdenum			
B_0	1156.16	1775.25	1712.34	1547.92	1174.48	1797.60	1735.22	1569.10
B_1	1450.55	1869.30	2027.58	1782.48	1291.20	1892.80	2051.95	1745.32
B_2	1522.50	1830.70	2051.00	1801.40	1543.43	1854.02	2075.64	1824.36
Mean	1376.40	1825.08	1930.31	1710.60	1336.37	1848.14	1954.27	1712.93
	S.E.(d)		C.D.(P=0.05)		S.E.(d)		C.D.(P=0.05)	
Zn	11.136		22.638		34.925		70.995	
B	11.136		22.638		34.925		70.995	
Mo	9.093		18.484		28.516		57.967	
Zn×B	19.289		39.210		60.491		122.967	
B×Mo	15.749		32.015		49.391		N.S.	
Zn×Mo	15.749		32.015		49.391		N.S.	
Zn×B×Mo	27.278		N.S.		85.547		N.S.	

maximum values in this case were 79.69 and 129.56 g ha^{-1} in without molybdenum whereas with molybdenum these values were 90.52 and 137.00 g ha^{-1} respectively.

The variation in stover manganese uptake under different level of zinc and boron in absence and presence of molybdenum is presented in Table. 4.54. Results were highly significant. Zn_2B_2 gave the highest manganese uptake and was the best treatment. The ranges of variation were from 69.76 to 123.99 g ha^{-1} and 98.67 to 164.67 g ha^{-1} in without and with molybdenum respectively. Addition of molybdenum increased the manganese uptake about 35.39 per cent over without molybdenum control during first year. Zn, B and Mo main effects and Zn × B, B × Mo, Zn × Mo were found to be significant.

During second year also the trends of results were Zn, B, Mo and Zn × Mo and Zn × B main effect and interaction were also found to be significant. In general the uptake values were somewhat higher during second year as compare to first year. Zn_2B_2 gave the highest manganese uptake and Zn_2B_1 registered a significant. Addition of molybdenum increased the uptake of manganese by about 34 per cent over control. They minimum and maximum values in this case were 64.00 and 125.17 in without molybdenum whereas with molybdenum these values were 99.35 and 165.55 g ha^{-1} respectively.

(a) Partitioning of Nitrogen uptake in Chickpea

Table 4.55 is a summary of preceding uptake Table 4.35 and 4.36 and is aimed to show the distribution of nitrogen in grain and stover and the total nutrients taken up by the crop for a particular yield level. It was revealed that during the first year the best treatment of (B_2) had the uptake of 71.95 kg and that in stover it was 56.74 kg ha^{-1} with a total uptake of 128.69 kg ha^{-1}. In case of zinc the highest value was 75.07 and 57.21 kg ha^{-1} in grain and stover, respectively. The total uptake in this case was 132.28 kg ha^{-1} in case of without molybdenum.

On molybdenum application the same treatments of boron and zinc gave 75.14 and 60.27 kg ha^{-1} uptake with in grain and stover respectively and total of 135.41 kg ha^{-1}. In case of zinc Zn_2 gave 77.61 kg ha^{-1} nitrogen in grain and 64.05 kg ha^{-1} in stover with a total of 141.66 kg ha^{-1}. The values in case of molybdenum application were uniformly higher than those in case of without molybdenum. With this data it is concluded that the nutrient treatments enhanced the uptake of nitrogen a key factor in maximizing the chickpea yields in (during first year).

Table. 4.55 is a summary, of preceding uptake data Table 4.35 and 4.36 to see the distribution of nitrogen in grain and stover and the total nutrients taken up by the crop for a particular yield level. It was revealed that during the second year the best treatment of (B_2) showed the uptake of 72.44 kg and that in stover it was 57.98 kg ha^{-1} with a total uptake of 130.42 kg ha^{-1}. In case of zinc the highest values were 75.68 and 58.61 kg ha^{-1} in grain and stover respectively in Zn_2. The total uptake in this case was 134.29 kg ha^{-1} in case of without molybdenum.

Table 4.53: Effect of Zn, B and Mo levels on manganese uptake (g ha^{-1}) in grain of Chickpea

Treatments	2012-13				2013-14			
	Without Molybdenum				Without Molybdenum			
	Zn_0	Zn_1	Zn_2	Mean	Zn_0	Zn_1	Zn_2	Mean
B_0	79.98	102.24	110.72	97.65	79.69	102.69	111.09	97.82
B_1	95.34	115.09	122.96	111.13	95.68	115.57	123.35	111.53
B_2	102.31	120.80	129.05	117.39	102.41	120.91	129.56	117.63
Mean	92.54	112.71	120.91	108.72	92.59	113.06	121.33	108.99
	With Molybdenum				With Molybdenum			
B_0	90.19	110.58	119.12	106.63	90.52	111.05	119.61	107.06
B_1	109.65	123.92	131.43	121.67	110.01	124.42	131.94	122.12
B_2	113.10	126.86	136.36	125.44	113.32	127.09	137.00	125.80
Mean	104.31	120.45	128.97	117.91	104.62	120.85	129.52	118.33
	S.E.(d)		C.D.(P=0.05)		S.E.(d)		C.D.(P=0.05)	
Zn	1.156		2.350		1.480		3.010	
B	1.156		2.350		1.480		3.010	
Mo	0.944		1.919		1.209		2.457	
Zn×B	2.002		N.S.		2.564		N.S.	
B×Mo	1.635		N.S.		2.094		N.S.	
Zn×Mo	1.635		N.S.		2.094		N.S.	
Zn×B×Mo	2.832		N.S.		3.626		N.S.	

Table 4.54: Effect of Zn, B and Mo levels on manganese uptake (g ha^{-1}) in stover of Chickpea

Treatments	2012-13				2013-14			
	Without Molybdenum				Without Molybdenum			
	Zn_0	Zn_1	Zn_2	Mean	Zn_0	Zn_1	Zn_2	Mean
B_0	69.76	93.39	103.90	89.02	64.00	94.41	105.00	87.80
B_1	82.11	100.55	121.37	101.34	83.08	101.59	122.56	102.41
B_2	93.57	112.16	123.99	109.91	94.58	113.26	125.17	111.00
Mean	81.81	102.03	116.42	100.09	80.55	103.09	117.58	100.41
	With Molybdenum				With Molybdenum			
B_0	98.67	127.39	144.87	123.64	99.35	128.14	145.69	124.39
B_1	117.70	139.22	164.51	140.48	103.94	140.00	165.37	136.44
B_2	120.09	142.51	164.67	142.42	120.83	143.30	165.55	143.23
Mean	112.15	136.37	158.02	135.51	108.04	137.15	158.87	134.69
	S.E.(d)		C.D.(P=0.05)		S.E.(d)		C.D.(P=0.05)	
Zn	1.098		2.232		1.400		2.846	
B	1.098		2.232		1.400		2.846	
Mo	0.896		1.822		1.143		2.323	
Zn×B	1.902		3.866		2.425		4.929	
B×Mo	1.553		3.156		1.980		N.S.	
Zn×Mo	1.553		3.156		1.980		4.024	
Zn×B×Mo	2.689		N.S.		3.429		N.S.	

On molybdenum application the same treatments of boron and zinc gave 76.03 and 60.93 kg ha^{-1} uptake of nitrogen in grain and stover respectively and total was 136.96 kg ha^{-1}. In case of zinc Zn_2 gave the highest value of 78.93 kg nitrogen in grain and 64.84 kg in stover with a total of 143.77 kg ha^{-1}. The values in case of molybdenum application were uniformly higher than those in case of without molybdenum. With this data, it is concluded that the nutrient treatments enhanced the uptake of nitrogen, a key factor in maximizing the chickpea yields in during second year Fig. 4.9.

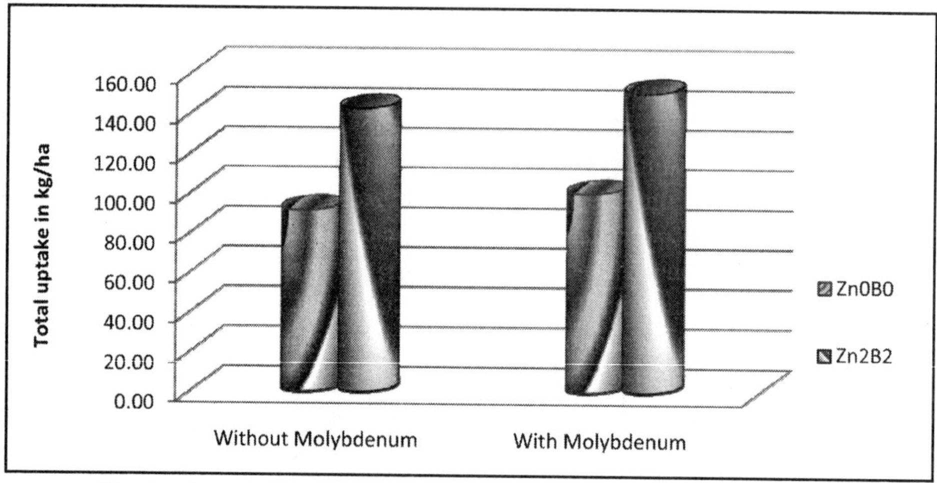

Fig. 4.9: Comparative performance of control and best treatment (Zn_2B_2) in respect of total nitrogen uptake of Chickpea

Table 4.55: Partitioning of nitrogen taken up by chickpea under different treatments and their total uptake kg ha^{-1}

2012-13						
	Without Mo			With Mo		
Treatments	Grain	Stover	Total	Grain	Stover	Total
B_0	61.84	47.43	109.27	64.93	52.39	117.32
B_1	68.65	52.37	121.02	72.43	58.92	131.35
B_2	71.95	56.74	128.69	75.14	60.27	135.41
Zn_0	57.76	45.25	103.01	62.99	49.17	112.16
Zn_1	69.61	54.08	123.69	71.90	58.37	130.27
Zn_2	75.07	57.21	132.28	77.61	64.05	141.66
2013-14						
	Without Mo			With Mo		
Treatments	Grain	Stover	Total	Grain	Stover	Total
B_0	62.40	48.60	111.00	66.01	53.28	119.29
B_1	69.23	53.46	122.69	73.74	57.67	131.41
B_2	72.44	57.98	130.42	76.03	60.93	136.96
Zn_0	58.24	46.24	104.48	63.94	47.65	111.59
Zn_1	70.15	55.20	125.35	72.91	59.40	132.31
Zn_2	75.68	58.61	134.29	78.93	64.84	143.77

(b) Partitioning of Phosphorous uptake in Chickpea

Table 4.56 is a summary uptake results as described before Table 4.37 and 4.38 to have an idea of the distribution of phosphorous in grain and stover and the total nutrients taken up by the crop for a particular yield level. It was revealed that during the first year the best treatment of boron (B_2) gave 7.65 kg phosphorous uptake and that in stover it was 10.30 kg ha^{-1} with a total uptake of 17.95 kg ha^{-1}. In case of zinc the highest value was 7.76 and 10.20 kg ha^{-1} in grain and stover respectively was given by Zn_2. The total uptake in this case was 17.96 kg ha^{-1} in case of without molybdenum.

In case molybdenum application the same treatments of boron and zinc gave 8.50 and 10.95 kg ha^{-1} in grain and stover respectively and total of 19.23 kg ha^{-1}. In case of zinc Zn_1 gave the highest of 8.61 kg phosphorous in grain and 11.55 kg in stover with a total of 20.07 kg ha^{-1}. The values in case of molybdenum application were somewhat higher than those in case of without molybdenum. From these findings it was concluded that the nutrient treatments enhanced the uptake of phosphorous like those of nitrogen the chickpea yields in during first year.

Table 4.56 is a summary of preceding uptake data Table 4.37 and 4.38. It shows the distribution of phosphorous in grain and stover and the total nutrients taken up by the crop for a particular yield level. It was revealed that during the second year the best treatment (B_2) gave 8.04 kg and that in stover it was 10.32 kg ha^{-1} with a total uptake of 18.28 kg ha^{-1}. In case of zinc the highest value was 8.60 and 11.09 kg ha^{-1} in grain and stover respectively in Zn_2. The total uptake in this case was 19.69 kg ha^{-1} in absence of molybdenum.

On molybdenum application the same treatments of boron and zinc gave 8.76 and 10.64 kg ha^{-1} in grain and stover respectively with a total of 19.08 kg ha^{-1}. In case of zinc Zn_2 gave 9.16 kg phosphorous in grain and 11.17 kg in stover with a total of 20.33 kg ha^{-1}. The values in case of molybdenum application were uniformly higher than those in case of without molybdenum. With this data it is concluded that the nutrient treatments enhanced the uptake of phosphorous which might be factor in maximizing the chickpea yields during second year Fig. 4.10.

(c) Partitioning of Potassium uptake in Chickpea

Table 4.57 is a summary preceding uptake values Table 4.39 and 4.40 to see the distribution of potassium in grain and stover and the total nutrients taken up by the crop for treatment wise. It was revealed that during the first year the best treatment (B_2) gave 11.27 kg and that in stover it was 48.45 kg ha^{-1} with a total uptake of 59.72 kg ha^{-1}. In case of zinc the highest value was 11.60 and 47.73 kg ha^{-1} in grain and stover, respectively. The total uptake in this case was 59.33 kg ha^{-1} in case of without molybdenum.

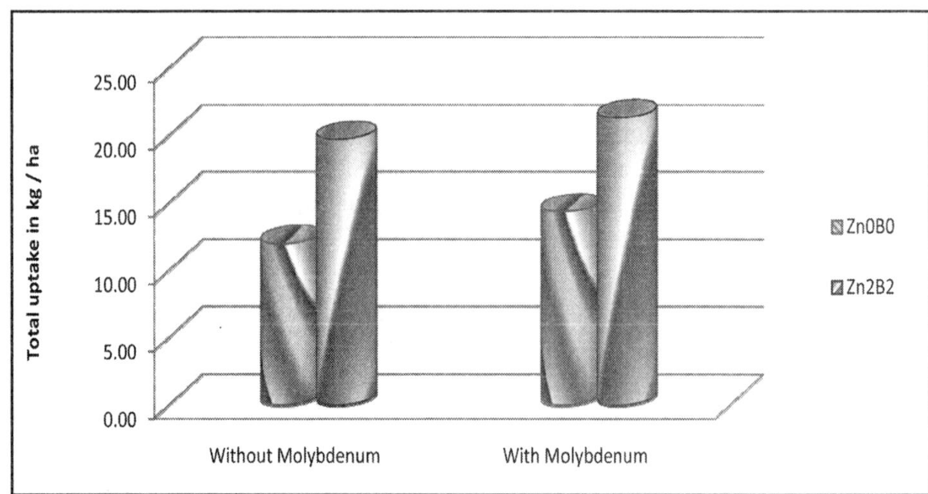

Fig. 4.10: Comparative performance of control and best treatment (Zn_2B_2) in respect of total phosphorous uptake of Chickpea

Table 4.56: Partitioning of phosphorous taken up by chickpea under different treatments and their total uptake kg ha[-1]

2012-13						
	Without Mo			With Mo		
Treatments	Grain	Stover	Total	Grain	Stover	Total
B_0	6.57	8.32	14.89	7.59	9.69	17.28
B_1	7.57	9.47	17.04	8.50	10.73	19.23
B_2	7.65	10.30	17.95	8.12	10.95	19.07
Zn_0	6.27	8.16	14.43	7.08	9.07	16.15
Zn_1	7.76	9.73	17.49	8.61	10.75	19.36
Zn_2	7.76	10.20	17.96	8.52	11.55	20.07
2013-14						
	Without Mo			With Mo		
Treatments	Grain	Stover	Total	Grain	Stover	Total
B_0	6.95	9.34	16.29	7.84	9.48	17.32
B_1	8.04	9.88	17.92	8.76	9.95	18.71
B_2	7.96	10.32	18.28	8.44	10.64	19.08
Zn_0	6.08	8.43	14.51	6.88	9.20	16.08
Zn_1	8.28	10.03	18.31	8.99	9.69	18.68
Zn_2	8.60	11.09	19.69	9.16	11.17	20.33

With molybdenum the same treatments of boron and zinc gave an uptake of 12.04 and 51.13 kg ha^{-1} of potassium in grain and stover respectively and total of 63.17 kg ha^{-1}. In case of zinc Zn_2 gave the highest value 12.19 kg potassium in grain and 52.77 kg in stover with a total of 64.96 kg ha^{-1}. The values in case of molybdenum application where uniformly higher than those in case of without molybdenum. The data showed that the nutrient treatments enhanced the uptake of potassium indicate of a maximizing factor in t chickpea yields in during first year.

Table 4.57 is a summary of preceding uptake data Table 4.39 and 4.40 to see the distribution of potassium in grain and stover and the total nutrients taken up by the crop for a particular yield level. It was revealed that during the second year the best treatment (B_2) gave 11.49 kg potassium and that in stover it was 49.05 kg ha^{-1} with a total uptake of 60.54 kg ha^{-1}. In case of zinc the highest value was 11.85 and 48.65 kg ha^{-1} in grain and stover respectively. The total uptake in this case was 60.50 kg ha^{-1} in case of without molybdenum.

On molybdenum application B_2 and Zn_2 gave 12.21 and 50.96 kg ha^{-1} uptake of potassium in grain and stover, respectively and total was 63.17 kg ha^{-1}. In case of zinc Zn_2 gave 12.37 kg potassium in grain and 53.52 kg in stover with a total of 65.89 kg ha^{-1}. The values in case of molybdenum application were uniformly higher than those in case of without molybdenum. With this data it is concluded that the nutrient treatments enhanced the uptake of potassium, a key factor in maximizing the chickpea yields during second year Fig. 4.11.

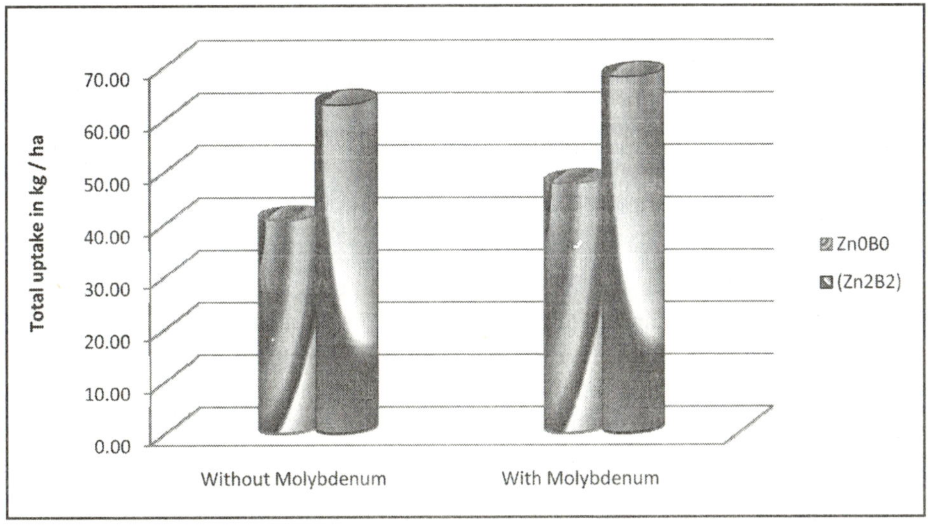

Fig. 4.11: Comparative performance of control and best treatment (Zn_2B_2) in respect of total potassium uptake of Chickpea

Table 4.57: Partitioning of potassium taken up by chickpea under different treatments and their total uptake kg ha^{-1}

			2012-13			
	Without Mo			With Mo		
Treatments	Grain	Stover	Total	Grain	Stover	Total
B_0	9.90	40.24	50.14	10.90	44.70	55.60
B_1	11.03	45.04	56.07	11.84	50.30	62.14
B_2	11.27	48.45	59.72	12.04	51.13	63.17
Zn_0	9.37	38.92	48.29	10.80	42.68	53.48
Zn_1	11.22	47.09	58.31	11.79	50.68	62.47
Zn_2	11.60	47.73	59.33	12.19	52.77	64.96
			2013-14			
	Without Mo			With Mo		
Treatments	Grain	Stover	Total	Grain	Stover	Total
B_0	10.13	40.98	51.11	10.93	45.31	56.24
B_1	11.27	45.83	57.10	12.09	48.65	60.74
B_2	11.49	49.05	60.54	12.21	50.96	63.17
Zn_0	9.58	39.49	49.07	10.89	41.09	51.98
Zn_1	11.46	47.71	59.17	11.96	50.30	62.26
Zn_2	11.85	48.65	60.50	12.37	53.52	65.89

(d) Partitioning of Sulphur uptake in Chickpea

Table 4.58 derived from Table 4.41 and 4.42 and shows the distribution of sulphur in grain and stover and the total nutrients taken up by the crop for a particular treatment. It was revealed that during the first year the best treatment of boron (B_2) was 14.97 kg uptake in grain that in stover it was 6.90 kg ha^{-1} with a total uptake of 21.87 kg ha^{-1}. In case of zinc the highest values were 15.37 and 7.00 kg ha^{-1} in grain and stover, respectively. The total uptake in this case was 22.37 kg ha^{-1} in case of without molybdenum.

On molybdenum application the same treatments of boron and zinc gave 16.08 and 7.15 kg ha^{-1} in grain and stover respectively and total of 23.20 kg ha^{-1}. In case of zinc Zn_2 gave maximum uptake of 16.00 kg sulphur in grain and 7.67 kg in stover with a total of 23.67 kg ha^{-1}. The values in case of molybdenum application were uniformly higher than those in case of without molybdenum. With this data it is concluded that the nutrient treatments enhanced the uptake of sulphur a key factor in maximizing the chickpea yields in during first year.

Table 4.58 is a summary preceding uptake Table 4.41 and 4.42 showing the distribution of sulphur in grain and stover and the total nutrients taken up by the crop for a particular yield level. It was revealed that during the second year the treatment of boron gave the maximum uptake of sulphur as 15.26 kg and that in stover it was 6.95 kg ha^{-1} with a total uptake of 22.12 kg ha^{-1}. In case of zinc the highest value was 15.63 and 7.05 kg ha^{-1} in grain and stover respectively at Zn_2. The total uptake in this case was 22.68 kg ha^{-1} in case of without molybdenum.

With molybdenum treatment the same treatments of boron and zinc gave the highest values of 16.37 and 7.37 kg ha^{-1} in grain and stover respectively and total of 23.65 kg ha^{-1}. In case of zinc, Zn_2 gave the highest uptake of 16.57 kg sulphur in grain and 7.80 kg in stover with a total of 24.37 kg ha^{-1}. The values in case of molybdenum application were higher than those in case of without molybdenum with this data it is concluded that the nutrient treatments increased the uptake of sulphur resulting in increase in chickpea yields in during second year Fig. 4.12.

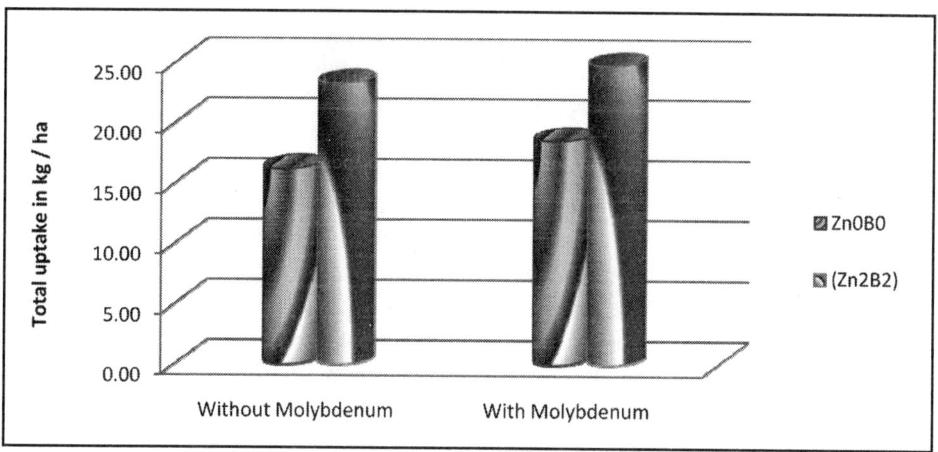

Fig. 4.12: Comparative performance of control and best treatment (Zn_2B_2) in respect of total sulphur uptake of Chickpea

Table 4.58: Partitioning of sulphur taken up by chickpea under different treatments and their total uptake kg ha^{-1}

	2012-13					
	Without Mo			With Mo		
Treatments	Grain	Stover	Total	Grain	Stover	Total
B_0	13.59	5.72	19.31	14.51	6.45	20.96
B_1	14.91	6.39	21.30	16.08	7.12	23.20
B_2	14.97	6.90	21.87	15.82	7.15	22.97
Zn_0	12.97	5.43	18.40	14.59	6.01	20.60
Zn_1	15.13	6.57	21.70	15.81	7.04	22.85
Zn_2	15.37	7.00	22.37	16.00	7.67	23.67
	2013-14					
	Without Mo			With Mo		
Treatments	Grain	Stover	Total	Grain	Stover	Total
B_0	13.76	5.85	19.61	14.82	6.48	21.30
B_1	15.26	6.51	21.77	16.37	6.89	23.26
B_2	15.17	6.95	22.12	16.28	7.37	23.65
Zn_0	13.19	5.55	18.74	14.74	5.78	20.52
Zn_1	15.37	6.70	22.07	16.16	7.16	23.32
Zn_2	15.63	7.05	22.68	16.57	7.80	24.37

(e) *Partitioning of Zinc Uptake in Chickpea*

Table 4.59 presents a summary preceding uptake data Table 4.43 and 4.44 to see the distribution of zinc in grain and stover and the total nutrients taken up by the crop for a particular yield level. It was observed that during the first year the best treatment of boron (B_2) gave 94.33 g and that in stover it was 68.56 g ha^{-1} with a total uptake of 162.89 g ha^{-1}. In case of zinc the highest value was 99.14 and 70.81 g ha^{-1} in grain and stover respectively. The total uptake in this case was 169.95 g ha^{-1} in case of without molybdenum.

On molybdenum application the same treatments of boron and zinc gave the highest of 100.07 and 74.73 g ha^{-1} in grain and stover, respectively with a total of 174.80 g ha^{-1}. In case of zinc Zn_2 gave 103.95 g zinc in grain and 81.60 g in stover with a total of 185.55 g ha^{-1}. The values in case of molybdenum application were in general uniformly higher than those in case of without molybdenum regardless of treatments. With this data it is evident that the nutrient treatments enhanced the uptake of zinc which might help in maximizing the chickpea yields in during first year.

Table 4.59 is a summary preceding uptake data Table 4.43 and 4.44 to see the distribution of zinc in grain and stover and the total nutrients taken up by the crop for a particular yield level. It was revealed that during the second year the best treatment of boron (B_2) gave 96.08 g in grain and that in stover it was 69.56 g ha^{-1} with a total uptake of 165.64 g ha^{-1}. In case of zinc the highest value was 100.88 g and 71.92 g ha^{-1} in grain and stover respectively. The total uptake in this case was 172.80 g ha^{-1} in case of without molybdenum.

On molybdenum application the same treatments of boron and zinc gave uptake of the highest values of 101.65 g and 75.46 g ha^{-1}, in grain and stover, respectively and total of 177.11 g ha^{-1}. In case of zinc Zn_2 gave highest of 105.88 g zinc in grain and 82.27 g in stover with a total of 188.15 g ha^{-1}. The values in case of molybdenum application were uniformly higher than those in case of without molybdenum with this data it is concluded that the nutrient treatments enhanced the uptake of zinc a key factor in maximizing the chickpea yields in during second year Fig. 4.13.

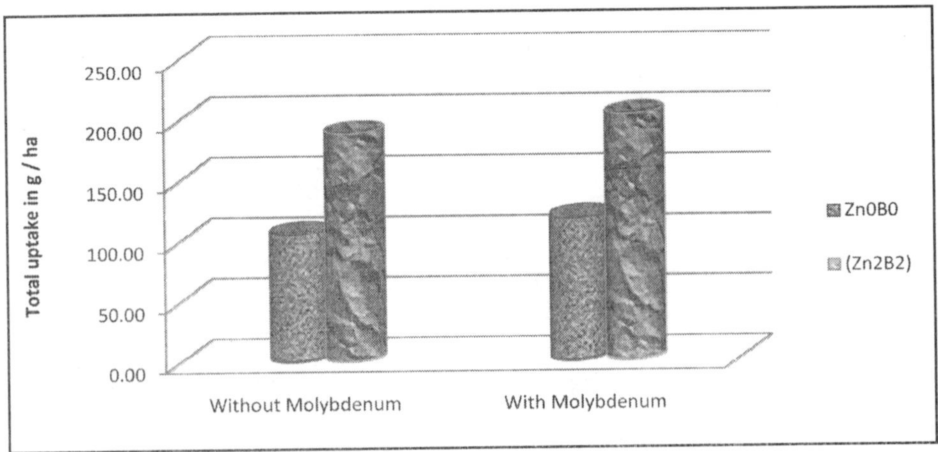

Fig. 4.13: Comparative performance of control and best treatment (Zn_2B_2) in respect of total zinc uptake of Chickpea

Table 4.59: Partitioning of zinc taken up by chickpea under different treatments and their total uptake g ha^{-1}

2012-13						
	Without Mo			With Mo		
Treatments	Grain	Stover	Total	Grain	Stover	Total
B_0	81.89	46.84	128.73	87.43	54.84	142.27
B_1	91.72	57.74	149.46	98.69	66.42	165.11
B_2	94.33	68.56	162.89	100.07	74.73	174.80
Zn_0	76.10	43.04	119.14	84.49	48.20	132.69
Zn_1	92.70	59.28	151.98	97.76	66.19	163.95
Zn_2	99.14	70.81	169.95	103.95	81.60	185.55
2013-14						
	Without Mo			With Mo		
Treatments	Grain	Stover	Total	Grain	Stover	Total
B_0	83.57	47.81	131.38	89.20	55.34	144.54
B_1	93.56	58.70	152.26	100.23	65.10	165.33
B_2	96.08	69.56	165.64	101.65	75.46	177.11
Zn_0	77.81	43.94	121.75	86.09	46.78	132.87
Zn_1	94.52	60.22	154.74	99.11	66.85	165.96
Zn_2	100.88	71.92	172.80	105.88	82.27	188.15

(f) Partitioning of Boron uptake in Chickpea

Table 4.60 are derived from Table 4.45 and 4.46 which shows the portioning of born in grain and stover. It was revealed that during the first year B_2 gave 120.26 g in grain and that in stover it was 106.59 g ha^{-1} with a total uptake of 226.85 g ha^{-1}. In case of zinc the highest value was 121.96 and 106.34 g ha^{-1} in grain and stover respectively, with a total uptake of 228.30 g ha^{-1} in case of without molybdenum.

On molybdenum application the same treatments of boron and zinc gave 127.91 and 114.18 g ha^{-1} in grain and stover respectively and total of 242.09 g ha^{-1}. In case of zinc Zn_2 gave 128.46 g in grain and 119.41 g in stover with a total of 247.87 g ha^{-1}. The values in case of molybdenum application were uniformly higher than those in case of without molybdenum. It is concluded that the nutrient treatments enhanced the uptake of boron which might be reason for enhanced yield.

Table 4.60 derived from Tables 4.45 and 4.46 showing the distribution of boron in grain and stover and also the total nutrients. It was noted that during the second year the best treatment B_2 gave 121.80 g and that in stover it was 109.04 g ha^{-1} with a total uptake of 230.84 g ha^{-1}. In case of zinc the highest value was 125.60 and 109.77 g ha^{-1} in grain and stover respectively by Zn_2. The total uptake in this case was 235.37 g ha^{-1} in case of without molybdenum.

On molybdenum treatment the same treatments of boron and zinc gave 129.48 and 117.32 g ha^{-1} in grain and stover respectively and total of 246.80 g ha^{-1}. In case of zinc Zn_2 gave 130.76 g boron in grain and 122.68 g in stover with a total of 253.44 g ha[-1]. The values in case of molybdenum application were uniformly higher than those in case of without molybdenum with this data it is concluded that the nutrient treatments enhanced the uptake of boron a key factor in maximizing the chickpea yields in during second year Fig. 4.14.

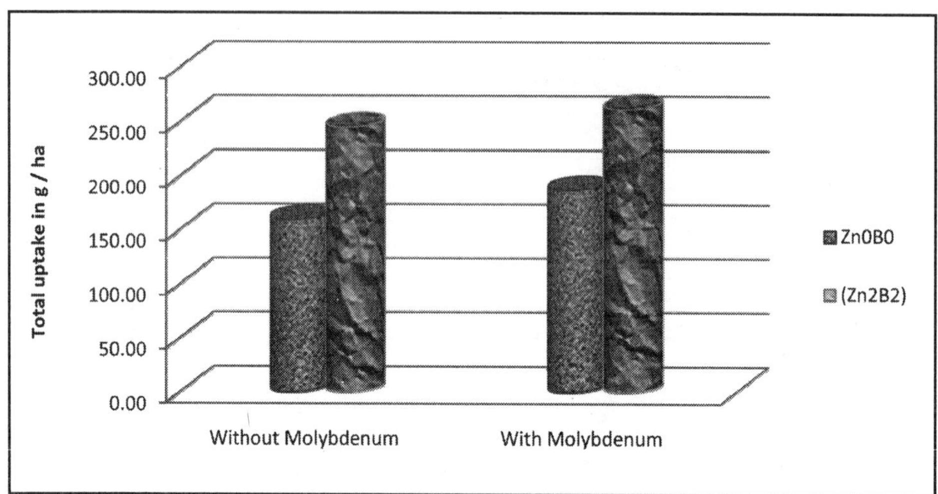

Fig. 4.14: Comparative performance of control and best treatment (Zn_2B_2) in respect of total boron uptake of Chickpea

Table 4.60: Partitioning of boron taken up by chickpea under different treatments and their total uptake g ha^{-1}

2012-13						
	Without Mo			With Mo		
Treatments	Grain	Stover	Total	Grain	Stover	Total
B_0	104.95	88.00	192.95	114.47	99.31	213.78
B_1	117.39	97.46	214.85	125.17	110.95	236.12
B_2	120.26	106.59	226.85	127.91	114.18	242.09
Zn_0	101.47	82.86	184.33	113.64	93.74	207.38
Zn_1	119.17	102.84	222.01	125.45	111.30	236.75
Zn_2	121.96	106.34	228.30	128.46	119.41	247.87
2013-14						
	Without Mo			With Mo		
Treatments	Grain	Stover	Total	Grain	Stover	Total
B_0	107.47	90.93	198.40	115.27	102.28	217.55
B_1	119.62	101.15	220.77	129.05	110.44	239.49
B_2	121.80	109.04	230.84	129.48	117.32	246.80
Zn_0	102.25	85.16	187.41	114.61	92.39	207.00
Zn_1	121.04	106.19	227.23	128.42	114.98	243.40
Zn_2	125.60	109.77	235.37	130.76	122.68	253.44

(g) Partitioning of Molybdenum ,uptake in Chickpea

Table 4.61 presents a summary preceding uptake data Tables 4.47 and 4.48 to see the distribution of molybdenum in grain and stover and the total nutrients taken up by the crop for a particular yield level. It was revealed that during the first year the best treatment of boron (B_2) gave 8.04 g and that in stover it was 1.76 g ha^{-1} with a total uptake of 9.80 g ha^{-1}. In case of zinc the highest value was 8.41 and 1.77 g ha^{-1} in grain and stover respectively. The total uptake in this case was 10.18 g ha^{-1} in case of without molybdenum.

On molybdenum application the same treatments of boron and zinc gave the highest of 8.99 and 1.94 g ha^{-1} in grain and stover, respectively with a total of 10.93 g ha^{-1}. In case of zinc Zn_2 gave 9.32 g molybdenum in grain and 2.06 g in stover with a total of 11.38 g ha^{-1}. The values in case of molybdenum application were uniformly higher than those in case of without molybdenum with this data it is concluded that the nutrient treatments enhanced the uptake of molybdenum which might help in maximizing the chickpea yields in during first year.

Table 4.61 is a summary preceding uptake data Table 4.47 and 4.48 to see the distribution of molybdenum in grain and stover and the total nutrients taken up by the crop for a particular yield level. It was revealed that during the second year the best treatment of boron (B_2) gave 8.22 g in grain and that in stover it was 1.78 g ha^{-1} with a total uptake of 10.00 g ha^{-1}. In case of zinc the highest value was 8.61 g and 1.79 g ha^{-1} in grain and stover respectively. The total uptake in this case was 10.40 g ha^{-1} in case of without molybdenum.

On molybdenum application the same treatments of boron and zinc gave uptake the highest values of 9.24 g and 1.95 g ha^{-1} in grain and stover respectively and total of 11.19 g ha^{-1}. In case of zinc Zn_2 gave highest of 9.58 g molybdenum in grain and 1.97 g in stover with a total of 11.55 g ha^{-1}. The values in case of molybdenum application were uniformly higher than those in case of without molybdenum Fig. 4.15.

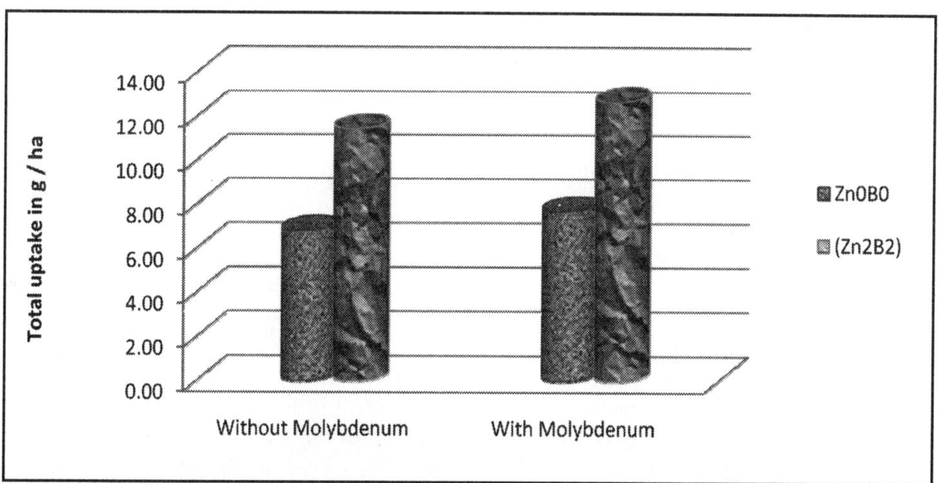

Fig. 4.15: Comparative performance of control and best treatment (Zn_2B_2 in respect of total molybdenum uptake in Chickpea

Table 4.61: Partitioning of molybdenum taken up by chickpea under different treatments and their total uptake g ha^{-1}

2012-13						
	Without Mo			With Mo		
Treatments	Grain	Stover	Total	Grain	Stover	Total
B_0	6.58	1.46	8.04	7.46	1.65	9.11
B_1	7.59	1.64	9.23	8.56	1.87	10.43
B_2	8.04	1.76	9.80	8.99	1.94	10.93
Zn_0	6.19	1.40	7.59	7.20	1.54	8.74
Zn_1	7.61	1.69	9.30	8.49	1.86	10.35
Zn_2	8.41	1.77	10.18	9.32	2.06	11.38
2013-14						
	Without Mo			With Mo		
Treatments	Grain	Stover	Total	Grain	Stover	Total
B_0	6.76	1.48	8.24	7.65	1.67	9.32
B_1	7.77	1.66	9.43	8.76	1.71	10.47
B_2	8.22	1.78	10.00	9.24	1.95	11.19
Zn_0	6.35	1.41	7.76	7.38	1.48	8.86
Zn_1	7.80	1.71	9.51	8.68	1.88	10.56
Zn_2	8.61	1.79	10.40	9.58	1.97	11.55

(h) Partitioning of Copper Uptake in Chickpea

Table 4.62 abridged from Tables 4.49 and 4.50 aimed see the distribution of copper in grain and stover and the total nutrients taken up by the crop for a particular yield level. It was revealed that during the first year B_2 gave of 65.17 g and that in stover it was 51.49 g ha^{-1} with a total uptake of 112.79 g ha^{-1}. In case of zinc Zn_2 gave the highest value was 74.92 and 51.47 g ha^{-1} in grain and stover respectively. The total uptake in this case was 126.39 g ha^{-1} in case of without molybdenum.

On molybdenum application the same treatments of boron and zinc gave 82.02 and 58.31 g ha^{-1} within grain and stover respectively and total of 138.87 g ha^{-1}. In case of zinc Zn_2 gave the maximum values of 90.21 g copper in grain and 62.57 g in stover with a total of 152.78 g ha^{-1}. The values in case of molybdenum application were uniformly higher than those in case of without molybdenum.

Table 4.62 is a summary of preceding uptake Tables 4.49 and 4.50 to see the distribution of copper in grain and stover and the total nutrients taken up by the crop for a particular yield level. It was revealed that during the second year the same gave treatments of 66.06 g and that in stover it was 52.41 g ha^{-1} with a total uptake of 114.56 g ha^{-1}. In case of zinc the highest value was 76.13 and 52.40 g ha^{-1} in grain and stover respectively. The total uptake in this case was 128.53 g ha^{-1} in case of without molybdenum.

On molybdenum application the same treatments of boron gave 83.34 and 59.07 g ha^{-1} in grain and stover respectively and total of 139.02 g ha^{-1}. In case of zinc Zn_2 gave 91.47 g copper in grain and 63.37 g in stover with a total of 154.84 g ha^{-1}. The values in case of molybdenum application were higher than those in case of without molybdenum Fig. 4.16.

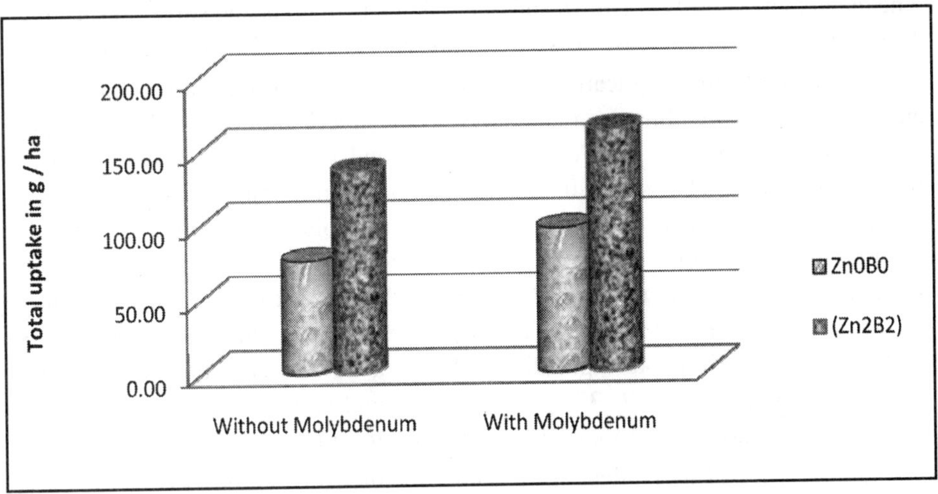

Fig. 4.16: Comparative performance of control and best treatment (Zn_2B_2) in respect of total copper uptake of Chickpea

Table 4.62: Partitioning of copper taken up by chickpea under different treatments and their total uptake g ha^{-1}

2012-13						
	Without Mo			With Mo		
Treatments	Grain	Stover	Total	Grain	Stover	Total
B_0	55.46	40.95	96.41	70.00	48.32	118.32
B_1	65.17	47.62	112.79	82.02	56.85	138.87
B_2	59.45	51.49	110.94	75.60	58.31	133.91
Zn_0	47.61	39.45	87.06	64.58	44.49	109.07
Zn_1	57.54	49.13	106.67	72.83	56.42	129.25
Zn_2	74.92	51.47	126.39	90.21	62.57	152.78
2013-14						
	Without Mo			With Mo		
Treatments	Grain	Stover	Total	Grain	Stover	Total
B_0	56.61	41.76	98.37	71.22	49.01	120.23
B_1	66.06	48.50	114.56	83.34	55.68	139.02
B_2	60.82	52.41	113.23	76.65	59.07	135.72
Zn_0	48.59	40.25	88.84	65.73	43.22	108.95
Zn_1	58.78	50.02	108.80	74.01	57.17	131.18
Zn_2	76.13	52.40	128.53	91.47	63.37	154.84

(i) *Partitioning of Iron uptake in Chickpea*

Table 4.63 is taken preceding uptake Tables 4.51 and 4.52 aimed at to see the distribution of iron in grain and stover and the total iron taken up by the crop. It was revealed that during the first year the best treatment of (B_2) and 160.07 g and that in stover it was 1603.06 g ha^{-1} with a total uptake of 1763.13 g ha^{-1}. In case of zinc the highest value was 161.78 and 1667.58 g ha^{-1} in grain and stover, respectively. The total uptake in this case was 1829.36 g ha^{-1} in case of without molybdenum.

On molybdenum application the same treatments of boron and zinc gave 181.52 and 1801.40 g ha^{-1} within grain and stover respectively and total of 1982.92 g ha^{-1}. In case of zinc, Zn_2 gave 182.76 g iron in grain and 1930.31 g in stover with a total of 2113.07 g ha^{-1}. The values in case of molybdenum application were uniformly higher than those in case of without molybdenum. Table 4.63 have been obtained by summarizing the Tables 4.51 and 4.52 to demonstrate the distribution of iron in grain and stover and the total iron taken up by the crop. It was revealed that during the second year the best treatment of (B_2) gave 160.39 g and that in stover it was 1628.47 g ha^{-1} with a total uptake of 1788.86 g ha^{-1}. In case of zinc the highest value was 162.37 and 1694.32 g ha^{-1} in grain and stover, respectively. The total uptake in this case was 1856.69 g ha^{-1} in case of without molybdenum.

In presence of molybdenum the same treatments of boron gave 182.22 g and 1824.36 g ha^{-1} in grain and stover respectively and total of 2006.58 g ha^{-1}. In case of zinc Zn_2 gave 183.48 g iron in grain and 1954.27 g in stover with a total of 2137.75 g ha^{-1}. The values in case of molybdenum treatments were uniformly higher than those in case of without molybdenum Fig. 4.17.

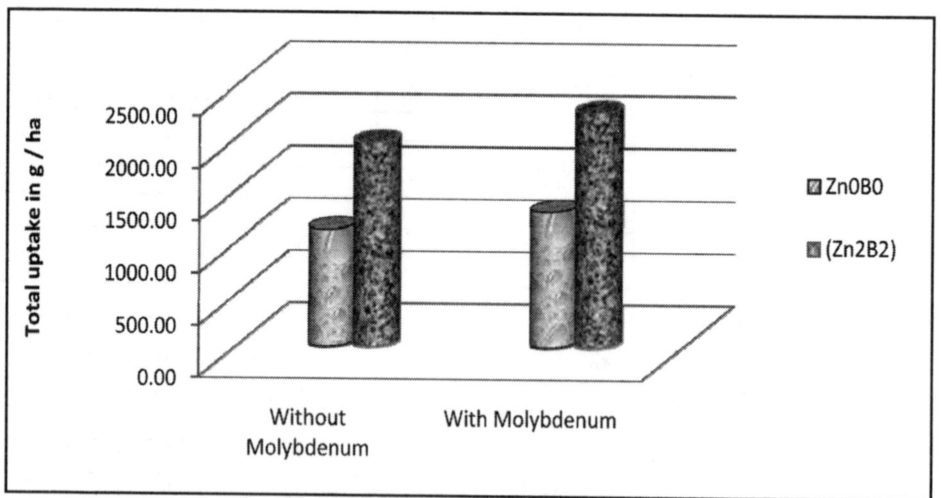

Fig. 4.17: Comparative performance of control and best treatment (Zn_2B_2) in respect of total iron uptake of Chickpea

Table 4.63: Partitioning of iron taken up by chickpea under different treatments and their total uptake g ha^{-1}

2012-13						
	Without Mo			With Mo		
Treatments	Grain	Stover	Total	Grain	Stover	Total
B_0	134.39	1351.88	1486.27	155.72	1547.92	1703.64
B_1	152.86	1518.51	1671.37	177.11	1782.48	1959.59
B_2	160.07	1603.06	1763.13	181.52	1801.40	1982.92
Zn_0	128.94	1216.51	1345.45	154.07	1376.40	1530.47
Zn_1	156.59	1589.36	1745.95	177.52	1825.08	2002.60
Zn_2	161.78	1667.58	1829.36	182.76	1930.31	2113.07
2013-14						
	Without Mo			With Mo		
Treatments	Grain	Stover	Total	Grain	Stover	Total
B_0	135.12	1376.05	1511.17	156.49	1569.10	1725.59
B_1	153.83	1543.21	1696.87	177.84	1745.32	1923.16
B_2	160.39	1628.47	1788.86	182.22	1824.36	2006.58
Zn_0	129.54	1238.73	1368.27	154.71	1336.37	1491.08
Zn_1	157.43	1614.69	1771.96	178.36	1848.14	2026.50
Zn_2	162.37	1694.32	1856.69	183.48	1954.27	2137.75

(j) Partitioning of Manganese uptake in Chickpea

Table 4.64 is a summary of preceding uptake Tables 4.52 and 4.54 to see the distribution of manganese in grain and stover and the total nutrients taken up by the crop for a particular yield level. It was revealed that during the first year the best treatment of (B_2) gave 117.39 g and that in stover it was 109.91 g ha^{-1} with a total uptake of 227.30 g ha^{-1}. In case of zinc the highest value was 120.91 and 116.42 g ha^{-1} in grain and stover, respectively was recorded in Zn_2. The total uptake in this case was 237.33 g ha^{-1} in case of without molybdenum.

On molybdenum application the same treatments of boron and zinc gave 125.44 and 142.42 g ha^{-1} within grain and stover respectively and total of 267.86 g ha^{-1}. In case of zinc Zn_2 gave 128.97 g manganese in grain and 158.02 g in stover with a total of 286.99 g ha^{-1}. The values in case of molybdenum application were uniformly higher than those in case of without molybdenum.

Table 4.64 is a summary of uptake Tables 4.53 and 4.54 showing the distribution of manganese in grain and stover and the total nutrients taken up by the crop for a particular yield level. It was revealed that during the second year the best treatment of (B_2) and 117.63 g and that in stover it was 111.00 g ha^{-1} with a total uptake of 228.63 g ha^{-1}. In case of zinc the highest value was 121.33 and 117.58 g ha^{-1} in grain and stover respectively, in Zn_2. The total uptake in this case was 238.91 g ha^{-1} in case of without molybdenum.

On molybdenum application B_2 gave 125.80 and 143.23 g ha^{-1} within grain and stover respectively and total of 269.03 g ha^{-1}. In case of zinc Zn_2 gave 129.52 g manganese in grain and 158.87 g in stover with a total of 288.39 g ha^{-1}. Molybdenum treatment gave higher values than control throughout Fig. 4.18.

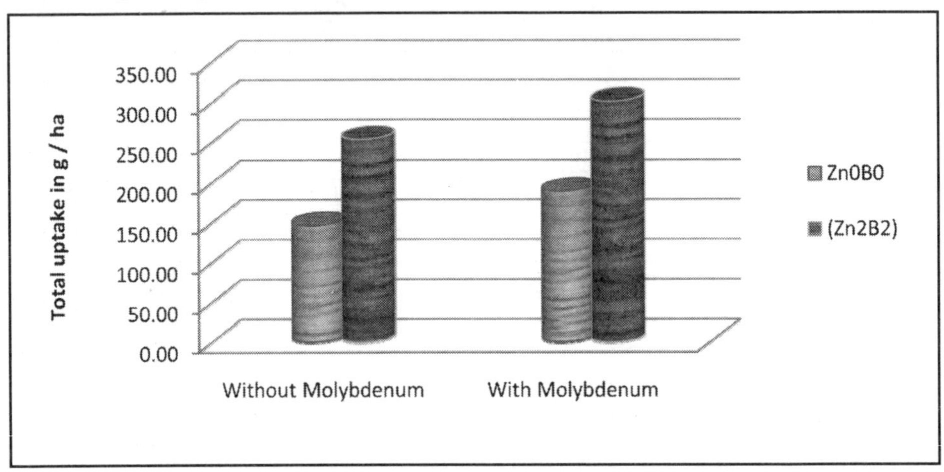

Fig. 4.18: Comparative performance of control and best treatment (Zn_2B_2) in respect of total manganese uptake of Chickpea

Table 4.64: Partitioning of manganese taken up by chickpea under different treatments and their total uptake g ha^{-1}

2012-13						
	Without Mo			With Mo		
Treatments	Grain	Stover	Total	Grain	Stover	Total
B_0	97.65	89.02	186.67	106.63	123.64	230.27
B_1	111.13	101.34	212.47	121.67	140.48	262.15
B_2	117.39	109.91	227.30	125.44	142.42	267.86
Zn_0	92.54	81.81	174.35	104.31	112.15	216.46
Zn_1	112.71	102.03	214.74	120.45	136.37	256.82
Zn_2	120.91	116.42	237.33	128.97	158.02	286.99
2013-14						
	Without Mo			With Mo		
Treatments	Grain	Stover	Total	Grain	Stover	Total
B_0	97.82	87.80	185.62	107.06	124.39	231.45
B_1	111.53	102.41	213.94	122.12	136.44	258.56
B_2	117.63	111.00	228.63	125.80	143.23	269.03
Zn_0	92.59	80.55	173.14	104.62	108.04	212.66
Zn_1	113.06	103.09	216.15	120.85	137.15	258.00
Zn_2	121.33	117.58	238.91	129.52	158.87	288.39

Crop Qualities

(a) Protein Content

Chickpea is a high protein crop like other legumes and protein is the principal product from nutritional point of view. In the present study an effort has been made to see the variation in protein content under the influence of different treatments. A summary of the results is given in Table 4.65 it was observed that protein content varied from 17.84 to 22.19 per cent and the lowest and the highest values were given by Zn_0B_0 and Zn_2B_2, respectively in case of without molybdenum during first year.

During the same year the values deviated between 18.00 and 22.25 per cent and the same treatments gave the best results as shown above. The increase in protein content due to molybdenum application was not significant. However, significant responses were obtained in case main effects of Zn and B.

During second year the trends of results were almost similar to those of first year that the protein values in general, were somewhat higher during this year as compared to those of first year. The effect of molybdenum during this year on protein content was positive and significant in addition the main effects of Zn and B were also significant.

During this year protein content ranged from 18.06 to 22.31 per cent and the lowest and the highest values were given by Zn_0B_0 and Zn_2B_2, respectively in case of without molybdenum and that in case of with molybdenum the minimum and maximum values 18.25 to 22.50 per cent, respectively were observed during second year.

(b) Protein Harvest

Pulses, in general, are important for dietary protein and protein is the target product of these crops and so also of chickpea. Therefore, in the present study, protein yields were calculated from grain yield and protein content. A summary of the results is given in Table 4.66. It was observed that protein yield increased with increasing levels of boron and zinc in both, without and with molybdenum. During first year it ranged from 384.64 to 448.86 kg ha^{-1} in B_0 and B_2 without molybdenum.

These treatments gave the lowest and highest values of 404.81 and 469.10 kg ha^{-1} with molybdenum. Similarly in case of zinc Zn_0 gave 359.99 kg ha^{-1} and in Zn_2 the yield was 468.83 kg ha^{-1} during first year in without molybdenum. In presence of molybdenum the lowest and highest values in Zn_0 and Zn_2 respectively were 393.22 and 484.65 kg ha^{-1}.

During second year the lowest and highest values were 388.83 and 451.83 kg ha^{-1} in B_0 and B_2. In case of zinc, Zn_0 and Zn_2 gave lowest and highest values as 363.55 and 472.55 kg ha^{-1} in case of no molybdenum control. On molybdenum treatment the values of B_0 and B_2 and Zn_0 and Zn_2 were 411.51 and 474.67 and 399.11 and 492.81 kg ha^{-1} in that order. A summary of performance of treatments in respect of protein harvest has been illustrated in Fig. 4.19(a) and 4.19(b).

Table 4.65: Effect of Zn, B and Mo levels on per cent protein in grain of Chickpea

Treatments	2012-13				2013-14			
	Without Molybdenum				Without Molybdenum			
	Zn_0	Zn_1	Zn_2	Mean	Zn_0	Zn_1	Zn_2	Mean
B_0	17.84	19.19	20.00	19.01	18.06	19.31	20.13	19.17
B_1	18.63	19.56	21.25	19.81	18.75	19.69	21.38	19.94
B_2	19.38	20.19	22.19	20.59	19.50	20.31	22.31	20.71
Mean	18.62	19.65	21.15	19.80	18.77	19.77	21.27	19.94
	With Molybdenum				With Molybdenum			
B_0	18.00	19.19	20.06	19.08	18.25	19.50	20.31	19.35
B_1	18.69	19.63	21.31	19.88	18.94	19.88	21.75	20.19
B_2	19.44	20.25	22.25	20.65	19.69	20.44	22.50	20.88
Mean	18.71	19.69	21.21	19.87	18.96	19.94	21.52	20.14
	S.E.(d)		C.D.(P=0.05)		S.E.(d)		C.D.(P=0.05)	
Zn	0.287		0.584		0.324		0.658	
B	0.287		0.584		0.324		0.658	
Mo	0.235		N.S.		0.264		N.S.	
Zn×B	0.498		N.S.		0.560		N.S.	
B×Mo	0.407		N.S.		0.458		N.S.	
Zn×Mo	0.407		N.S.		0.458		N.S.	
Zn×B×Mo	0.704		N.S.		0.793		N.S.	

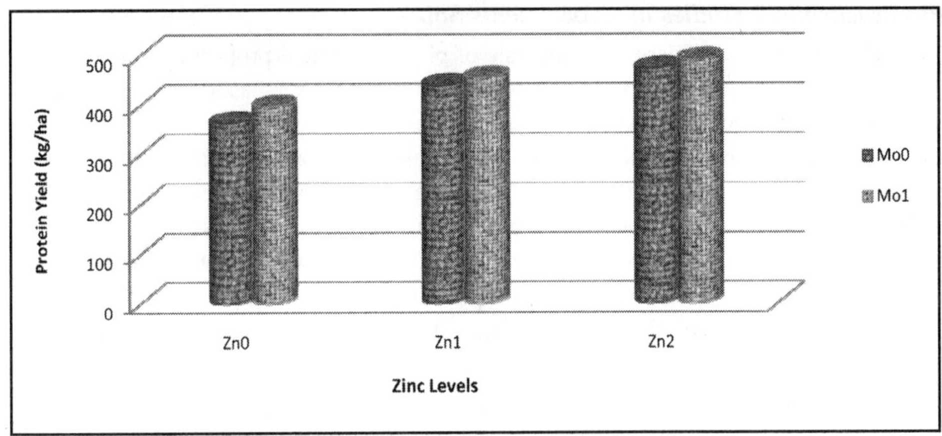

Fig. 4.19(a): Comparative protein yield performance of zinc levels in without and with molybdenum treatments of chickpea

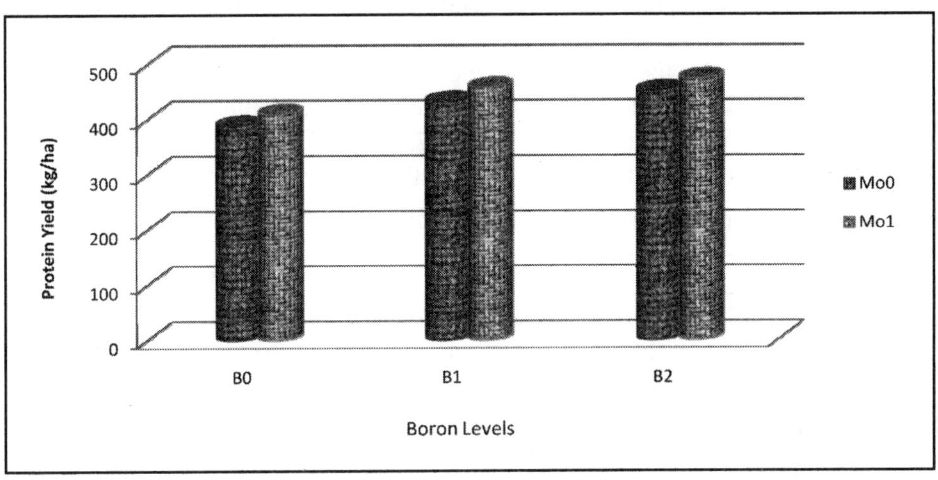

Fig. 4.19(b): Comparative protein yield performance of boron levels in without and with molybdenum treatments of chickpea

Table 4.66: Comparative protein harvest performance kg ha^{-1} of zinc and boron levels in without and with molybdenum treatments of chickpea

Treatments	2012-13		2013-14	
	Without Molybdenum	With Molybdenum	Without Molybdenum	With Molybdenum
B_0	384.64	404.81	388.83	411.51
B_1	427.90	452.27	431.70	460.33
B_2	448.86	469.10	451.83	474.67
Zn_0	359.99	393.22	363.55	399.11
Zn_1	434.92	449.26	438.24	455.63
Zn_2	468.83	484.65	472.55	492.81

Physicochemical Studies of Experiments Soil

This study encompasses the analysis of physiochemical properties in relation to different nutrients applied and crop grown in two consecutive seasons in the prevalent monoculture practice of chickpea – fallow – chickpea in the years 2012-13 and 2013-14. The parameters analyzed included pH, EC organic carbon, available nitrogen, available phosphorus, available potassium, available sulphur, available zinc, available boron, available molybdenum, available copper, available iron and available manganese before and after the harvest the crop aimed at recording the variation in soil characteristics and dynamics of nutrients due to crop growth. The data presented here for all the physicochemical properties are reported on the basis of composite analysis and no statistical treatments of data were necessary. The results are given as below:

A Physicochemical Properties

A (a) pH

The data relating to pH of the soil in 1:2.5 soil: water extract for the year 2012-13 and 2013-14 are given in Table 4.67. The results showed that in all the cases pH varied between 7.00 and 8.00 in normal neutral range conducive to crop growth. pH did not appear to vary with fertilizer treatments, and the treatment effects did not show any regular trend in respect of pH indicating that there was no perceptible effect of different treatments on soil pH. It ranged from 7.19 to 7.23 and 7.21 to 7.23 before the crop during first and second year, respectively. After the crop it ranged from 7.20 to 7.24.

Table 4.67: Effect of Zn, B and Mo levels on soil pH (1:2.5) of the experimental field

Treatments	2012-13		2013-14	
	Before crop	After crop	Before crop	After crop
$Mo_0 Zn_0 B_0$	7.20	7.20	7.21	7.21
$Mo_0 Zn_0 B_1$	7.22	7.23	7.23	7.23
$Mo_0 Zn_0 B_2$	7.22	7.22	7.22	7.23
$Mo_0 Zn_1 B_0$	7.21	7.22	7.22	7.23
$Mo_0 Zn_1 B_1$	7.22	7.23	·7.23	7.24
$Mo_0 Zn_1 B_2$	7.22	7.23	7.23	7.24
$Mo_0 Zn_2 B_0$	7.23	7.22	7.22	7.23
$Mo_0 Zn_2 B_1$	7.20	7.22	7.22	7.23
$Mo_0 Zn_2 B_2$	7.20	7.21	7.22	7.23
$Mo_1 Zn_0 B_0$	7.22	7.23	7.23	7.23
$Mo_1 Zn_0 B_1$	7.21	7.22	7.23	7.24
$Mo_1 Zn_0 B_2$	7.19	7.20	7.21	7.22
$Mo_1 Zn_1 B_0$	7.20	7.21	7.22	7.23
$Mo_1 Zn_1 B_1$	7.21	7.21	7.22	7.23
$Mo_1 Zn_1 B_2$	7.20	7.21	7.22	7.22
$Mo_1 Zn_2 B_0$	7.23	7.23	7.23	7.24
$Mo_1 Zn_2 B_1$	7.22	7.23	7.23	7.24
$Mo_1 Zn_2 B_2$	7.23	7.23	7.23	7.24

A (b) EC

The data relating to EC of the soil in 1:2.5 soil: water extract are given in Table 4.68. The results showed that in all the cases an EC varied between 0.26 and 0.30 in normal neutral range conducive to crop growth. However, the treatment effects did not show any regular trend in respect of EC indicating that there was no perceptible effect of different treatments on soil EC. It ranged from 0.27 to 0.30 and 0.26 to 0.29 before the crop during first and second year, respectively. After the crop it ranged from 0.26 to 0.30.

Table 4.68: Effect of Zn, B and Mo levels on soil EC (1:2.5) dSm^{-1} of the experimental field

Treatments	2012-13		2013-14	
	Before crop	After crop	Before crop	After crop
Mo_0 Zn_0 B_0	0.27	0.27	0.26	0.26
Mo_0 Zn_0 B_1	0.29	0.28	0.28	0.28
Mo_0 Zn_0 B_2	0.28	0.27	0.28	0.27
Mo_0 Zn_1 B_0	0.29	0.28	0.28	0.27
Mo_0 Zn_1 B_1	0.30	0.28	0.28	0.28
Mo_0 Zn_1 B_2	0.30	0.29	0.29	0.29
Mo_0 Zn_2 B_0	0.27	0.27	0.26	0.26
Mo_0 Zn_2 B_1	0.28	0.28	0.26	0.26
Mo_0 Zn_2 B_2	0.27	0.27	0.27	0.28
Mo_1 Zn_0 B_0	0.30	0.29	0.29	0.29
Mo_1 Zn_0 B_1	0.27	0.27	0.26	0.26
Mo_1 Zn_0 B_2	0.28	0.28	0.29	0.29
Mo_1 Zn_1 B_0	0.28	0.27	0.28	0.28
Mo_1 Zn_1 B_1	0.29	0.29	0.28	0.28
Mo_1 Zn_1 B_2	0.28	0.28	0.27	0.28
Mo_1 Zn_2 B_0	0.30	0.30	0.29	0.29
Mo_1 Zn_2 B_1	0.30	0.30	0.29	0.29
Mo_1 Zn_2 B_2	0.29	0.29	0.28	0.28

B Chemical Properties

B (a) Organic Carbon

Table 4.69 describe the changes in organic carbon. The results showed that there were enhancements in organic carbon with incase in boron and molybdenum doses both in case of without and with molybdenum uniformly. Addition of molybdenum increased the organic carbon. It ranged from 0.25 to 0.30 and 0.31 to 0.33 per cent in case of boron and 0.27 to 0.27 and 0.31 to 0.33 per cent in case of zinc in control and molybdenum treatments during first year. In 0.28 to 0.30 per cent zinc and 0.28 to 0.30 per cent boron in absence of molybdenum and 0.33 to 0.34 per cent zinc and 0.34 to 0.33 per cent boron in presence of molybdenum during second year. In the analysis of post harvest samples the results indicated that zinc, boron and molybdenum tended to increase the organic carbon after the crop, to a small extent.

Table 4.69: Effect of Zn, B and Mo levels on per cent organic carbon of the experimental field soil

Post Harvest (2012-13)								
	Without Molybdenum				With Molybdenum			
Treatments	Zn_0	Zn_1	Zn_2	Mean	Zn_0	Zn_1	Zn_2	Mean
B_0	0.25	0.25	0.26	0.25	0.31	0.30	0.32	0.31
B_1	0.27	0.26	0.27	0.27	0.31	0.33	0.34	0.33
B_2	0.30	0.30	0.29	0.30	0.32	0.33	0.33	0.33
Mean	0.27	0.27	0.27	0.27	0.31	0.32	0.33	0.32
Post Harvest (2013-14)								
	Without Molybdenum				With Molybdenum			
Treatments	Zn_0	Zn_1	Zn_2	Mean	Zn_0	Zn_1	Zn_2	Mean
B_0	0.26	0.27	0.30	0.28	0.33	0.33	0.35	0.34
B_1	0.28	0.28	0.29	0.28	0.32	0.34	0.34	0.33
B_2	0.29	0.31	0.30	0.30	0.33	0.33	0.34	0.33
Mean	0.28	0.29	0.30	0.29	0.33	0.33	0.34	0.33
Initial soil organic carbon status based on composite analysis were 0.25 and 0.26 % during first and second year								

B (b) Available Nitrogen

Table 4.70 describe the changes in available nitrogen. The results showed in that boron and zinc levels molybdenum increased the available nitrogen. The available nitrogen ranged from 175 to 177 and 178 to 180 kg ha^{-1} in case of boron and 175 to 177 and 178 to 180 kg ha^{-1} in case of zinc in control and molybdenum treatments, respectively during first year. during second year 176 to 183 kg ha^{-1} in case of zinc and 178 to 182 kg ha^{-1} in case of boron in absence of molybdenum and 180 to 187 kg ha^{-1} in case of zinc and 182 to 185 kg ha^{-1} in case of boron in presence of molybdenum, respectively. In the analysis of post harvest samples the results indicated that zinc, boron and molybdenum tended to increase the available nitrogen after the crop.

Table 4.70: Effect of Zn, B and Mo levels on available nitrogen (kg ha^{-1}) soil of the experimental field

Post Harvest (2012-13)								
	Without Molybdenum				With Molybdenum			
Treatments	Zn_0	Zn_1	Zn_2	Mean	Zn_0	Zn_1	Zn_2	Mean
B_0	173	175	177	175	176	178	179	178
B_1	175	177	176	176	179	181	180	180
B_2	176	178	178	177	178	182	180	180
Mean	175	177	177	176	178	180	180	179
Post Harvest (2013-14)								
	Without Molybdenum				With Molybdenum			
Treatments	Zn_0	Zn_1	Zn_2	Mean	Zn_0	Zn_1	Zn_2	Mean
B_0	175	177	181	178	179	181	185	182
B_1	175	180	182	179	180	184	186	183
B_2	178	181	186	182	182	185	189	185
Mean	176	179	183	179	180	183	187	183

Initial soil available nitrogen status based on composite analysis were 173 and 175 kg ha^{-1} during first and second year

B (c) Available Phosphorous

As shown in Table 4.71, increasing doses of zinc had a depressing effect on soil phosphorous indicating an antagonistic effect between phosphorous and zinc. Conversely, boron seemed to have an increasing effect on available phosphorous. It was also evident that addition of molybdenum tended to increase the phosphorous content over no molybdenum before crop. During both the years in initial and post harvest results. It ranged from 7.90 to 8.53 and 8.40 to 8.56 kg ha^{-1} during first year without and with molybdenum respectively. The corresponding values were 7.44 to 8.59 in control and 8.50 to 8.65 kg ha^{-1} in molybdenum treatments.

B (d) Available Potassium

Table 4.72 describe the changes due to different treatments in available potassium. The results showed that there were enhancements in available potassium by the use of boron and molybdenum doses both in case of without and with molybdenum uniformly. Addition of molybdenum available potassium ranged from 178 to 182 and 179 to 184 kg ha^{-1} in case of boron and 179 to 182 and 181 to 183 kg ha^{-1} in case of zinc in control and molybdenum treatments during first year. During second year it ranged from 180 to 184 kg ha^{-1} due to zinc and 180 to 183 kg ha^{-1} due to boron in absence of molybdenum and 183 to 187 kg ha^{-1} in zinc treatment and 182 to 186 kg ha^{-1} in boron treatment in presence of molybdenum during second year. Zinc, boron and molybdenum tended to increase the available potassium after the crop.

Table 4.71: Effect of Zn, B and Mo levels on available phosphorus (kg ha^{-1}) soil of the experimental field

Post harvest (2012-13)								
	Without Molybdenum				With Molybdenum			
Treatments	Zn_0	Zn_1	Zn_2	Mean	Zn_0	Zn_1	Zn_2	Mean
B_0	8.00	7.95	7.90	7.95	8.50	8.48	8.40	8.46
B_1	8.53	8.50	8.48	8.50	8.55	8.48	8.50	8.51
B_2	8.42	8.38	8.35	8.38	8.56	8.52	8.50	8.53
Mean	8.32	8.28	8.24	8.28	8.54	8.49	8.47	8.50
Post harvest (2013-14)								
	Without Molybdenum				With Molybdenum			
Treatments	Zn_0	Zn_1	Zn_2	Mean	Zn_0	Zn_1	Zn_2	Mean
B_0	8.05	7.48	7.44	7.66	8.60	8.50	8.50	8.53
B_1	8.55	8.59	8.58	8.57	8.64	8.65	8.60	8.63
B_2	8.46	8.52	8.52	8.50	8.60	8.55	8.60	8.58
Mean	8.35	8.20	8.18	8.24	8.61	8.57	8.57	8.58
Initial soil available phosphorous based on composite analysis were 8.00 and 8.05 kg ha^{-1} during first and second year								

Table 4.72: Effect of Zn, B and Mo levels on available potassium (kg ha^{-1}) soil of the experimental field

Post harvest (2012-13)								
	Without Molybdenum				With Molybdenum			
Treatments	Zn_0	Zn_1	Zn_2	Mean	Zn_0	Zn_1	Zn_2	Mean
B_0	176	177	180	178	178	179	180	179
B_1	179	182	183	181	182	181	183	182
B_2	181	183	183	182	184	183	185	184
Mean	179	181	182	181	181	181	183	182
Post harvest (2013-14)								
	Without Molybdenum				With Molybdenum			
Treatments	Zn_0	Zn_1	Zn_2	Mean	Zn_0	Zn_1	Zn_2	Mean
B_0	177	179	184	180	180	181	186	182
B_1	180	183	183	182	184	186	187	186
B_2	182	184	184	183	185	186	187	186
Mean	180	182	184	182	183	184	187	185
Initial soil available potassium based on composite analysis were 176 and 177 kg ha^{-1} during first and second year								

B (e) Available Sulphur

As shown in Table 4.73 increasing level of boron and zinc resulted in linear increase in available sulphur (SO_4^-) form and addition of molybdenum also increased the sulphur content over no molybdenum control. This trend was observed during both the years. B_2Zn_2 came out to be best treatment in both without and with molybdenum during both the years. The ranges of variation were 7.96 to 8.53 and 7.97 to 8.76 mg kg^{-1} in control and molybdenum treatment respectively, during first year. During second year it ranged from 8.02 to 8.33 mg kg^{-1} in control and 8.04 to 8.40 mg kg^{-1} in presence of molybdenum.

Table 4.73: Effect of Zn, B and Mo levels on available sulphur (mg kg^{-1}) soil of the experimental field

Post Harvest (2012-13)								
	Without Molybdenum				With Molybdenum			
Treatments	Zn_0	Zn_1	Zn_2	Mean	Zn_0	Zn_1	Zn_2	Mean
B_0	7.96	8.19	8.29	8.15	7.97	8.20	8.30	8.16
B_1	8.00	8.20	8.30	8.17	8.30	8.50	8.67	8.49
B_2	8.27	8.50	8.53	8.43	8.57	8.58	8.76	8.64
Mean	8.08	8.30	8.37	8.25	8.28	8.43	8.58	8.43
Post Harvest (2013-14)								
	Without Molybdenum				With Molybdenum			
Treatments	Zn_0	Zn_1	Zn_2	Mean	Zn_0	Zn_1	Zn_2	Mean
B_0	8.02	8.22	8.30	8.18	8.04	8.25	8.37	8.22
B_1	8.13	8.23	8.30	8.22	8.30	8.33	8.38	8.34
B_2	8.20	8.30	8.33	8.28	8.33	8.36	8.40	8.36
Mean	8.12	8.25	8.31	8.23	8.22	8.31	8.38	8.31
Initial soil available sulphur based on composite analysis were 7.96 and 8.02 mg kg^{-1} during first and second year								

B (f) Available Zinc

The data with respect to soil available zinc under different nutrient treatment are shown in Table 4.74. As a general trend it was observed that increasing levels of boron and zinc increased the available zinc content linearly both in control and molybdenum treatments and this trend was maintained during both the years. However, the values were somewhat higher during second year than those of first year. The ranges of variation were from 0.54 to 0.70 and 0.55 to 0.72 mg kg^{-1} in control and molybdenum treatments during first year. Parallel to this the ranges were 0.56 to 0.72 and 0.58 to 0.74 mg kg^{-1}, respectively, in control and molybdenum treatments during second year.

Table 4.74: Effect of Zn, B and Mo levels on available zinc (mg kg^{-1}) soil of the experimental field

Post Harvest (2012-13)								
	Without Molybdenum				With Molybdenum			
Treatments	Zn_0	Zn_1	Zn_2	Mean	Zn_0	Zn_1	Zn_2	Mean
B_0	0.54	0.59	0.64	0.59	0.55	0.60	0.66	0.60
B_1	0.57	0.62	0.67	0.62	0.58	0.63	0.69	0.63
B_2	0.60	0.65	0.70	0.65	0.61	0.67	0.72	0.67
Mean	0.57	0.62	0.67	0.62	0.58	0.63	0.69	0.63
Post Harvest (2013-14)								
	Without Molybdenum				With Molybdenum			
Treatments	Zn_0	Zn_1	Zn_2	Mean	Zn_0	Zn_1	Zn_2	Mean
B_0	0.56	0.61	0.66	0.61	0.58	0.63	0.68	0.63
B_1	0.59	0.63	0.69	0.64	0.61	0.65	0.71	0.66
B_2	0.62	0.67	0.72	0.67	0.64	0.69	0.74	0.69
Mean	0.59	0.64	0.69	0.64	0.61	0.66	0.71	0.66
Initial soil available zinc based on composite analysis were 0.54 and 0.56 mg kg^{-1} during first and second year								

B (g) Available Boron

Table 4.75 exibits the effect of zinc and boron levels in absence and presence of molybdenum on available boron content of soil for both the years. Wherein, as a common trend during both the years increasing levels of zinc and boron resulted in a regular increase in available boron and addition of molybdenum also increased the available boron over control. However, the boron content during second year was slightly higher than the first year. The minimum and maximum values of available boron were 0.35 and 0.38 mg kg^{-1} in control and that in molybdenum treatment corresponding values 0.35 and 0.39 mg kg^{-1} in during first year.

Similarly these values were 0.35 and 0.39 mg kg^{-1} in control and 0.35 and 0.40 mg kg^{-1} in control and molybdenum treatments, respectively during second year. The above values were observed in B_0Zn_0 and B_2Zn_2 during both the years.

B (h) Available Molybdenum

Table 4.76 shows the data on available molybdenum content of soil during first and second year. It was observed that the increase in the available molybdenum due to boron and zinc levels did not show any consistent trend of variation during both years. In control during first year it varied from 0.042 to 0.046 mg kg^{-1} without molybdenum and with molybdenum the minimum and maximum values were 0.045 to 0.047 mg kg^{-1}.

Table 4.75: Effect of Zn, B and Mo levels on available boron (mg kg^{-1}) soil of the experimental field

Post Harvest (2012-13)								
	Without Molybdenum				With Molybdenum			
Treatments	Zn_0	Zn_1	Zn_2	Mean	Zn_0	Zn_1	Zn_2	Mean
B_0	0.35	0.35	0.35	0.35	0.35	0.35	0.35	0.35
B_1	0.36	0.36	0.36	0.36	0.37	0.37	0.37	0.37
B_2	0.38	0.38	0.38	0.38	0.38	0.38	0.39	0.38
Mean	0.36	0.36	0.36	0.36	0.37	0.37	0.37	0.37
Post Harvest (2013-14)								
	Without Molybdenum				With Molybdenum			
Treatments	Zn_0	Zn_1	Zn_2	Mean	Zn_0	Zn_1	Zn_2	Mean
B_0	0.35	0.35	0.36	0.35	0.35	0.35	0.35	0.35
B_1	0.37	0.38	0.37	0.37	0.38	0.37	0.37	0.37
B_2	0.39	0.39	0.39	0.39	0.39	0.37	0.40	0.39
Mean	0.37	0.37	0.37	0.37	0.37	0.37	0.37	0.37
Initial soil available boron based on composite analysis were 0.35 and 0.35 mg kg^{-1} during first and second year								

During second year the values were somewhat higher than those of first year. The ranges of variation during second year were 0.044 to 0.047 mg kg^{-1} in control and 0.046 to 0.049 mg kg^{-1} in case of molybdenum treatment.

Initial soil available molybdenum based on composite analysis were 0.042 and 0.044 mg kg^{-1} during first and second year

B (i) Available Copper

The trends of result in case of available copper under the influence of different treatments are shown in Table 4.77. The trends of result were common to those described above for boron. The ranges of variation were 0.43 to 0.49 and 0.44 to 0.52 mg kg^{-1} in control and molybdenum treatments, respectively during first year. During second year the corresponding variation were 0.44 to 0.53 and 0.47 to 0.56 mg kg^{-1}. During both the years the combination treatment B_1Zn_2 in control B_2Zn_2 in molybdenum treatment gave the highest values.

Table 4.76: Effect of Zn, B and Mo levels on available molybdenum (mg kg^{-1}) soil of the experimental field

Post Harvest (2012-13)								
Without Molybdenum					With Molybdenum			
Treatments	Zn_0	Zn_1	Zn_2	Mean	Zn_0	Zn_1	Zn_2	Mean
B_0	0.042	0.043	0.044	0.043	0.045	0.045	0.046	0.045
B_1	0.043	0.044	0.044	0.044	0.045	0.046	0.047	0.046
B_2	0.045	0.046	0.046	0.046	0.046	0.047	0.047	0.047
Mean	0.043	0.044	0.045	0.044	0.045	0.046	0.047	0.046
Post Harvest (2013-14)								
Without Molybdenum					With Molybdenum			
Treatments	Zn_0	Zn_1	Zn_2	Mean	Zn_0	Zn_1	Zn_2	Mean
B_0	0.044	0.045	0.045	0.045	0.046	0.047	0.047	0.047
B_1	0.045	0.047	0.047	0.046	0.047	0.048	0.048	0.048
B_2	0.045	0.046	0.047	0.046	0.048	0.048	0.049	0.048
Mean	0.045	0.046	0.046	0.046	0.047	0.048	0.048	0.048
Initial soil available molybdenum based on composite analysis were 0.042 and 0.044 mg kg^{-1} during first and second year								

Table 4.77: Effect of Zn, B and Mo levels on available copper (mg kg^{-1}) soil of the experimental field

Post Harvest (2012-13)								
Without Molybdenum					With Molybdenum			
Treatments	Zn_0	Zn_1	Zn_2	Mean	Zn_0	Zn_1	Zn_2	Mean
B_0	0.43	0.45	0.47	0.45	0.44	0.48	0.50	0.47
B_1	0.46	0.47	0.49	0.47	0.47	0.49	0.51	0.49
B_2	0.47	0.48	0.45	0.47	0.50	0.51	0.52	0.51
Mean	0.45	0.47	0.47	0.46	0.47	0.49	0.51	0.49
Post Harvest (2013-14)								
Without Molybdenum					With Molybdenum			
Treatments	Zn_0	Zn_1	Zn_2	Mean	Zn_0	Zn_1	Zn_2	Mean
B_0	0.44	0.47	0.50	0.47	0.47	0.49	0.54	0.50
B_1	0.47	0.48	0.53	0.49	0.49	0.49	0.54	0.51
B_2	0.50	0.48	0.52	0.50	0.53	0.53	0.56	0.54
Mean	0.47	0.48	0.52	0.49	0.50	0.50	0.55	0.52
Initial soil available copper based on composite analysis were 0.43 and 0.44 mg kg^{-1} during first and second year								

B (j) Available Iron

The data in Table 4.78 depict the variation in available iron content of soil affected by different treatments. Variations in available iron content during first year, it showed a range of variation from 4.64 to 5.16 mg kg^{-1} and B_2Zn_2 gave the highest value and without molybdenum during first year. On molybdenum treatment the values varied from 4.80 to 5.08 mg kg^{-1} and Zn_2B_2 gave the highest value during first year.

During second year the variations were recorded in Zn_0B_0 with molybdenum treatments the available iron showed a range of 5.23 to 5.57 mg kg^{-1} and the latter value was observed in Zn_2B_2. Addition of both Zn and B tended to increase the available iron content and the values were further increased due to molybdenum in pre sowing and post harvest stags. However, crop removal did not show any decline in available iron.

Table 4.78: Effect of Zn, B and Mo levels on available iron (mg kg^{-1}) soil of the experimental field

Post Harvest (2012-13)								
	Without Molybdenum				With Molybdenum			
Treatments	Zn_0	Zn_1	Zn_2	Mean	Zn_0	Zn_1	Zn_2	Mean
B_0	4.64	4.80	4.84	4.76	4.80	4.92	4.95	4.89
B_1	4.66	4.82	4.87	4.78	4.92	4.97	4.98	4.96
B_2	5.09	5.08	5.16	5.11	4.98	4.99	5.08	5.02
Mean	4.80	4.90	4.96	4.88	4.90	4.96	5.00	4.96
Post Harvest (2013-14)								
	Without Molybdenum				With Molybdenum			
Treatments	Zn_0	Zn_1	Zn_2	Mean	Zn_0	Zn_1	Zn_2	Mean
B_0	4.90	5.03	5.23	5.05	5.23	5.35	5.39	5.32
B_1	4.96	5.13	5.29	5.13	5.29	5.48	5.55	5.44
B_2	5.18	5.27	5.31	5.25	5.40	5.50	5.57	5.49
Mean	5.01	5.14	5.28	5.14	5.31	5.44	5.50	5.42
Initial soil available iron based on composite analysis were 4.64 and 4.90 mg kg^{-1} during first and second year								

B (k) Available Manganese

The data in Table 4.79 in case of available manganese no definite trend in the data were observed under different treatments in without molybdenum during first year. In this case varied from 20.08 22.32 mg kg^{-1} in the highest value was obtained Zn_0B_2. On molybdenum treatment the maximum available manganese was observed in

Zn_2B_1. However, the differences due to different treatment were not marked similarly during second year there was no definite trend of results either in absence or with molybdenum.

Table 4.79: Effect of Zn, B and Mo levels on available manganese (mg kg^{-1}) soil of the experimental field

Post Harvest (2012-13)								
	Without Molybdenum				With Molybdenum			
Treatments	Zn_0	Zn_1	Zn_2	Mean	Zn_0	Zn_1	Zn_2	Mean
B_0	20.08	21.16	21.58	20.94	20.06	20.50	21.72	20.76
B_1	20.68	21.44	20.68	20.93	20.50	20.77	22.44	21.24
B_2	22.32	21.62	20.42	21.45	20.92	22.18	21.34	21.48
Mean	21.03	21.41	20.89	21.11	20.49	21.15	21.83	21.16
Post Harvest (2013-14)								
	Without Molybdenum				With Molybdenum			
Treatments	Zn_0	Zn_1	Zn_2	Mean	Zn_0	Zn_1	Zn_2	Mean
B_0	22.16	22.68	23.22	22.69	21.46	21.46	22.20	21.71
B_1	22.26	23.42	22.54	22.74	21.68	21.78	22.45	21.96
B_2	23.04	22.20	21.72	22.32	21.22	21.40	22.54	21.72
Mean	22.49	22.77	22.49	22.58	21.45	21.55	22.40	21.80

Initial soil available manganese based on composite analysis were 20.08 and 22.16 mg kg^{-1} during first and second year

5 DISCUSSION

The problem "Studies on the dynamics of select micronutrients in soil, plant and their responses on chickpea (*Cicer arietinum* L.) under rainfed conditions", was conducted on the aspects of soil physiochemical properties and field scale experimentation. The soil was normal sandy loam deficient in organic carbon, available nitrogen, sulphur, zinc, boron, molybdenum and medium in phosphorous various treatments of zinc, boron and molybdenum were tested. Zn and B with three levels were tested as Zn_0, Zn_1, Zn_2 and B_0, B_1, B_2 and their combinations in absence and presence of molybdenum in a randomized block design with three replications and eighteen treatments on Agricultural Research Farm, Rajaula of Mahatma Gandhi Chitrakoot Gramodaya Vishwavidyalaya Chitrakoot, Satna (M.P.) during rabi 2012-13 and 2013-14 with chickpea variety Awarodhi.

The observation were recorded on growth characters *viz*; plant height, number of branches plant^{-1}, number of nodules plant^{-1}, nodule dry weight (mg) plant^{-1} were recorded at three stages of crop growth *i.e.* 30, 60 and 90 DAS, number of pods plant^{-1}, number of grains pod^{-1}, test weight (weight of 100 grains in g). The observations were also recorded on grain and stover yields at the harvest of crop and the data on harvest index were calculated therefrom.

After the harvest grain and stover samples were analysed for N, P, K, S, Zn, B, Mo, Cu, Fe, Mn and uptake of nutrients was calculated. For quality assessment the grain were analysed treatment-wise for protein content and harvest of protein was calculated to havc an idea about the amount of edible protein obtainable from different treatments.

Growth Parameters

Plant Height

Plant height is an index of growth and vigour. In the present study the plant height in different treatments were recorded at 30, 60 and 90 DAS. The results showed that the plant height was most affected by different stages. At 60 DAS there was a magnitude increase over 30 DAS by about 80 per cent and from 60 DAS to 90 DAS the increased was 50 per cent regardless of different treatments.

In molybdenum treatments the corresponding increase was 82 per cent and 45 per cent from 30 to 60 DAS and from 60 to 90 DAS respectively. Thus, it was evident that the period between 30 and 60 DAS was most vigorous stage of plant growth. It was further indicated that the growth rate was further increased from 80 to 82 per cent due to molybdenum treatment. This period might be considered as the prime growth period with a small enhancement by molybdenum treatment, on the basis of mean of two years. The crop duration from sowing to harvesting was of 162 days during first year and 173 days in second year. Ninety days span in both crops might be considered as the growth period and the rest as developmental period (about 75 days).

The addition of both zinc and boron increased the plant height significantly at 30 DAS both increase of without and with molybdenum but at 60 DAS only zinc had significant increasing affect on plant height both without and with molybdenum. At 90 DAS the effects of Zn and Mo were significant. However, with molybdenum the increase in plant height was significant at the three stages of study (30, 60 and 90 DAS), unlike the reports of (Ashokan and Raj; 1974 who reported that the plant height increased with the different levels of boron. Khan *et al.* 2003 reported that under rainfed condition the plant height was increased due to zinc application. Similar results have been reported by Hafiz; 2004) who reported that chelated zinc increase the plant height in chickpea. Similar results have been reported by (Thiyagarajan *et al.* 2003 and Singh *et al.* 2008) reported that the plant height was increased significantly at 60 and 90 DAS but this increase was not significant at 30 DAS. In the present study effect of molybdenum application was significant at all the three stages of 30, 60 and 90 DAS. Tripathi *et al.* (1997) reported that sulphur and zinc application increased the yield of gram significantly and their interactions were also significant on growth and yield.

The increase in plant height due to zinc application has been reported by (Tiwari *et al.* 2007; Bozoglu *et al.* 2007 and Kaisher *et al.* 2010) reported the significant increase in plant height in mungbean. In chickpea has been reported by (Shil *et al.* 2007; Quddus *et al.* 2011 and Ceyhan *et al.* 2007) the increase in plant height due to combined use of B and Mo application. These workers assigned the reason for increase plant height along with other characters that the molybdenum is required for the formation of nitrate reductase enzyme and in legume it plays an important role in symbiotic nitrogen fixation.

Number of Branches Plant^{-1}

In chickpea branches are important components for pod formation, grain setting and yield. In the present study the branching pattern of chickpea variety Awarodhi has been studied at 30, 60 and 90 DAS under the different treatments. On an average basis there was about three time increase in number of branches from 30 DAS to 60 DAS. The magnitude of increase in branch number was 17 per cent from 60 to 90 DAS on the basis of mean of two years in control. However, in molybdenum treatment the percentage increase was about 13 per cent in the span from 60 to 90 DAS. Thus, it was evident that maximum increase in number of branches occurred in the period between 30 and 60 DAS which may be considered as the peak growth period of the crop. Zn, B and Mo application increased the number of branches plant^{-1} significantly. At 30 DAS Zn × B interaction was also significant during first year and Zn × B × Mo at 60 DAS during first and second both the years, significant.

The increase in number of branches due to application of Zn, B and Mo on branching growth and metabolism of chickpea has been reported by several workers (Hafiz, 2004; Bozoglu *et al.* 2007; Karwasra and Anil Kumar 2007; and Gupta, *et al.* 2012). Singh *et al.* (2008) reported that application of Zn, B and Mo increased the branching in black gram.

The type of results might be due to fundamental roles of Zn, B and Mo in the growth and metabolism of chickpea. Moreover the balanced and combined use of these nutrients might have been resulted in balanced nutrition of the crop. The results of present study are in agreement with those of above workers.

Number of Nodules Plant^{-1}

Nodules harbour *Rhizobia* which help in biological N-fixation and therefore, the numbers of healthy nodules are indices of better N-fixing capacity of the crop. The nodule number was recorded at 30, 60 and 90 DAS. It was evident that, in general highest number of nodules was recorded up to 60 DAS at 30 DAS the number of nodules was lower at 90 DAS it was lowest. The results might be due to the fact that 30 DAS was fairly early for formation of nodules and at 60 DAS it attained the maximum number. During a period between 60 and 90 DAS the crop growth was seemingly nearing the completion of the growth with the start of developmental period resulting in degeneration of nodules towards maturity.

The present study revealed that the number of nodules plant^{-1} was almost doubled at 60 DAS in relation to 30 DAS both, in case of presence and absence of molybdenum during both the years with a drastic reduction at 90 DAS.

At 30 DAS only the main effects of Zn and Mo were significant but at 60 DAS the main effects of Zn, B and Mo had significant increase in nodule number. At 90 DAS Zn, B, Mo and Zn × B had significant increasing effect during first year. During second year the increasing effects of Zn, B and Mo were significant at 30 DAS and at 60 and 90 DAS in addition to Zn, B and Mo and Zn × B interactions were also significant. The magnitude of degeneration in nodules was less severe at 90 DAS during second year against first year. Thus, it was clear that addition on Zn, B and Mo had, in general increasing effect on number of nodules plant^{-1}. The increase in the number of nodules plant^{-1} has been reported by several workers in chickpea due to boron (Ashokan and Raj 1974; Harris and Gilman 1950; Guhey *et al.* 2008) and due to molybdenum (Deo, *et al.* 2002 and Thiyagarajan *et al.* 2003) reported that combined use of Zn, Fe, B and Mo increased the nodule were in number in chickpea. Similar results have been observed by Khan *et al.* (2014) due to addition of Fe and Mo. Several other workers have reported positive responses of Zn, B and Mo in chickpea (Das *et al. 2012* and Abraham and Abraham 2011) have been reported that application of P, B and Mo in chickpea. In our study the results showed that Zn, B and Mo increased the nodule number in chickpea. Singh *et al.* (2008) reported that application of S and Mo increased the nodules number significantly in black gram. The outcome of this study is corroborated with the above workers.

Nodules Dry Weight Plant^{-1}

The number of nodule plant^{-1} does not give the complete idea of nodule contribution and assessment of its weight of major important in the present investigation the weight was recorded at 30, 60 and 90 DAS in all the treatments during both the years. The results indicated that regardless of different treatments the nodule weight was increased by about two times at 60 DAS as compare to 30 DAS and also three times greater than those of 90 DAS *i.e.* at 60 DAS the nodule weight was maximum. The drastic decrease in nodule weight at 90 DAS might be due to a transition period between growth and development the above trend continued in control and molybdenum treatments both.

Main effects of Zn, B and Mo were significant during both the years. However, during second year Zn × B interaction was also significant at 90 DAS. It was therefore clear that balanced used of these micronutrients increased the nodule dry weight significantly. A combination of Zn_2B_2 without Mo gave the highest weight of 12.5 mg plant^{-1} at 30 DAS. At 60 DAS Zn_2B_2 gave 26.30 mg plant^{-1} and at 90 DAS the same treatment gave the highest weight of 11.26 mg plant-^{1}. Zn_2B_2 gave the corresponding values of 12.36, 29.41 and 11.87 mg plant^{-1} at 30, 60 and 90 DAS respectively. Nodule weight is a quantitative character it's increased due to Mo application might be due to increase in chlorophyll synthesis and its favourable effect on plant growth. Singh *et al.* (2008) several investigations have reported due to Zn, Fe, B and Mo increased the nodule dry weight significantly Thiyagarajan *et al.* (2003). Khan *et al.* (2014) reported that nodule dry weight was significantly increased with the use Mo and Fe in chickpea. Das *et al.* (2012) reported increase in nodule weight of chickpea due to Zn, B and Mo. Abraham and Abraham (2011) have been reported that application of P, B and Mo in increasing in nodule dry weight of chickpea. Gad and El-Moez (2013) reported that Mo application increased the nodule dry weight in cowpea.

Number of Pods Plant^{-1}

Pod number is a direst indication of grain yield and therefore, it appears relevant to study this character as affected by different nutrients. The observation was recorded at the physiological stage of maturity *i.e.,* the grain formation was complete but the moisture content was intact. The results indicated that on the basis of mean of two years Zn_1B_2 gave the highest number of 86.58 in control and with molybdenum Zn_1B_2 gave a mean value of 87.53. The main effects of Zn, B and Mo and the interaction Zn × B were significant indicating that Zn, B and also Mo resulted in an increase in pod number.

Similar findings have been reported by (Hafiz 2004; Ceyhan, *et al.* 2007; Guhey *et al.* 2008; Gitanjali *et al.* 2010) due to addition of B, Gupta, *et al.* (2012) due to Mo, Bozoglu *et al.* (2007) due to Zn and Mo, Khan *et al.* (2014) with the use Mo and Fe, Shil *et al.* (2007) due to B and Mo, (Valenciano *et al.* 2010; Valenciano *et al.* 2011; due to Zn, B and Mo; Thiyagarajan *et al.* 2003) due to Zn, Fe, B, Mo and Abraham and Abraham (2011) have been reported that application of P, B and Mo in increasing in number of pods plant^{-1} in chickpea. Quddus *et al.* (2011) due to Zn and B in increasing in number of pods plant^{-1} in mungbean. Gad and El-Moez 2013) reported that Mo application increased the number of pods in cowpea. Singh *et al.* (2008) due to application of molybdenum in black gram. Our results collaborated with the findings of above workers.

Number of Grains Pod^{-1}

The variations in number of grains pod^{-1} were small but significant. There was only slight increase in grain number due to Mo application during both the years. During first year Mo application gave 4 per cent and during second year 5.6 per cent increase in grain number over control. The main effects of Zn, B and Mo during first year and B and Mo during second year were significant over control rest of the interactions were not significant. The overall range of variation in grain number of pod^{-1} was recorded from 1.24 to 1.50 with Mo during first year and during second year it ranged from 1.26 to 1.52. The ranges of variation under Mo application were from 1.35 to 1.58 and 1.42 to 1.65 during first and second year, respectively.

Thus, it was inferred that addition of these micronutrients exerted a favourable effect on number of grains pod^{-1}. The findings are corroborated by those reported by (Mishra 2001; Hafiz 2004; due to boron, Khan *et al.* 2014 due to Fe and Mo, Thiyagarajan *et al.* 2003; due to Zn, Fe, B, Mo, Valenciano *et al.* 2010; Valenciano *et al.* 2011; due to Zn, B, Mo in chickpea and Quddus et al. 2011) due to Zn and B in mungbean respectively.

Test Weight g of 100 Seeds

Test weight expressed as weight of 100 grains in (g) indicates the grain size and boldness. The grains with higher test weight might get premium price in the market. Moreover, it is the yield contributory character, thus higher test weight is desirable. In the present study the main effects of Zn, and B during first year and Zn, B and Mo during second year gave significant increase in seed size, rest of the factors were not significant. The overall range of variation in case of without Mo was observed from 18.20 to 20.80 (g) and 18.22 to 20.86 (g) during first and second years, respectively. In presence of Mo the corresponding range was observed form 18.71 to 20.93 (g) and 18.73 to 21.06 (g) per 100 grains in respective years.

Similar reports have been observed by (Hafiz 2004; Ceyhan, *et al.* 2007; due to B; Khan *et al.* 2014 due to Fe and Mo; Shil *et al.* 2007 due to B and Mo; Bozoglu *et al.* 2007 due to Zn and Mo; Abraham and Abraham 2011 due to B and Mo; Thiyagarajan *et al.* 2003) reported increased test weight due to Zn, Fe, B, Mo application in chickpea.

A number of investigators have reported increased test weight due to Zn, B and Mo (Valenciano *et al.* 2010; Valenciano *et al.* 2011; Singh *et al.* 2008; Gad and EI-Moez, 2013; Quddus *et al.* 2011).

Yields

Grain Yield

The general mean yield of chickpea under the present study was 2170 kg ha^{-1} indicating that the grain yield level was considerably high. Main effects of Zn, B and Mo were significant but their interactions were not significant. Among the B levels both B_1 and B_2 were significantly superior to B_0 but B_1 and B_2 were at par during first and second years respectively in absence of Mo. Addition of boron resulted in 6 to 7 per cent increase in yield. Both Zn_1 and Zn_2 were significantly superior to control but they were not significant among themselves during both the years in presence and absence of Mo. Addition of zinc resulted in increase in grain yield between 8.5 to 9.0 per cent, there was about 5 per cent increase in grain yield due to addition of Mo over no Mo (control). The mean yield varied from 1933.33 to 2216.67 kg ha^{-1} and from 2023.33 to 2180.00 kg ha^{-1} due to Zn and B in absence of molybdenum. The corresponding yield values were 2101.67 to 2285.00 and 2121.67 to 2271.67 kg ha^{-1} in presence of molybdenum during first year. The mean yield varied from 1936.67 to 2221.67 kg ha^{-1} and from 2028.33 to 2181.67 kg ha^{-1} due to Zn and B in absence of molybdenum. The corresponding yield values were 2105.00 to 2290.00 and 2126.67 to 2273.33 kg ha^{-1} in presence of molybdenum during second year.

In view of very less cost of the fertilizer of Zn, B and Mo this magnitude of increase appears to be economical. Several investigators have reported increase in yield due to Zn, B and Mo fertilization in pulses. Similar reports have been obtained by (Tripathi *et al.* 1997 due to Zn; Sakal *et al.* 1996; Hafiz 2004; Harris and Gilman 1950; Ceyhan *et al.* 2007 due to B; Deo, *et al.* 2002; Gupta *et al.* 2012 due to Mo; Khan *et al.* 2014 due to Fe, Mo; Bozoglu *et al.* 2007 due to Zn, Mo; Shil *et al.* 2007 due to B, Mo; Abraham and Abraham 2011 due to B and Mo; Das *et al.* 2012; Valenciano *et al.* 2010; Valenciano *et al.* 2011 due to Zn, B, Mo; Singh, *et al.* 2004 due to Zn, Fe, Mo; Thiyagarajan *et al.* 2003) due to Zn, Fe, B, Mo in chickpea, (Poongothai *et al.* 2004 due to Zn, B, Mo; Singh *et al.* 2008) due to S, Mo in Blackgram, Gad and EI-Moez (2013) due to Mo in cowpea, Quddus *et al.* (2011) due to Zn, B in mungbean. Thus our results showing increased grain yield due to Zn, B and Mo are in conformity with these of above investigators.

Stover Yield

Significant increases in the stover yield due to Zn, B and Mo levels were observed during both the years. The ranges of variation in stover yield were observed from 1980.00 to 2591.33 kg ha^{-1} in without molybdenum and that from 2145.00 to 2930.00 kg ha^{-1} in case of with molybdenum during first year. The corresponding values were 2000.00 to 2745.00 kg ha^{-1} in without molybdenum and 2155.00 to 2940.00 kg ha^{-1} with molybdenum during second year. Zinc application resulted in the highest yield of stover followed by boron and then by molybdenum. On the basis of mean of two years it was observed that Zn_1 and Zn_2 resulted in nearly 17 and 21 per cent increase in stover yield as compared to control (Zn_0). Whereas, the magnitude of increase in stover yield was about 7 and 12 per cent in case of B_1 and B_2 respectively over control (B_0). Molybdenum resulted in 6.55 per cent increase in stover yield over control (Mo_0). Thus it appeared that the application of these nutrients was appreciably beneficial with regard to stover yield. Several investigators reported similar results (Tripathi *et al.* 1997 due to Zn; Hafiz 2004 due to B; Pingoliya *et al.* 2014 due to Fe; Shil *et al.* 2007 due to B and Mo, Das *et al.* 2012 due to Zn, B, Mo; Singh, *et al.* 2004 due to Zn, Fe, Mo; Thiyagarajan *et al.* 2003 due to Zn, Fe, B, Mo; Singh *et al.* 2008 due to S, Mo).

Harvest Index (%)

Application of Zn and B resulted in significant decrease in harvest index indicating that stover was a better sink for photosynthates for chickpea crop. Molybdenum gave significant difference only during first year but the same was not significant during second year. The trends were similar in without and with molybdenum. These results are agreement with reports of (Valenciano *et al.* 2010 and Valenciano *et al.* 2011) due to Zn, B, Mo in chickpea.

Concentration of Nutrients

Nitrogen

Only the main effects of Zn and B were significant. In case of B, nitrogen content varied from 3.06 to 3.30 per cent and that in case of Zn it varied from 2.99 to 3.39 per cent on the basis of mean of two years in absence of Mo in grain. However, it could be remarked that in general, nitrogen content was chickpea grain was considerably high. In case of B, nitrogen content varied from 3.08 to 3.32 per cent and that in case of Zn it varied from 3.01 to 3.42 per cent on the basis of mean of two years in presence of Mo in grain.

Zn and B levels tended to increase the stover nitrogen content in chickpea in presence and absence of molybdenum. Only the main effect of Zn and B were significant. In case of B, nitrogen content varied from 2.10 to 2.19 per cent and that in case of Zn it varied from 2.07 to 2.23 per cent in absence of molybdenum. However, it could be observed that, in general, nitrogen content was chickpea grain was considerably high. In case of B, nitrogen content varied from 2.13 to 2.23 per cent and that in case of Zn it varied from 2.11 to 2.26 per cent in presence of Mo. These results are in agreement with the reports of (Singh, *et al.* 2004; due to Zn, Fe, Mo and Thiyagarajan *et al.* 2003; due to Zn, Fe, B, Mo).

Phosphorous

Addition of Zn and B tended to increase the grain phosphorous content in chickpea in without and with molybdenum. Only the main effect of Zn, B and Mo were significant during both the years but only first year Zn × B interaction was significant. In case of B phosphorous content varied from 0.33 to 0.36 per cent and that in case of Zn it varied from 0.32 to 0.37 per cent in without Mo. In case of B, phosphorous content varied from 0.37 to 0.38 per cent and that in case of Zn it varied from 0.34 to 0.39 per cent in presence of Mo in grain.

Both, without and with molybdenum, the phosphorous content in stover increased due to main effects of zinc and boron significantly. In case of B, phosphorous content varied from 0.37 to 0.40 per cent and that in case of Zn it varied from 0.38 to 0.40 per cent in absence of Mo. In case of B phosphorous content varied from 0.39 to 0.40 per cent and that in case of Zn it varied from 0.39 to 0.41 per cent in presence of Mo in stover. These results are agreement with reports of (Singh, *et al.* 2004; due to Zn, Fe, Mo and Thiyagarajan *et al.* 2003; due to Zn, Fe, B, Mo).

Potassium

Zn and B levels tended to increase the grain potassium content in chickpea in without and with Mo only the main effect of Zn, B and Mo were significant both the years but only second year Zn × B interaction was significant. In case of B potassium content varied from 0.50 to 0.53 per cent and that in case of Zn it varied from 0.49 to 0.53 per cent on the basis of mean of two years in without Mo in grain. In case of B potassium content varied from 0.51 to 0.54 per cent and that in case of Zn it varied from 0.52 to 0.54 per cent with molybdenum.

In case of potassium content of stover in without and with Mo, only the main effects of Zn, B and interaction Zn × B were significant during both the years but the effect of Mo was significant only during first year. In case of B, potassium content varied from 1.77 to 1.86 per cent and that in case of Zn it varied from 1.78 to 1.86 per cent on the basis of mean of two years in without Mo. In case of B potassium content varied from 1.81 to 1.88 per cent and that in case of Zn it varied from 1.82 to 1.87 per cent in with Mo. These results are in agreement with the reports of Thiyagarajan *et al.* (2003) due to Zn, Fe, B, Mo.

Sulphur

Zn and B increased the grain sulphur content in chickpea in presence and absence of molybdenum. Only the main effect of Zn, B and Mo were significant both the years but Zn × B interaction was significant during first year only. In case of B, sulphur content varied from 0.68 to 0.70 per cent and that in case of Zn it varied from 0.68 to 0.70 per cent in absence of Mo in grain. In case of B sulphur content varied from 0.69 to 0.72 per cent and that in case of Zn it varied from 0.70 to 0.71 per cent in presence of Mo.

Similar trends of results were observed in stover. In case of B sulphur content varied from 0.25 to 0.26 per cent and that in case of Zn it varied from 0.25 to 0.27 per cent without Mo in stover. In case of B, sulphur content varied from 0.26 to 0.27 per cent and that in case of Zn it varied from 0.26 to 0.27 per cent in with Mo in stover. These results are agreement with reports of Thiyagarajan *et al.* (2003) due to Zn, Fe, B, Mo in sulphur increases of chickpea and Singh, *et al.* (2004) due to Zn, Fe, Mo in sulphur increases of blackgram.

Zinc

Sequential addition of Zn and B tended to increase the grain zinc content in chickpea in presence and absence of molybdenum and only the main effect of Zn, B, Mo and interaction Zn × B were significant both the years. It varied from 40.73 to 43.52 mg kg^{-1} and from 39.74 to 45.04 mg kg^{-1} due to boron and zinc, respectively. In case of B, zinc content varied from 41.50 to 44.30 mg kg^{-1} and that in case of Zn it varied from 40.52 to 45.84 mg kg^{-} in presence of Mo in grain.

The treatment effects in stover were similar to those reported for grain. In case of B zinc content varied from 20.50 to 26.13 mg kg^{-1} and that in case of Zn it varied from 19.59 to 27.34 mg kg^{-1} in without Mo in stover. In case of B, zinc content varied from 21.93 to 27.35 mg kg^{-1} and that in case of Zn it varied from 20.59 to 28.74 mg kg^{-1} in with Mo in stover. These results are agreement with reports of Singh, *et al.* (2004) due to Zn, Fe, Mo in zinc.

Boron

It varied from 52.22 to 55.48 mg kg^{-1} and from 52.50 to 55.76 mg kg^{-1} due to boron and zinc without Mo in grain. Whereas on addition of Mo the ranges of variation were from 54.00 to 56.62 mg kg^{-1} and from 54.19 to 56.65 mg kg^{-1} due to boron and zinc, respectively.

Zn and B tended to increase the stover boron content in chickpea in without and with molybdenum and only the main effect of Zn, B and Mo were significant both the years but during only second year interaction Zn × Mo was also significant. In case of B, boron content varied from 38.46 to 41.17 mg kg^{-1} and that in case of Zn it varied from 38.00 to 41.50 mg kg^{-1} in without Mo in stover. In case of B, boron content varied from 40.59 to 42.50 mg kg^{-1} and that in case of Zn it varied from 40.50 to 42.50 mg kg^{-1} in presence of Mo.

Molybdenum

The trends of variation in molybdenum content due to different treatments were similar in both, grain and stover. Effect of Zn, B, Mo and interaction Zn × B were significant both the years without Mo. In case of B, molybdenum content varied from 3.28 to 3.71 mg kg^{-1} and that in case of Zn it varied from 3.23 to 3.83 mg kg^{-1} in grain. In case of B, molybdenum content varied from 3.54 to 4.00 mg kg^{-1} and that in case of Zn it varied from 3.46 to 4.13 mg kg^{-1} in presence of Mo in grain.

In case of B, molybdenum content stover varied from 0.64 to 0.67 mg kg^{-1} and that in case of Zn it varied from 0.64 to 0.69 mg kg^{-1} on the basis of mean of two years in without Mo. In case of B, molybdenum content varied from 0.67 to 0.72 mg kg^{-1} and that in case of Zn it varied from 0.66 to 0.73 mg kg^{-1} in with Mo. These results are agreement with reports of Singh, *et al.* (2004) due to Zn, Fe, Mo in molybdenum content increases of chickpea and Singh, *et al.* (2008) in molybdenum content increases of blackgram.

Copper

Addition of Zn and B tended to increase the grain copper content in chickpea in presence and absence of molybdenum only the main effect of Zn, B, Mo and interaction Zn × B were significant. In case of B, copper content varied from 27.42 to 30.08 mg kg^{-1} and that in case of Zn it varied from 24.80 to 34.04 mg kg^{-1} on the basis of mean of two years in absence of Mo in grain. In case of B, copper content varied from 33.08 to 36.22 mg kg^{-1} and that in case of Zn it varied from 30.92 to 39.70 mg kg^{-1} in presence of Mo.

In case of in Mo treatment stover B, copper content varied from 18.03 to 19.73 mg kg^{-1} and that in case of Zn it varied from 18.03 to 19.93 mg kg^{-1} in without Mo. Main effects of Zn, B and Mo and interaction Zn x Mo were significant during both the years. In case of B, copper content varied from 19.53 to 21.48 mg kg^{-1} and that in case of Zn it varied from 19.07 to 22.10 mg kg^{-1} in with Mo.

Iron

Zn and B levels tended to increase the grain iron content in chickpea in presence and absence of molybdenum. Only the main effect of Zn, B, Mo and interaction Zn × B were significant both the years. In case of B, iron content varied from 66.30 to 73.33 mg kg^{-1} and that in case of Zn it varied from 66.63 to 72.93 mg kg^{-1} in absence of Mo. In case of B, iron content varied from 73.33 to 79.93 mg kg^{-1} and that in case of Zn it varied from 73.27 to 80.03 mg kg^{-1} in presence of Mo.

Similar trends of results were obtained in stover. In case of B, iron content varied from 591.34 to 619.50 mg kg^{-1} and that in case of Zn it varied from 554.50 to 645.67 mg kg^{-1} in without Mo. In case of B, iron content varied from 624.00 to 664.33 mg kg^{-1} and that in case of Zn it varied from 589.00 to 681.33 mg kg^{-1} with Mo. These results are agreement with reports of (Singh, *et al.* 2004; due to Zn, Fe, Mo and Pingoliya *et al.* 2014; due to Fe) in iron content increases of chickpea.

Manganese

Only the main effect of Zn, B and Mo were significant in grain manganese content. In case of B, manganese content varied from 48.04 to 53.77 mg kg^{-1} and that in case of Zn it varied from 47.71 to 54.53 mg kg^{-1} absence of Mo in grain. On molybdenum treatment of B, manganese content varied from 50.14 to 55.21 mg kg^{-1} and that in case of Zn it varied from 49.55 to 56.46 mg kg^{-1} presence of Mo.

Similar trends of results were obtained in stover. In case of B, manganese content varied from 38.38 to 41.92 mg kg^{-1} and that in case of Zn it varied from 36.68 to 44.92 mg kg^{-1} in without Mo in stover. In case of B, manganese content varied from 49.75 to 52.32 mg kg^{-1} and that in case of Zn it varied from 47.88 to 55.62 mg kg^{-1} in with Mo.

Uptake of Macronutrients

The uptake of nutrients is a direct index of nutrients absorbed by the plants for a particular yield target. Uptake values are the function of nutrient concentration and crop yield. It provides a fundamental idea of management of nutrients for a given yield target. In the present study the results are discussed on the basis of pooled average of two years data in relation to the variants under investigation the results are discussed below:-

Nitrogen

Nitrogen uptake varied from 58.00 to 73.58 kg ha^{-1} Zn_1 and Zn_2 resulted in significant increase in uptake of nitrogen due to Zn, B and Mo levels, which was of the order of 24.48 and 29.97 per cent over control by Zn_1 and Zn_2 respectively. B_1 and B_2 showed 10.98 and 16.23 per cent increase over B_0 and the results were significant. The ranges are variation was observed from 62.12 to 72.20 kg ha^{-1} Zn_1 and Zn_2 increased the uptake by 14.09 and 23.32 per cent and B_1 and B_2 increased the uptake by 11.64 and 15.46 per cent with molybdenum treatment, respectively.

Addition of molybdenum also increased the uptake of nitrogen in grain to the tune of 5.34 per cent. The trends of variation in nitrogen uptake by stover was similar to that described for grain but magnitude of increase due to Zn_2 was comparatively higher (26.58%) and so also in B_2 (19.45%) over control in absence of molybdenum. On addition of Mo the stover nitrogen uptake showed higher increase in Zn_1 (21.65%), Zn_2 (33.13%), B_1 (10.33%) and B_2 (14.69%) over their respective controls. Thus, it was indicated that the per cent age magnitude of nitrogen uptake comparatively higher in Mo treatment over its control. The mean nitrogen uptake was about 25 per cent higher in grain than stover, indicating that grain was a better sink of protein than that of stover and greater part of nitrogen goes in seed. These results are agreement with reports of (Das *et al.* 2012; Zn, B, Mo, Singh, *et al.* 2004; Zn, Fe, Mo and Thiyagarajan *et al.* 2003; Zn, Fe, B, Mo).

Phosphorous

Phosphorous uptake in grain ranged from 6.18 to 8.18 kg ha^{-1} and the corresponding range under boron was between 6.76 and 7.81 kg ha^{-1}. It was revealed that the magnitute of increase due to Zn_1 (30%) and Zn_2 (32%) was higher in absence of Mo and the corresponding figures of Zn_1 and Zn_2 were lower (26% and 27%) respectively under Mo treatment. The same trend was observed in case of boron wherein, with Mo the increase was 12 per cent and 7 per cent due to B_1 and B_2. It appeared that addition of Mo lowered the magnitude of uptake probably because of antagonistic effect of Zn and B on grain phosphorous.

The ranges of variation in stover phosphorous uptake due to Zn were 8.3 to 10.65 kg ha^{-1} and due to B 8.83 to 10.31 kg ha^{-1} without Mo. On addition of Mo the corresponding ranges of variation were from 9.14 to 11.36 kg ha^{-1} and 9.59 to 10.80 kg ha^{-1} in Zn and B respectively. Addition of Mo reduced the per cent age magnitude of increase by about (4%). These results are agreement with reports of (Thiyagarajan *et al.* 2003; Zn, Fe, B, Mo, Das *et al.* 2012; Zn, B, Mo and Singh, *et al.* 2004; Zn, Fe, Mo).

Potassium

Potassium uptake values were much higher in stover as compared to grain; in general, it was about 4 times higher irrespective of Zn and B levels. There was 14 and

18 per cent increase in uptake in Zn_1 and Zn_2, respectively and B_1 and B_2 recorded 10 and 12 per cent increase over control. The overall range of variation in K uptake by grain was 10 to 12 kg ha^{-1}. The magnitude of increase in K uptake by stover was 21 and 25 per cent in Zn_1 and Zn_2 and 11 and 17 per cent in B_1 and B_2 over their respective controls. The uptake ranged from 40.55 to 50.00 kg ha^{-1}. Molybdenum application resulted in increase in K uptake to the tune of 7.5 to 8 per cent in grain and stover over no molybdenum control.

The role of K in providing mechanical rigidity in stem and lignifications of stem tissues is reported to be improved by K application. This may be abscribed to the higher K concentration and uptake in chickpea stem and justifies the use of K along with balanced application of the macro and micronutrient for better crop growth and yield as observed in the present study.

Sulphur

The results revealed that sulphur uptake varied from 13.88 to 15.90 kg ha^{-1} due to Zn application. There was 12.5 and 14.6 per cent increase in S uptake due to Zn_1 and Zn_2 over control. It ranged from 14 to 16 kg ha^{-1} uptake of S under B treatment wherein, the magnitude of increase was about 10 per cent due to B_1 and B_2 both over control in chickpea grain. Addition of molybdenum also increased S uptake by 7 per cent in grain and this value was 8 per cent higher in stover over no molybdenum (control). S uptake was about 2.5 times higher in grain over stover.

S uptake in stover ranged from 5.7 to 7.4 kg ha^{-1} and 6.1 to 7.1 kg ha^{-1} in case of Zn and B levels, respectively. S uptake was increase by 21 per cent in Zn_1 and 30 per cent in Zn_2 respectively. Similarly the magnitude of increase was 10 per cent and 16 per cent due to B_1 and B_2 over their control. The high S absorption and its deposition in grain is understandable because S is a component of protein and since the protein content is higher in chickpea grain S content and its uptake is higher moreover there are many other nonprotein S compounds of metabolic importance like vitamins, glucotothione, plastocyanine, ferredoxin are S compounds. Therefore, adequate S uptake is essential for better crop growth and yield.

Uptake of Micronutrients

Zinc

In general, application of Zn and B resulted in significant increase in Zn uptake grain and stover both. The highest uptake values were observed in case of Zn_2 and B_2 having (102.5 and 98 mg kg^{-1}) by Zn_2 and B_2 respectively. With corresponding increase by 26 per cent and 15 per cent in grain and same treatment the highest increase of 68.52 per cent and 40.75 per cent due to Zn_2 and B_2. The magnitude of per cent increase in grain was higher in stover. Mo application resulted in 7 per cent and 12 per cent increase in Zn uptake over without Mo.

Boron

B uptake varied from 108 to 126 mg kg^{-1} due to Zn and from 111 to 125 mg kg^{-1} due to B. However, Mo resulted in 7 per cent increase in grain and 10 per cent in stover. The B content in stover under Zn application varied from 88.5 to 115 mg kg^{-1}. Whereas, in case of B application B uptake had the lowest and the highest values of 95 and 112 mg kg^{-1}. Zn_2 and B_2 gave the highest magnitude of increase 30 per cent and 18 per cent. The clear responses of Zn and B application were noted in chickpea because these nutrients elements are vital for protein synthesis cell division and structural organization.

Molybdenum

Uptake of Mo varied from 6.78 to 8.98 mg kg^{-1} in case of Zn and 7.12 to 8.63 mg kg^{-1} in B chickpea grain. In stover the uptake varied from 1.46 to 1.90 mg kg^{-1} and 1.57 to 1.86 mg kg^{-1} in Zn and B respectively. In case of Zn the uptakes increase by 32 per cent and in B 21 per cent in grain and the maximum increase in stover 30 per cent and 18.5 per cent in Zn and B respectively. Mo application resulted an average increase of 11 per cent in grain and stover. Remarkably the Mo application in micro-quantity resulted in spectular increase in Mo uptake and the grain content about 7 time's higher Mo uptake over that of stover. Significance of molybdenum nutrition might be ascribed to its vital role in nitrogen fixation and nitrification, in pulses.

Copper, Iron and Manganese

Significant increases were observed in the uptake of Cu, Fe and Mn due to Zn, B and Mo application and the trends of results were similar both in grain and stover. The uptake of Cu and Mn uptakes were higher in grain than that in stover. Conversely the Fe content in stover was nearly nine times higher in stover as compared to that of grain Zn_2 and B_2 gave the highest values over other levels both in grain and stover in respect of all the three minerals. Resulting in about 40 per cent increase in uptake of Cu. Similarly about 30 per cent and 35 per cent in case of iron and manganese respectively due to Zn_2 over control. B_2 resulted in 15 per cent, 17 per cent and 19 per cent in the mean uptake of Cu, Fe and Mn, respectively. Addition of molybdenum resulted increase in the uptake values 21 per cent, 14 per cent and 22 per cent, respectively in Cu, Fe and Mn. The minimum and maximum values of Cu, Fe and Mn in average (grain+ stover) were 49.25 and 70.33, 716.93 and 991.47 and 97.08 and 131.46 mg kg^{-1} in zinc treatments. In case of boron treatments the uptake values in grain for Cu, Fe and Mn in average (grain+ stover) were 54.18 and 61.73, 803.36 and 942.69 and 104.26 and 124.11 mg kg^{-1}. It was revealed that application of Zn, B and Mo resulted in appreciable increase in the uptake values because the treatments had increasing effect on both, concentration and yield. These results are agreement with reports of (Pingoliya *et al.* 2014; Singh, *et al.* 2004).

Total uptake of Nutrients

The highest yielding treatment *i.e.*, Zn_5, B_2 and Mo_{400} resulted in 2224.73 kg ha^{-1} grain and 2618.69 kg ha^{-1} stover yield. In an effort to yield maximization it was observed that the total nutrients absorbed by the crop (grain + stover) were: nitrogen 164.44, phosphorous 19.39, potassium 64.30, sulphur 23.75 kg ha^{-1}, zinc 181.41,boron 247.56, molybdenum 11.27, copper 146.38, iron 2060.08 and manganese 278.07 g ha^{-1}.

Crop Qualities

Protein Content

The pulses are the potential sources of dietary protein and go a long way in solving protein, calorie malnutrition like the syndromes of kwashiorkor and marasmus. Pigeonpea is a pioneer pulse crop and contributes for a sizable dietary protein supply. Driven with this concept, an attempt has been made in present study to examine the extent of improvement in protein content and protein harvest due to balanced nutrition including Zn, B and Mo along with recommended doses of macronutrients. We have observed that mean protein content was increased expressed in per cent age values Zn_2 and B_2 gave 13 per cent and 8 per cent. However, the Mo application affected only a marginal increased in protein per cent age. Thus it was clear that a major improvement in chickpea quality in terms of protein could be brought about by application of 5 kg ha^{-1} zinc and 2 kg ha^{-1} boron.

Similarly the protein harvest also increased sizably as a result of increase in nitrogen concentration and grain yield. These results are agreement with reports of (Hafiz 2004; Ceyhan, *et al.* 2007; Gitanjali *et al.* 2010; Pingoliya *et al.* 2014; Thiyagarajan *et al.* 2003; Singh, *et al.* 2004; Singh *et al.* 2008; Deo, *et al.* 2002; Gupta, *et al.* 2012; Gad and EI-Moez 2013).

Nutrient Dynamics in Soil in Relation to the Application of Macro and Micronutrients

The soil of experimental plot was sandy loam with near neutral pH, low EC, organic carbon, available nitrogen, phosphorous, sulphur, zinc, boron, molybdenum and medium in available potassium. With this back ground, plot-wise samples were analysed after Zn, B and Mo application before crop. After harvest similar plot-wise analysis was done to compare the dynamics of nutrients before and after the crops during both the years.

The results revealed that pH, EC, organic carbon, available P, K, Zn, B, Mo, Cu, Fe and Mn were not affected due to crop removal. The available nitrogen was slightly increased during second year. This might be due to addition of organic residues and enhanced fixation of nitrogen in soil under the influence of Zn, B and Mo.

Sulphur was slightly reduced after crop during second year as compared to first year. The reason for this decrease in available S, could not be clearly defined.

It was inferred conclusively that there was no decline in the status of nutrients in the soil due to crop removal. This suggested sustainability in overall dynamics of nutrients in soil.

SUMMARY AND CONCLUSION

The study entitled "Micronutrients in Soil and Plants (Study of Chickpea under Rainfed)", was under taken with a field scale experiment conducted during rabi seasons of 2012-13 and 2013-14 on a sandy loam soil deficient in Zn, B and Mo on Agricultural Research Farm, Rajaula of Mahatma Gandhi Chitrakoot Gramodaya Vishwavidyalaya Chitrakoot, Satna (M.P.) with chickpea variety Awarodhi the envisaged objectives of the study were as follows:

1. Analysis of surface soil of experimental plot for Zn, B and Mo before and after the crop.
2. Conducting the field scale experiments to see the effect of Zn, B and Mo application on the growth and yield of chickpea.
3. Analysis of plants for Zn, B and Mo contents to calculate the total uptake of nutrients.
4. To study the effect of Zn, B and Mo & their interactions on the grain and straw yields.
5. To see the effect of Zn, B and Mo & their interaction on the nodulation of the crop.

The experiment was laid out in factorial RBD with eighteen treatments and three replications. The soil analysis was conducted in initial soil for physicochemical parameter of soil including the important macro and micronutrient on composite basis. Before sowing NPKS were applied as basal uniformly, variable doses of three levels of each zinc (0, 2.5 and 5 kg ha^{-1}) and boron (0, 1 and 2 kg ha^{-1}) and two levels of molybdenum (0 and 400 g ha^{-1}) were applied and plot wise samples were analyzed for physicochemical parameters of soil.

Growth observations viz. plant height, number of branches $plant^{-1}$, number of nodules $plant^{-1}$, nodules dry weight (mg) $plant^{-1}$ were recorded at 30, 60 and 90 DAS (days after sowing). At the maturity, number of pods $plant^{-1}$, number of grains pod^{-1}, test weight (weight of 100 grains in g), grain yield, stover yield and harvest index were recorded.

The plants were analyzed for N, P, K, S, Zn, B, Mo, Cu, Fe and Mn and their respective concentration and grain; stover yields uptake values their calculated. Chickpea grains were analyzed for protein (N x 6.25) content to assess the effect of treatments on protein content. With the help of protein per cent and grain yield the protein yield was also calculated as the protein amount obtainable in different treatments. The results obtained therefrom, are summarized below:

Growth and yield Attributes

1. Plant height was significantly increased due to the main effects of Zn, B and Mo at 30, 60 and 90 DAS except that the effect of B was not significant at 30 DAS. The mean plant heights during first year were 13.72, 24.57 and 36.39 cm at 30, 60 and 90 DAS respectively and that in second year these values were 13.83, 25.24 and 36.89 cm at 30, 60 and 90 DAS respectively.
2. Addition of molybdenum had also increasing effect on plant height.
3. Number of branches varied significantly with different treatments at 30 DAS. The increase was significant only for the main effects of Zn and Zn x B interaction. At 60 DAS Zn, B, Mo and Zn x B, B x Mo and Zn x Mo increased the number of branches significantly and at 90 DAS main effects of Zn, B and Mo gave significant increase in branches plant^{-1} during first year. However, during second year main effects of Zn, B and Mo were significant at 30 and 90 DAS. At 60 DAS main effects of Zn, B, Mo and interaction Zn x B, B x Mo, Zn x Mo were significant.
4. Mean number of branches were 4.20, 12.20 and 14.05 plant^{-1} during first year. Similarly during second year the mean numbers were 4.19, 12.29 and 14.41 plant^{-1} respectively at 30, 60 and 90 DAS.
5. Number of nodules plant^{-1} were significantly increased due to main effects of Zn, B and Mo at all the three stages and Zn x B interaction was significant only 90 DAS during first year. Similar results were obtained during second year at all the three stages.
6. The mean nodule numbers were 4.74, 10.14 and 3.03 and 4.77, 10.31 and 4.03 during first and second year at 30, 60 and 90 DAS. The treatment effects were significant.
7. Nodules dry weight plant^{-1} was significantly increased due to Zn, B and Mo. The main effects of Zn, B and Mo were significant at all the three stages and in addition Zn x Mo interaction was significant at 30 and 90 DAS during first year. The mean nodule dry weights were 10.69, 25.24 and 8.22 mg plant^{-1} during first year. Similarly during second year the main effects of Zn, B and Mo were significant at all the three stages, in addition, Zn x B interaction was also significant at 90 DAS. The mean nodule dry weights were 10.90, 25.78 and 11.12 mg plant^{-1} at 30, 60 and 90 DAS respectively during second year.
8. Except Zn x B x Mo interaction in second year all the main and interaction had significant increasing effect on number of pods plant^{-1}. The mean values were 80.61 and 83.05 during first and second year respectively.

9. Number of grains pod^{-1} was significantly increased by the main effects of Zn, B and Mo except that effect of Zn was significant only during second year. The interactions were not significant. The mean numbers were 1.44 and 1.46 grain pod^{-1} during first and second year.
10. Almost all the growth attributing characters gave the highest values at the combination dose of Zn_2B_2 in presence of molybdenum.
11. The test weight was significantly increased due to main effects of Zn and B during first year and those of Zn, B and Mo during second year. No interactions were found significant. The mean values were 19.85 and 19.90 (g) test weight during first and second year. A combination of Zn_2B_2 with molybdenum gave the highest test weight.
12. The grain yield was significantly increased due to main effects of Zn, B and Mo but there interactions were not significant. The mean yield was 2171.95 and 2175.84 kg ha^{-1} during first and second years respectively. The addition of Zn, B and Mo resulted in 9%, 7% and 5% respectively increase in yield over control on the basis mean of two years. The grain yield varied from 1800.00 to 2260.00 kg ha^{-1} without molybdenum and 1805.00 to 2265.00 kg ha^{-1} during first and second year and on addition of molybdenum the minimum and maximum values were 1950.00 and 2125.00 kg ha^{-1} during first year and 1955.00 and 2330.00 kg ha^{-1} during second year. Combination of Zn_2B_2 gave the highest yield in all the cases.
13. In case of stover, the yield varied from 1980.00 to 2725.00 kg ha^{-1} without molybdenum and 2145.00 to 2930.00 kg ha^{-1} with molybdenum during the first year. The corresponding values 2000.00 to 2745.00 kg ha^{-1} without molybdenum and 2155.00 to 2940 kg ha^{-1} with molybdenum during second year. Zn_2B_2 gave the highest stover yield. On the basis of mean of two years, addition of Zn, B and Mo increased the yield by 21%, 12% and 6.55% over control. The main effects of Zn, B and Mo were significant during both the years. During second year the interaction Zn x B and Zn x Mo were also significant during second year.
14. Harvest index was significantly decreased due to application of Zn, B and Mo. The main effects and interaction of all the tree nutrients were significant except Zn X B and Zn x B x Mo during first year and Mo during second year.

Concentration and uptake of Nutrients

1. On the basis of mean of two years concentration of N, P, K, S were 3.18, 0.35, 0.51 and 0.69% and Zn, B, Mo, Cu, Fe and Mn were 42.34, 54.16, 3.51, 28.34, 70.11 and 51.06 mg kg^{-1} in without molybdenum and similar results were 3.20, 0.37, 0.53, 0.71% and 43.14, 55.47, 3.79, 34.25, 77.04 and 52.94 mg kg^{-1} in with molybdenum in grain.
2. On the basis of mean of two years concentration of N, P, K, S were 2.15, 0.39, 1.83 and 0.26% and Zn, B, Mo, Cu, Fe and Mn were 23.35, 40.12, 0.66, 19.08, 608.23 and 40.50 mg kg^{-1} in without molybdenum and similar results were 2.18,

0.40, 1.85, 0.26% and 24.58, 41.56, 0.69, 20.69, 649.22 and 51.30 mg kg^{-1} in with molybdenum in stover.

3. Concentrations of nutrients were significantly increased by application of Zn, B and Mo and their interactions in most cases.
4. Uptake values of nutrients were a function of their concentration and yields of seed and stover.
5. The uptake values were significantly increased due to application of nutrients. The highest values of all nutrients were recorded by Zn_2B_2 in presence of molybdenum. The highest uptake values on the basis of mean of two years without molybdenum were N 67.76, P 7.46, K 10.85, S 14.61 kg ha^{-1} and Zn 90.19, B 115.25, Mo 7.50, Cu 60.60, Fe 149.45 and Mn 108.86 g ha^{-1} in grain.
6. On addition of molybdenum the corresponding values were N 71.38, P 8.21, K 11.67, S 15.65 kg ha^{-1} and Zn 96.22, B 123.56, Mo 8.45, Cu 76.47, Fe 171.82 and Mn 118.12 g ha^{-1} in grain.
7. The uptake values were significantly increased due to application of nutrients. The highest values of all nutrients were recorded by Zn_2B_2 in presence of molybdenum. The highest uptake values on the basis of mean of two years without molybdenum were N 52.77, P 9.61, K 44.94, S 6.39 kg ha^{-1} and Zn 58.20, B 98.86, Mo 1.63, Cu 47.13, Fe 1503.55 and Mn 100.25 g ha^{-1} in stover.
8. On addition of molybdenum the corresponding values were N 57.24, P 10.24, K 48.51, S 6.91 kg ha^{-1} and Zn 65.32, B 109.09, Mo 1.80, Cu 54.55, Fe 1711.77 and Mn 135.10 g ha^{-1} in stover.
9. On the basis of mean of two years grain protein per cent was 19.87 without molybdenum and 20.01 with molybdenum. The main effects of Zn and B were significant and Mo and interaction were not significant.

Conclusion and Recommendation

From the results emerging out of the study it is concluded that under the given set of experimental conditions the chickpea yields can be optimized with an appropriate balance in macro and micronutrients and it is recommended that the farmers under rainfed areas should apply 20 kg N, 40 kg P, 20 kg K and 30 kg S ha^{-1} along with 5 kg Zn, 2 kg B and 400 g ha^{-1} molybdenum to obtain about 2200 kg ha^{-1} yield.

BIBLIOGRAPHY

A.O.A.C. (1970). Official Method of Analysis. Association of Official Analytical Chemists, Washtington, D.C., USA: 174.

Abraham Shalu Ann and Abraham Thomas (2011). Response of Chickpea (*Cicer kabulium*) to different methods of P Application, Bio-inoculants and Micronutrients. *Legume Res.,* 34 (2): 117-122.

Anonymous (2003). Boron Fact Sheet. Incitec Pivot Limited 70 Southbank Bvd, Melbourne 3006. www.incitecpivot.com.au.

Anonymous (2006). Pulses in *Ibid.* pp. 913-919.

Anonymous (2006). Soil Fertility Fertilizers and Integrated Nutrient Use in *"Hand Book of Agriculture"*, ICAR, New Delhi pp. 416.

Argust, P. (1998). Distribution of Boron in the Environment. *Biol Trace Element Research,* 66: 153-166.

Arora, H., Bharadwaj, S.S. and Sharma, B.D. (2004). Effect of Ionic Strength of NaCl and $CaCl_2$ Supporting Electrolytes on Boron Adsorption by Soils of North-Western India. *Journal of the Indian Society of Soil Science,* 52(2): pp. 140-147.

Asad, A. Blamey, F.P.C. and Edward, D.G. (2002). Dry Matter Production and Boron Concentration of Vegetative and Reproductive Tissues of Canola and Sunflower Plants Grown in Nutrient Solutions. *Plant and Soil,* 243: 252.

Ashokan, S. and Raj, P. (1974). Effects of Forms and Levels of B Application on Groundnut. *Madras Agric. J.,* 61(8): 467-471.

Begum, M., Narayanwamy, G., Rai, R.K. and Biswas, D.R. (2007). Influence of Integrated Nutrient Management in Nitrogen, Maize Cropping System. *Journal of the Indian Society of Soil Science*, 52(2), pp. 175-183.

Benton, J.J. (2003). Agronomic Handbook; Management of Crops, Soils and their Fertility. *CRC Press* LLC. USA.

Berger, K.C. and Pratt, P.F. (1963). Advances in Secondary and Micronutrient Fertilization in *"Fertilizer Technology and Usage"* (M.H. Mc Vicker, G.L. Bridger and I.B. Nelson eds.) *Soil Science Society of America Madison,* pp. 281-340.

Berger, K.C. and Trong, E. (1939). Boron Determination in Soil and Plant. *Ind. Eng. Chem. Anal. Ed.,* 11: 540-544.

Bingham, F.T., Peryal, F.J. and Rhodes, J.D. (1981). Boron Tolerance Character of Wheat. Proceedings Int. American Salinity and Water Management Technology, Juarez, Mexico, December 11-12 pp: 207-216.

Blevin, D.G. (1999). Why Plants Need Phosphorus?, *Better Crops*, 83(2): 20-30.

Bolanos, L., Lukaszewski, K., Bonilla, I. and Blevins, D. (2004). Why Boron? *Plant Physiology and Biochemistry* 42: 907-912.

Bouyoucos. G.J., (1962). Hydrometer method Improved for making Particle Size Analysis of Soil. *Agron. Journal,* 54-464.

Bozoglu, Hatice; Ozcelik, Huseyin; Mut, Zeki and Pesken, Erkut (2007.) Response of Chickpea (*Cicer arietinum* L.) to Zinc and Molybdenum Fertilization. *Bangladesh J. Bot.,* 36(2): 145-149.

Brady, N.C. (1995). Micronutrient Elements in *"Nature and Properties of Soil".* Prentice-Hall of India Pvt. Ltd., New Delhi - 110001 pp. 383-385.

Brown, P.H. and Hu, H. (1998). Boron Mobility and Consequent Management in Different Crops. *Better Crops* 82: 28-31.

Brown, P.H. and Shelp, B.J. (1997). Boron Mobility in Plants. *Plant and Soil* 193: 85-101.

Brown, P.H., I. Cakmak and Q. Zhang (1993). Form and Function of Zinc in Plants. Chap 7 in Robson, A.D. (ed.) *Zinc in Soils and Plants,* Kluwer Academic Publishers, Dordrecht. pp. 90-106.

Brown, P.H., Bellaloui, N., Hu, H. and Dandekar A. (1999). Transgenically Enhanced Sorbitol Synthesis Facilitates Phloem Boron Transport and Increases Tolerance of Tobacco to Boron Deficiency. *Plant Physiology* 110: 17-20.

Ceyhan, E., Onder, M., Harmankaya, M., Hamurcu, M. and Gezgin, S. (2007). Response of Chickpea Cultivars to Application of Boron in Boron-deficient Calcareous Soils. *Communications in Soil Science and Plant Analysis,* 38 (17/18): 2381-2399.

Chandel, S.R.S. (1990). "A Hand Book of Agricultural Statistics" Achal Prakashan Mandir 117/574, Pandu Nagar, Kanpur pp. 843-853.

Chaudhary, D.R. and Shukla, L.M. (2004). Boron States of Arid Soils of Western Rajasthan in Relation to their Characteristics. *Indian Soc. Soil Sci.,* 52(2) pp. 194-199.

Chaudhary, I.A. and Cornfield, A.H. (1966). Determination of Total Sulphur in Soil and Plant Material. *Analyst*, 91: 528-530.

Chen, X., Zhu, D., Cheng, D. and Liu, W. (2002). Effect Adsorption Desorption of Boron on Surface Properties of Soil. *Acta pedologica Sinica,* 39: 145-151.

Chesnin, L. and Yien, C.H. (1951). Turbidimetric Determination of Available Sulphur. *Proc. Soil Soc. Amer.*, 14: 149-151.

Das Shrila, Pareek Navneet, Raverkar K.P., Chandra R. and Kaustav Aditya (2012). Effectiveness of Micronutrient Application and Rhizobium Inoculation on Growth and Yield of Chickpea. *Intl. J. Agric. Env. Biotech.,* 5(4): 445-452.

Das, D.K. (1988). *Ibid* pp. 333, 340.

Das, D.K. (1999). Quality of Irrigation Water in *"Introductory Soil Science", Kalyani Publishers*, New Delhi, pp. 243.

Deo, C. and Kothari, M.L. (2002). Effect of Modes and Levels of Molybdenum Application on Grain Yield Protein Content and Nodulation of Chickpea Grown on Loamy Sand Soil. *Communications in Soil Science and Plant Analysis,* 33 (15-18). pp. 2905-2915.

Dhane, S.S. (2011). Scenario of Micronutrients in Agriculture and Retrospective. *Journal of the Indian Society of Soil Science* 58: 81-87 (Supplement).

Dobermann A. and Fairhurst, T. (2000). Rice Nutrient Disorders & Nutrient Management. Handbook Series. Potash & Phosphate Institute (PPI), Potash & Phosphate Institute of Canada (PPIC) and Int. Rice Res. Institute. 191 p.

Dugger, W.M. (1983). Encyclopedia of Plant Physiol, New Ser. 15 B pp. 626-650 Springer- Verlag Berlin, New York.

Gad Nadia; and El-Moez M.R. Abd (2013). Influenced of Molybdenum on Nodulation, Nitrogen Fixation and Yield of Cowpea. *Journal of Applied Sciences Research,* 9(3): 1498-1504.

Gitanjali, B., Khurana, N., Chatterjee, C. (2010). Impact of Boron Deficiency on Changes in Biochemical Attributes, Yield, and Seed Reserves in Chickpea. *Communications in Soil Science and Plant Analysis.* 41 (2): 211-218.

Goldberg S. and Chuming, S. (2007). New Advances in Boron Soil Chemistry. F.Xu *et al* (ed.) *Advances in Plant and Animal Boron Nutrition*, 313-330 Springer Science + Business Media B.V, Netherlands.

Goldberg, S. (1997). Reactions of Boron with Soils. *Plant and Soil* 193: 35-48.

Govt. of M.P. (2014). *Agricultural Statistics*, Department of Agriculture. Govt of M.P., Bhopal, India, 2011.

Graham, R., J.S. Archer, S.C. and Hynes (1992). Selecting Zinc-efficient Cereal Genotypes for Soils of Low Zinc Status. *Plant and Soil,* 146: 241-250.

Grigg's, J.L. (1953). Determination of Available Molybdenum of Soils. *New Zealand Journal of Science Technology* 34, 183-189.

Guhey, A., Sha, R.A., Khan, M.I. Kuruwanshi, V.B. (2008). Effect of Boron Application on Germination, Nodulation, Chlorophyll Content, flower Drop & Seed Yield in Chickpea (*Cicer arietinum* L.). *Advances in Plant Sciences,* 21 (1): 333-335.

Gupta, S.C. and Gangwar, S. (2012). Effect of Molybdenum, Iron and Microbial Inoculants on Symbiotic Traits, Nutrient Uptake and Yield of Chickpea. *Journal of Food Legumes*, 25 (1). pp. 45-49.

Gupta, U.C. (1993). Boron and its Role in Crop Production, CRC Press Florida pp. 237.

Gupta, U.C. (1993). Sources of Boron, In: Gupta UC, (Ed.) Boron and its Role in Crop Production 87-104. CRP Press, Florida, USA.

Hafiz, S.I. (2004). Response of Chickpea Crop to Biofertilization and Foliar Spraying with Zinc under different Levels of N and P Fertilization in Newly Reclaimed Sandy Soils. *Annals of Agricultural Research, Moshtohor,* 42(3): 933-948.

Harris, H.C. and Gilman (1950). Effect of B on Peanuts. *Soil Sci.* 84: 233-242.

Hou, L.J., Evans, L.J. and Spiers, G.A. (1994). Boron Fractionation in Soils. *Communication in Soil Science and Plant Analysis* 25: 1841-1853.

Jackson, M.L. (1967). Soil Chemical Analysis Prentice Hall of India Pvt. Ltd. Delhi.

Jackson. M.L., (1973). Soil Chemical Analysis. Prentice Hall Inc. Englewood Eliffs, New Jersey. 68-91.

Jain, V.K. (2011). Fundamentals of Plant Physiology, pp. 106-107.

Kaisher, M.S. Ataur Rahman, M., Amin, M.H.A., Amanullah, A.S.M. and Ahsanullah, A.S.M. (2010). Effects of Sulphur and Boron on the Seed Yield and Protein Content of Mungbean. *Bangladesh Research Publications Journal*, 3 (4) 1181-1186.

Karwasra, R.S. and Anil, Kumar (2007). Effect of Phosphorus and Zinc Application on Growth, Biomass and Nutrient Uptake by Chickpea in Calcareous Soils. *Haryana Journal of Agronomy,* 23(1/2): 111-112.

Katyal, J.C. and Randhawa, N.S. (1983). Micronutrients, Fertilizer and Nutrition Bulletin 7 FAO. pp. 82.

Katyal, J.C. and Rattan, R.K. (2003). Secondary and Micronutrients. Research Gaps and Future needs. *Fertilizer News* 48 (4), 9-14 and 17-20.

Keren, R. and Binghum, F.T. (1985). Boron in Water, Soils and Plants. *Advances in Soil Science*, 37: 427-438.

Keren, R., Bingham, F.T. (1985). Boron in Water, Soil, Plants. *Advances in Soil Science. Springer-Verlag New York, Inc.*, 1: 230-276.

Khan Nawaj, Tariq Muhammad, Ullah Khitab, Muhammad Dost, Khan Imran, Rahatullah Kamran, Ahmed Nazeer and Ahmed Saeed (2014). The Effect of Molybdenum and Iron on Nodulation, Nitrogen Fixation and Yield of Chickpea Genotypes (Cicer arietinum L), *Journal of Agriculture and Veterinary Science*, 1 (1) III: 63-79.

Khan, H.R., McDonald, G.K. and Rengel, Z. (2003). Zn Fertilization Improves Water use Efficiency, Grain yield and Seed Zn Content in Chickpea. *Plant and Soil,* 249 (2): 389-400.

Kochher, P.L. (1977). 'Mineral Nutrition of Plant' A Text Book of Plant Physiology 10th Ed. Atma Ram and Sons, New Delhi, pp. 129-145.

Kochian, L.V. (1993). Zinc Absorption from Hydroponic Solution by Plant Roots. Chap 4 in Robson, A.D. (ed.) *Zinc in Soils and Plants,* Kluwer Academic Publishers, Dordrecht. pp. 45-58.

Lindsay, W.L. and Norvell, W.A. (1978). Development of a DTPA Test for Zinc, Iron, Manganese and Copper. *Soil Science of America Journal,* 42: 421-428.

Marschner, H. (1986). "Mineral Nutrition of Higher Plants" *Academic Press,* New York, pp. 298.

Marschner, H. (1995). *Mineral Nutrition of Higher Plants* (2nd edn.) Academic Press, London. 889 pp.

Matoh, T. and Ochiai, K. (2005). Distribution and Partitioning of Newly takeup Boron in Sunflower. *Plant and Soil* 278: 351-360.

Mishra, S.K. (2001). Salt Tolerance of Different Cultivars of Chickpea as Influence by Zinc Fertilization. *Journal of the Indian Society of Soil Science*, 49 (1):135-140.

Mortvedt J.J., Woodruff J.R. (1993). Technology and Application of Boron Fertilizers for Crops. In: U.C. Gupta (ed.) Boron and its Role in Crop Production 157-176. *CRC Press, Boca Raton*, FL.

Murthy, I.Y., L.N. (2006). Boron Sorption Studies in Differentially Fertilized Black Soil. *J. Indian Soc. Soil Sci.,* 54(3) pp. 290-293.

Nadia Gad; and M.R. Abd El-Moez (2013). Influenced of Molybdenum on Nodulation, Nitrogen Fixation and Yield of Cowpea. *Journal of Applied Sciences Research,* 9(3): 1498-1504.

Nilnond, C. Nippa, P.; Charason, N. and Wichai, P. (1986). Soil Fertility Assessment in Southern Thailand, Transactions of XIII-Congress of International Society of Soil Science Vol. III, Hamburg, Aug. 13-20 pp. 887-888.

Noguchi, K., Dannel, F., Pfeffer, H., Romheld, V., Hayashi, H. and Fujiwara, T. (2000). Defect in Root-shoot Translocation of Boron in Arabidopsis Thaliana Mutant bor1-1. *J. of Plant Physiology* 156: 751-755.

Olsen, S.R., Cole, C.V.; Watanabe, F.S. and Dean, L.A. (1954). Estimation of Available Phosphorus in Soils by Extraction with Sodium Bicarbonate. *U.S. Dep. Agri. Washington*, D.C. Cir. 939.

Pingoliya K.K., Dotaniya M.L. and Lata M. (2014). Effect of Iron on Yield, Quality and Nutrient uptake of Chickpea (Cicer arietinum L.) *African Journal of Agricultural Research*, Vol. 9 (37), pp. 2841-2845.

Poongothai S., Savithri P. and Chitdeshwari T. (2004). Effect of Multimicronutrients on the Yield and Nutrient" uptake by Blackgram. *Agricultural Science Digest,* 24 (l): 67-68.

Quddus, M.A.; Rashid, M.H.; Hossain, M.A. and Naser, H.M. (2011). Effect of Zinc and Boron on yield and yield Contributing Characters of Moogbeam in Low Ganges River Floodplain Soil at Madaripr, Bangladesh. *Bangladesh J. Agril. Res.,* 36(1): 75-85.

Reeve, R.C., Pillsbury, N. and Wilcox, L.V. (1955). Reclamation of Saline and High Boron Soils in Coachella Valley of California, *Hilgardia,* 24: 69-91.

Sakal, R; Singh, A.P.; Singh, R.B. and Bhogal, N.S. (1996).Twenty Years of Research on Micro and Secondary Nutrients in Soils and Crops of Bihar. Research Bulletin, Department of Soil Science Faculty of Agriculture, Rajendra Agriculture University Pusa, Samstipur, Bihar, India pp. 1-207.

Saleem M., Khanif Y.M., Fauziah Ishak, Samsuri A.W. and Hafeez, B. (2011). Importance of Boron for Agriculture Productivity: A Review. *International Research Journal of Agricultural Science and Soil Science*, 1(8) pp. 293-300.

Saxena, H.K. and Mehrotra, O.N. (1984). Effect of B and Mo is Presence and Absence of P and Ca on Groundnut. *J. Agric. Res.,* 18(2): 91-94.

Sharma, C.P. (2006). Plant Micronutrients. Science Publishers, Enfield, USA.

Shil, N.C.; Noor, S. and Hossain, M.A. (2007). Effects of Boron and Molybdenum on the Yield of Chickpea. *J Agric Rural Dev.,* 5(1&2), 17-24.

Shorrocks, V.M. (1997). The Occurrence and Correction of Boron Deficiency. *Plant and Soil,* 193: 121-148.

Shukla (2011). Macro Role of Micronutrients. Training Course on Enhancement of Soil Health for Sustaining Crop Productivity and Improving Environmental Quality. Centre of Advanced Faculty Training, Department of Soil Science. Punjab Agricultural University, Ludhiana.141 004 pp. 89-102.

Singh, H.P., Sharma, K.L. Venkateswarlu, B. and Neelaveni, K. (1999). Fertilizer use in Rainfed Areas, Problems and Potentials. *Fertilizer News*, 44(5): 27-30 and 33-38.

Singh, K.B. and Saxena, M.C. (1999). *Chickpea* the Tropical Agriculturalist Series, Macmillan, London 134pp.

Singh, M.V. (2001). Micronutrients Status of Indian Soils and Crop Responses to their Application. Paper Presented in National Seminar on Biofertilizers and Micronutrients New Delhi.

Singh, Mahavir, Chaudhary, S.R., Sharma, S.R., and Rathore, M.S., (2004). Effect of some Micronutrients on Content and uptake by Chickpea *(Cicer arietinum). Agricultural Science Digest,* 24 (4): 268-270.

Singh, R.P., Bisen, Jay Singh, Yadav, P.K., Singh, S.N., Singh, R.K. and Singh, J. (2008). Integrated use of Sulphur Molybdenum on Growth, yield and Quality of Black Gram (*Vigna mungo* L.). *Legume Research*, 31 (3): 214-217.

Singh, R.P., Bisen, Jay Singh, Yadav, P.K., Singh, S.N., Singh, R.K. and Singh, J. (2008). Integrated use of Sulphur and Molybdenum on Growth, yield and Quality of Black Gram (*Vigna mungo* L.). *Legume Res.,* 31 (3): 214-217.

Singh, R.P., Dass, S.K. and Reddy, Y.V.R. (1988). Soil Fertility and Fertilizer Management in Semi Arid Tropical India. Proc. Colloquium held at ICISAT Centre, Patancheru, India, International Fertilizer Development Centre pp. 109-118.

Singh, S.S. and Kanwar, J.S. (1963). Boron and some Other Characteristics of well Water and their Effect on Boron Content of Soils in Patti (Amritser). *Journal of the Indian Society of Soil Science,* II: 283-286.

Srinivasarao, C., Wani, S.P., Sahrawat, K.L. and Pardhasaradhi, G. (2008). Zinc, Boron and Sulphur Deficiencies are holding Back the Potential of Rainfed Crops in Semi-arid India: Experiences from Participatory Watershed Management. *International Journal of Plant Production,* 2 (1): 89-99.

Stangolius, J.C., Brown, P.H., Bellaloui, N., Reid, R.J. and Graham, R.D. (2001). The Efficiency of Boron Ulitisation in Canola. *Australian J. Plant Physiol.*, 28: 1109-1114.

Subbiah, B.V. and Asija, G.L. (1956). A Rapid Procedure for the Determination of Available Nitrogen in Soils. *Curr. Sci.,* 25: 259-260.

Takano, J., Yamagami, M., Noguchi, K., Hayashi, H. and Fujiwara, T.M. (2001). Preferential Translocation of Boron to Young Leaves in Arabidopsis Thaliana Regulated by the BOR1 Gene. *Soil Science and Plant Nutrition,* 47: 345-357.

Tanaka, M. and Fujiwara, T. (2008). Physiological Roles and Transport Mechanism of Boron: Perspective from Plants. *Eur. J. Physiol.*, 456: 671-677.

Tandon, H.L.S. (1992). Management of Nutrient Interaction in Agriculture. FDCO, New Delhi.

Tandon, H.L.S. (2002). Soil Nutrients and Soil Fertility in *"Fertilizer Guide. Fertilizer Development and Consultation Organization"* 204-204A Bhanot Corner, 1-2 Pamposh Enclave, New Delhi-110048 (India) pp. 29 and 32.

Tariq, M., Kakar, K.M. and Shah, Z. (2005). Effect of Boron Zinc Interaction on the yield, yield Attributes and Availability of each to Wheat (*Triticum aestivum* L.) Grown on Calcareous Soils. *Soil and Environment,* 24: 103-108.

Thiyagarajan T.M.; Backiyavathyand M.R. and Savithri P. (2003). Nutrient Management for Pulses-a review. *Agricultural Reviews*, 24(1): 40-48.

Tisdale, S.L., Nelson, W.R., Beaton, J.D. and Havlin, J.I. (1993). Micronutrients and other Beneficial Elements in Soils and Fertilizers in *"Soil Fertility and Fertilizers"* V. ed. Prentice Hall, New Jersey 07458, pp. 304-363.

Tisdale, S.L., Nelson, W.R., Beaton, J.D. and Havlin, J.I. (2012). Micronutrients and other Beneficial Elements in Soils and Fertilizers in *"Soil Fertility and Fertilizers"* 7th. ed. Prentice Hall, New Jersey 07458, USA.

Tiwari, J.K. and Dwivedi, K.N. (2007). Effect of Sulphur and Zinc on yield and Mineral Nutrition of Pigeonpea in Inceptisols. *Ann. Plant Soil Research,* 9 (1): 35-38.

Tiwari, K.N. (1995). Bharatiya Mittian in *"Urvarrk and Khad", ICAR,* New Delhi, pp. 1-18.

Tiwari, K.N. and Tiwari, A. (1996). *Tikau Kheti Santulit Urvarak Upyog.* Samadhan Gramya Vikas Sansthan. Impact Printing Press 7/193 Swaroop Nagar, Kanpur pp. 82 and 143.

Tripathi, H.C., Singh, R.S. and Mishra, V.K. (1997). Response of Gram (*Cicer arietinum*) to Sulphur and Zinc Fertilization. *Indian Journal of Agricultural Science,* 67: 541-542.

Valenciano J.B.; Boto J.A. and Marcelo V. (2010). Response of Chickpea (*Cicer arietinum* L.) yield to Zinc, Boron and Molybdenum Application under Pot Conditions, *Span J Agric Res.,* 8(3), 797-807.

Valenciano J.B.; Boto J.A. and Marcelo V. (2011). Chickpea (Cicer arietinum L.) Response to Zinc, Boron and Molybdenum Application under Field Conditions. *New Zealand Journal of Crop and Horticultural Science*, 39: (4) 217-229.

Venkateswarlu, S. (1987). In *"15 Years of Dryland Agricultural Research"*. Souvenir CRIDA Hyderabad, pp. 42-58.

Walkley, A. and Black, I.A. (1934). An Examination of the Degtjareff method for Determining Soil Organic matter and Proposed Modification of the Chromic Acid Titration method. *Soil Science,* 37, 29-30.

Welch, R.M. (1995). Micronutrient Nutrition of Plants. *Critical Reviews in Plant Science,* 14: 49-82.

Zerrari, N., Moustaoui, D. and Verloo, M. (1999). The Forms of Boron in Soil, Effect of Soil Characteristics and Availability for the Plants. *Agrochimica,* 43: 77-88.

INDEX